# SENSE OF PLACE

# SENSE
## OF
# PLACE

## American
## Regional
## Cultures

EDITED BY

BARBARA ALLEN

& THOMAS J. SCHLERETH

THE UNIVERSITY PRESS OF KENTUCKY

*Sense of Place* has been selected
as a Publication of the American Folklore Society,
New Series, Ralph B. Mullen, General Editor

*Editorial and Sales Offices:* Lexington, Kentucky 40508

**Library of Congress Cataloging-in-Publication Data**

Sense of place : American regional cultures / edited by Barbara Allen
& Thomas J. Schlereth.
    p.  cm.
Includes bibliographical references.
ISBN 0-8131-1730-5 (alk. paper) :
1. United States—Social life and customs—20th century.
2. Regionalism—United States.  3. Folklore—United States.
I. Allen, Barbara, 1946-  .  II. Schlereth, Thomas J.
E169.S448  1990
306.4'0973—dc20                       90-44010

*These essays are intended to honor*
*William Lynwood Montell,*
*whose work as a folklorist and oral historian*
*in the Upper Cumberland region*
*of Kentucky and Tennessee serves*
*as a model of regional scholarship.*

# Contents

# Regional Studies in American Folklore Scholarship

BARBARA ALLEN

A sense of place, a consciousness of one's physical surroundings, is a fundamental human experience. It seems to be especially strong where people in a neighborhood, a community, a city, a region, possess a collective awareness of place and express it in their cultural forms. In the United States, this consciousness of place has most often been identified with regions, large and small, within which distinctive cultures have developed. These regional cultures and the regional consciousness that both shapes and is shaped by them are the subject of the essays in this book.

While regional studies as an interdisciplinary field is a relatively recent development in American scholarship, regionalism has long been a theme, although often a muted one, in the work of American geographers, economists, sociologists, political scientists, anthropologists, historians, literary scholars, and folklorists. Perhaps because so many researchers in such diverse fields have concerned themselves with region, definitions of the concept are abundant. In chapter 1 of *American Regionalism*, for instance, Howard Odum and Harry Estil Moore list forty-one definitions of *region*, among them:

> A complex of land, water, air, plant, animal and man regarded in their special relationship as together constituting a definite, characteristic portion of the Earth's surface.

> An area within which the combination of environmental and demographic factors have created a homogeneity of economic and social structure.

> Any part of a national domain sufficiently unified physiographically and socially, to have a true consciousness of its own customs and ideals, and to possess a sense of distinction from other parts of the country.[1]

Devising a single formulation that will satisfy all regionalists clearly cannot be done, for each discipline involved in regional studies conceives of the *nature* of region somewhat differently. While geographers regard regions primarily as chunks of physical space, economists prefer to think of them as systems of human activity. Historians see them as the products of events or experiences over time; anthropologists, as areas marked by the presence of one or more culture traits.

Beneath the surface of this diversity, however, lie several elements that virtually all regionalists would agree are fundamental to a region. The first of these is *place:* a region is at its heart a geographical entity. What makes a region more than an arbitrarily designated spot on earth is its human dimension. "A region is a reservoir of energy," according to the French geographer Paul Vidal de la Blache, "whose origins lie in nature but whose development depends upon man."[2] Thus, the second element of a region is the *people* who live there and organize their lives within the context of the environmental conditions and natural resources of that place. Because the relationship between a place and its residents evolves through time, the third component of a region is *the history* of residents' shared experiences in and with that place. For Odum and Moore, this dimension fosters an organic unity in a region, comprising "the land and the people, culturally conditioned *through time* and spatial relationships."[3] The final element in a region is *distinctiveness*, both from the areas surrounding it and from the whole (e.g., the nation) of which the region is a part. That distinctiveness may lie in economic and social structure and systems, in historical development and experiences, in cultural patterns, or in all three. Whatever the bases for its identity, argues Rupert Vance, a region "sufficiently unified to have a consciousness of its customs and ideas . . . thus possesses a sense of identity distinct from the rest of the country."[4] That identity, according to Louis Wirth, stems from the fact that people living under similar conditions and in a state of interdependence develop similar traits and a sense of belonging. "Thus," he writes, "regions develop a conception of themselves and acquire a more or less stereotyped conception in the minds of others who think about them or have relations with them."[5] The idea of regional consciousness and regional identity—a regional sense of self—crops up in virtually every serious discussion of regions and regionalism. It is at the basis of the concept of vernacular region, that is, "a *region* perceived to exist by its inhabitants and other members of the population at large."6 Writing about New England as a region, George Pierson points out that even though "no matter how you measure it—geographically, economically, racially, or religiously—there is no New England region today," the *idea* of the region persists; in the face of this idea, Pierson concludes that New England is a region "of heart and mind."7

As Pierson suggests, regional identity is as much a matter of subjective perception as of objective observation. "A region may be described loosely," says V.B. Stanbery, "as an area of which the inhabitants instinctively feel themselves a part." In his introduction to *Land of the Millrats*, a study of the folk cultures of the Calumet region of northwestern Indiana, Richard Dorson follows the same line of reasoning. "The folk region," he says, "lies in the mind and spirit as much as in physical boundaries." James Shortridge echoes this sentiment in his study of vernacular regions in Kansas. "For people trying to discern general cultural or humanistic areas for planning and other purposes," he writes, "perceived regions are the ones that matter." A full understanding of the nature of a region, then, may best be achieved by adopting the perspective of residents to see a place from the inside rather than the outside, to understand "the totality of perceptions and knowledge of a place gained by residents through their long experience of it, and intensified by their feelings for it." The key to getting at this insiders' view is investigating its regional culture, which provides the vehicle for inhabitants to express both personally and collectively their sense of regional identity and regional consciousness. This esoteric view of the regional experience is most richly manifested, according to Archie Green, when people in a region "use its lore to mark [regional] consciousness."8

The essays gathered together here are all concerned in some way with this sense of place as expressed in American regional cultures. This is an appropriate focus for a tribute to Lynwood Montell, whose academic career has been devoted to the study of the Upper Cumberland region of south central Kentucky and northern Tennessee. Each of the authors represented here, like Montell, writes about a particular region, and, also like him, employs a folkloristic perspective in doing so. As regional folklorists, all are part of a long-established tradition in American folklore scholarship.9

While European folklorists have long been involved in regional ethnology and folklife studies, the study of regional folk culture has been slow to develop among their American counterparts. The reasons that folklorists in the United States did not adopt the folklife model until recently derive from the differences between the European and American contexts within which folklore studies originated.[10] The focus of European regional ethnology and folklife has traditionally been on rural peasant or ethnic groups with deep roots in a specific place. Because time depth has been seen as the defining quality of the cultures being studied, folklife scholars have relied on archaeology as well as ethnographic fieldwork and have tended to focus more attention on material culture than on verbal or customary lore.

In contrast, American folklorists were far more interested from the beginning in verbal than in material culture. At least part of this interest stemmed from their training as literary scholars. But it also reflected the idea prevalent among Americans in general then—as it is even yet—that the United States lacked the rich historical and cultural heritage of Old World nations although remnants of it— dying relics of an ancient tradition—were to be found in the folk culture of groups transplanted to the United States. Those remnants were largely verbal and behavioral rather than artifactual. Further, the population of the United States, perceived as comprising immigrant stock, seemed to offer no direct analogue to the European peasant class bound to the land both economically and historically. Although African-Americans, first in legal bondage and later in economic peonage, constituted a kind of peasantry in the South, they clearly lacked the historical relationship with the land they lived on that characterized their European counterparts. The indigenous peoples of the North American continent, on the other hand, were closely identified with the land, but few had been agrarianists (as peasants were by definition), and by the end of the nineteenth century when American folklore scholarship began to be systematized, their ties with the land had been almost completely disrupted by displacement, removal, and the reservation system.

Finally, and perhaps most critically, there had not yet evolved in the United States a sense of regions as culturally distinct entities.[11] Americans in the nineteenth century were, of course, keenly aware of sectional divisions between North and South, for the Civil War was still within living memory. And in the 1890s Frederick Jackson Turner had drawn Americans' attention to the West as the keystone of national destiny. But the recognition of North, South, and West as sections of the country was limited largely to their roles in American political and economic life; regionalism as a historical or cultural force did not become a defining component of national identity as did immigration and its concomitant ethnic pluralism.

It is not surprising, then, that American folklorists concentrated their attention on folklore within immigrant and ethnic groups (including Native Americans). Doing so was in line not only with a general American perception that the United States was a nation of immigrants but also with the conception of folklore as survivals persisting from earlier stages of cultural development or as static items transmitted through generations of tradition bearers. Not until folklore came to be seen as dynamic rather than static, as actively generated rather than passively transmitted, has there been room for the idea that the expressive behavior of people in a *particular place* is necessarily shaped to some degree by their interactions with their physical environment.[12]

All these ideas about folklore in general and American folklore in particular are clearly reflected in the editorial statement published in the initial issue of the *Journal of American Folklore* (1888), which described the purposes of the journal:

(1) For the collection of the fast-vanishing remains of Folk-Lore in America, namely:
   (a) Relics of Old English Folk-Lore (ballads, tales, superstitions, dialect, etc.)
   (b) Lore of Negroes in the Southern States of the Union.
   (c) Lore of the Indian Tribes of North America (myths, tales, etc.)
   (d) Lore of French Canada, Mexico, etc.
(2) For the study of the general subject, and publications of the results of special students in this department.

The emphasis on racial and ethnic groups notwithstanding, contributions dealing with folklore from particular locales appeared in the journal's pages from the beginning. Between 1888 and 1900, more than a dozen articles or notes were published on folklore in various regional settings, including New England, Maryland's Eastern Shore, the Rio Grande Valley, the Carolina mountains, and middle Tennessee.[13] In fact, a small but relatively steady stream of such pieces flows through the journal up through the 1940s. The collection of folklore in regional and local settings was also going on beyond the pages of the journal during this same period, bolstered by the establishment of a dozen state and regional folklore publications.[14]

In keeping with the function of cultural salvage that folklorists saw themselves as performing—rescuing "fast-vanishing remains" by preserving them in print—much of this work consisted solely or primarily of texts. Collections of songs and ballads were especially numerous; a premier example is Cecil Sharp's collection of traditional ballads in the southern Appalachians. Other researchers conducted multigenre surveys of folklore on a county, state, or regional basis. Frank C. Brown of North Carolina, for instance, compiled voluminous materials on folksongs, narratives, customs, and beliefs between 1913 and 1943, while Vance Randolph began his voracious collecting in the Ozarks in the 1920s.[15]

The works dealing with regional folklore from the 1880s through the 1940s clearly reflect prevailing conceptions of the nature of folklore and approaches to its study. The concentration on texts to the virtual exclusion of all else reveals folklorists' notion that folklore items—songs, stories, games, beliefs—had an existence independent of the folk among whom they circulated. Because the item itself was of paramount concern, its geographical or social provenience was deemed secondary, useful in establishing transmission or migration patterns but otherwise incidental. As a result, there is no consistency in the kinds of geographical units within which collections are made. They range in size from a single county (e.g., Adams County, Illinois, in which Harry M. Hyatt worked) to an entire state (such as Nebraska, represented by the work of Louise Pound) and from regions contained entirely within one state ("Egypt" in southern Illinois) to regions that cross state lines (the Ozarks).[16]

Much of the ostensibly regional folklore gathered during this period was actually collected from ethnic groups within particular regions, such as Pennsylvania Germans, southern blacks, and Hispanics in New Mexico. In these collections, the ethnic element is represented as dominating regional culture; indeed, the boundaries of the region are often seen as coterminous with the settlement patterns of that group. For all intents and purposes, regional culture in these works was ethnic in nature.[17]

This lack of consistency in the basis for collecting regional folklore signals a general disregard for the nature of region as a framework within which folklore could be studied. A particularly clear indication of this state of affairs is a volume proposed in 1945 on "Regional American Folklore," to be edited by Stith Thompson and to include twenty-seven chapters on such diverse subjects as "The Maritime Provinces," "Pioneer Days in the Middle West," "Sailors on Lakes and Sea," and "The World of Children."[18] Archie Green, commenting on this period of regional folklore scholarship, points out, "It has been easy for us to collect within territorial bounds, but difficult to use place as a cluster point for theory."[19] Part of the reason for this neglect of the relationship between the folklore collected and its regional context lay in the assumption that folklore comprises static items transmitted more or less intact through generations of tradition bearers. This notion does not preclude change as an item moves along the chain of transmission; the historic-geographic school of folklore scholarship, after all, is predicated on changes effected in folklore items as they "travel" through time and space. But it does not provide a theoretical basis for recognizing and interpreting folklore created in response to local or regional experience. The nearest approach to this position comes in Carl von Sydow's concept of oikotypes, which are region-specific redactions of more widespread folklore items adapted to local conditions, especially environmental ones.[20] Even in von Sydow's scheme, however, there is the assumption that folklore is introduced into, not generated within, local settings.

By the late 1940s, however, there were indications that the study of regional folklore was about to be transformed. One of the first hints of change came in 1947 in an article by Herbert Halpert published as part of an assessment of North American folklore research. Surveying the field of American regional folklore, Halpert cited the lack of a clear-cut definition of region among folklorists as the primary limitation of work done thus far. In his own fieldwork in the Pine Barrens of New Jersey for his doctoral dissertation in the early 1940s, Halpert carefully prefaced the folktale texts he had gathered with a description of the region as a self-conscious entity. Folklorists must begin to heed the relationship between lore and locale, Halpert argued, especially in light of "the development of regional consciousness [that] is [now] part of a growing nation-alism," as witnessed by Odum and Moore's *American Regionalism*.[21]

*American Regionalism*, in fact, represented a groundswell of in-terest in American regions and regional culture in the 1930s, which manifested itself on a variety of fronts. It appeared in the work of

American historians and geographers, among them Walter Prescott Webb, whose magisterial treatment of the Great Plains as a distinctive culture area appeared in 1931; in the literary and art criticism of the New Regionalists, such as the Southern Agrarians; in government programs, notably the Federal Writers' Project, whose original mission had been to produce a series of regional guides; in the popular press, represented, for instance, in the multivolume American Folkways Series under the general editorship of Erskine Caldwell, each book dealing with a different American region or subregion; and in academic enterprises such as the conference "Regionalism in America" at the University of Wisconsin in 1949. (A parallel development in folklore circles was the Western Folklore Conference initiated at the University of Denver in 1941 and continuing through 1955.) All this activity drew attention to regions as cultural as well as geographical, economic, or political entities and suggested various frameworks for their systematic study.[22]

A folklorist who was involved in this new regionalism from the beginning was Benjamin A. Botkin.[23] His interest in regional folk culture was intense and enthusiastic, grounded in a conception of folklore as living expression shaped by present experience, rather than as moribund relics of the past. Because regional folklore was a vital expression of local experience, he argued, it afforded the creative artist an invaluable source of material from which genuine regional art could be made. In 1929 Botkin initiated *Folk-Say*, an annual compendium of poems and stories based on or drawn from regional folk tradition, particularly the Southwest, to serve as a living laboratory for his theory.

Botkin's commitment to the idea of folk materials as grounded in contemporary experience and to the artist's right to appropriate those materials in creative works led him into conflict with those who thought of folklore as a legacy from the past to be preserved in pristine form. As a result, his view of regional folklore did not have widespread impact on other folklorists.[24]

In fact, ideas and concepts from the newly emerging field of regional studies filtered only gradually into folklorists' approach to the subject; indeed, their full impact would not be felt for another twenty years. But several straws indicate that by the 1950s the wind was blowing in a new direction. One such indication was Richard M. Dorson's *Bloodstoppers and Bearwalkers: Folk Traditions of the Upper Peninsula*. Dorson was attracted to this region both because of its isolation from mainstream American culture—a "remote and rugged land" which had become a "storyteller's paradise"—and because "the Peninsula contains in minuscule the nation's folk culture," especially in its mix of ethnic groups.[25] These characterizations seem rooted in a recognition of the Upper Peninsula as a distinct region; further, the chapter divisions of the book according to occupations and local history as well as ethnic groups suggest that the key forces shaping the region, including geography and natural resources, settlement patterns, economic structure, and history, also shaped its folk culture. While Dorson does not articulate it explicitly, the message of *Bloodstoppers and Bearwalkers* is that the folklore of the Upper Peninsula is truly a regional product, a response to residents' experiences there.

However unaware Dorson may have been of the implications of his work, *Bloodstoppers and Bearwalkers* represents a shift from the prevailing image of regional folklore as old stock transplanted in new ground (although that idea is very much in evidence in the book) to the idea of region as seedbed for folk culture. This shift reflected a reformulation of the notion that folklore was a survival from and a relic of the past into a conception of folklore as a contemporary response to historical events and experiences. Dorson develops this idea more fully in *American Folklore*, in which he argues that American folklore can best be interpreted as an outgrowth of the major historical forces—for example, the colonial experience, the frontier, immigration—that had shaped the nation.[26] Within this broad theoretical framework, however, Dorson still also clung to the older concept of folklore as historical artifact; in his chapter on "Regional Folk Cultures," for instance, he describes them as "relics" and "pockets," "nooks and byways" isolated from the cultural mainstream—places where folk cultures imported with the ethnic groups occupying these regions could persist uninfluenced by technology, mass media, and other elements of urbanized American culture.[27]

Another work published in the 1950s, however, is pivotal in moving regional folklore studies from simply collecting folklore *within* a region to studying the folklore *of* a region: *"With His Pistol in His Hand": A Border Ballad and Its Hero*, by Americo Paredes.[28] In this study of balladry along the Lower Rio Grande border between Mexico and the United States, Paredes argues eloquently that the *corrido* (folk ballad) was a product of historical and cultural forces in that region, and he demonstrates in an elegant analysis that, in spite of its ultimate European ancestry, the border ballad is truly an indigenous element of regional folklife, a *product* of the regional experience.

The full emergence of an emphasis in regional folklore studies on exploring the "relationship of land to lore," in Archie Green's words, came with the revolution in folklore studies in the 1960s that involved a profound reconceptualization of folklore as a process (of which a folklore item was simply an outcome) and a concomitant shift from a concern with folklore as traditional item to folklore as a dynamic, creative response to and expression of a group's shared beliefs, values, and experiences, shaped by individuals out of traditional materials and patterns in particular contexts for particular purposes.[29] This broadening of the conception of folklore brought with it correspondingly expanded notions of the nature of folk groups—notions that could include the idea of people bound together by a consciousness of living together in the same place.

The impact of this paradigmatic shift in the discipline on the study of regional folklore was heralded by Suzi Jones in her article "Regionalization: A Rhetorical Strategy," in which she argues that the changes effected in folklore as people move from one place to another reflect adaptations to local regional environments; regionalization is the process by which folklore is transformed through people's response to *place*. What differentiates Jones's argument from von Sydow's idea of oikotypification is that she grounds it in the theoretical view of folklore as a rhetorical device used in interaction to achieve a variety of social purposes. Folklore is often "regionalized," Jones suggests, to demonstrate familiarity with the local environment and thereby to mark boundaries between insiders and outsiders.[30]

While Jones's argument is still fundamentally item-centered—a large part of her essay, for instance, is taken up with a discussion of which genres lend themselves most readily to regionalization—she offers a clear definition of regional folklore that recognizes it as a response to experience. Commenting on folklorists' vague designation of various groups as regional, she writes that the term "regional folk group" should be used only "in instances where people share a body of folklore because they live in a certain geographical area; their geographical location is a primary basis for a shared identity that is expressed in their lore, and they themselves are conscious of their regional identity."[31]

Jones' article serves not only as a bridge between text-centered folklore scholarship, which prevailed through the 1950s, and pro-cess-centered scholarship, which has come to dominate in recent years, but also calls particular attention to the connections between folkloristic and geographic approaches to the idea of region and regional culture. In fact, geographers had been using folk cultural materials as data in regional studies for a number of years. The pioneer in this regard is universally acknowledged as Fred Kniffen who, in 1936, published a study of domestic folk architecture in Louisiana; in subsequent work he traced the distribution of folk house types as indicators of cultural diffusion along regional lines. Henry Glassie followed Kniffen's lead in *Pattern in the Material Folk Culture of the Eastern United States*, identifying five distinctive cultural regions in that part of the country on the basis of the distribution and diffusion patterns of a variety of folk architectural and artifactual forms. In Texas, Terry Jordan examined a broad range of folk materials in documenting the vernacular cultural regions of that state.[32]

While Kniffen, Glassie, and Jordan focused on material culture, other scholars have used verbal and customary folklore in identify-ing regional cultural patterns. The linguistic atlas approach, ex-emplified in Han Kurath's three-volume *Linguistic Atlas of New England*, sought to delineate regions by mapping dialect.[33] In an innovative adaptation of the linguistic atlas method in the 1970s, several geographers, including Joseph Brownell, Ruth Hale, John Shelton Reed, Terry Jordan, and Wilbur Zelinsky, identified Amer-ican "perceptual" or "vernacular" regions by documenting the dis-tribution of locally used regional names on the grounds that residents' own names for the region in which they live can offer a valid measure of a region's geographical outlines. In the 1960s, E. Joan Wilson Miller drew upon Vance Randolph's folklore collec-tions to plot subregions in the Ozarks according to the distribution of such items as folktales and folk beliefs. This particular use of folk materials, Herbert Halpert had suggested, was desirable in order to "distinguish the limits of the zones which have homogeneous repertories of songs, stories, beliefs, riddles, and proverbs; like styles of singing and dancing; similar types of building structures, craft designs, agricultural and occupational practices."[34]

The folklorist W.F.H. Nicolaisen, a close observer of cultural geographers' use of regional folk materials, argued in a series of articles published in the 1970s that folklorists ought to concern themselves with exploring the questions raised by the existence of

regions plotted according to cultural data—questions ranging from
the relevance of Carl von Sydow's concept of oikotype to the expression of regional consciousness through folklore.[35] Geographers
were beginning to ask similar questions in the 1960s and 1970s,
revolving around issues such as environmental perception, the
construction of symbolic landscapes, and the concept of sense of
place. In an effort to extend geographical conceptions of the relationship between human beings and their physical environments
beyond the strictly instrumental and functional, these studies
focused on the cultural and symbolic meaning ascribed to landscape and place as expressed in literature and art. Clearly, what
geographers had to say with regard to perception of place and the
symbolic meaning of landscape had implications for folklorists
interested in defining folk regions on grounds that correspond to
the reality of residents' experience. Indeed, Suzi Jones argued that
the work of humanistic geographers, such as Yi-Fu Tuan's book
*Topophilia: A Study of Environmental Perception, Attitudes, and Values,*
should be "requisite reading for anyone studying folklore in a
regional context and trying to understand the interactions between
the people, the lore, and the regional environment."[36]

The maturing of regional folklore studies in recent years is
apparent in a number of ways. In the public sector, several regional
folklore centers have been created, including the Center for Southern Folklore in Memphis, the Southwest Folklore Center in Tucson,
and the Western Folklife Center in Salt Lake City. The American
Folklife Center of the Library of Congress has undertaken a number
of regional culture projects since 1976, among them studies of the
Blue Ridge Parkway area of Virginia and North Carolina, the ranching community of Paradise Valley in northern Nevada, and the New
Jersey Pinelands Reserve.[37] In the scholarly literature, there are
fewer collections of texts and more analytical studies of the relationship between people and place as manifested in regional folk
culture.[38]

The essays gathered here represent this mature stage of regional
folklore scholarship. At the heart of each is a concern with how
people construct a sense of place, of region, for themselves through
cultural expression. The authors explore this issue on a variety of
regional fronts, which span the United States from one coast to the
other and range in size from the expanse of the American West to
the confines of Barnegat Bay in southern New Jersey. Equally diverse are the forms of cultural expression that the authors examine,

encompassing narrative, musical, material, and customary expressions of regional culture and regional consciousness. And they raise critical questions about cultural responses to natural forces on a regional basis; about the impact of historical factors on regional culture; about the role of regional consciousness in shaping residents' responses to events and experiences; about the construction of regional identity to distinguish insiders from outsiders through folk cultural expression; and, above all, about the creative response to local experience that symbolizes regional consciousness in an astonishing variety of verbal, behavioral, and material forms.

# Folklore and Reality
# in the American West

## BARRE TOELKEN

*Barre Toelken opens this collection of essays by considering the most fundamental question raised by the study of regional culture: what is the relationship between people's experiences in a particular place and their cultural expressions of those experiences? Using examples drawn from the "invisible," or folk, culture of the American West, Toelken argues that key elements of the western regional experience, such as harsh environmental conditions and conflict between whites and Native Americans, are clearly articulated in a variety of folkloric forms. Because these forms express the historical realities of life in the West, Toelken points out, folklore is a sensitive tool for understanding the region as a shaping force in residents' lives.*

The title of this essay suggests a kinship between folklore and reality in the West and is not meant to bring up (once again) a contrast or dialectic between "fact" and "fiction" or The Real versus The Fanciful in the American West, even though these terms are sometimes amusing ways of appreciating the creative attempts of writers and scholars to characterize the western experience. Rather, I want to pay serious attention to the ways in which everyday people who live in the West have created a sense of reality out of shared cultural values and have expressed those abstractions in the traditional genres we too simplistically call "folklore." Of course, there are many cultures in the West, each with distinctive values, worldviews, and traditions, and each with distinctive senses of daily reality (not monolithic, of course, but known to and participated in by most typical members of the group). I will focus here mainly on the Euro-American dimension because of its substantial impact on our subsequent sense of what the West is and was, but I trust that others interested in Native American, African-American, Hispanic, and Asian cultures in the West will note the parallels in the way vernacular expressions carry and express the perceived realities of life among those groups.

What Japanese folklorist Yanagita Kunio called "invisible culture" consists of the everyday people who "perform" their culture to each other on the live vernacular level and who thus seldom achieve notoriety or acclaim, or become individually recognized writers and philosophers: these are the housewives, fishermen, farmers, tradespeople, artisans, longshoremen, children, and the like. Yanagita calls them "invisible" not because their numbers or their importance can be conceived of as inconsiderable but because their thoughts and works seldom appear in the books, libraries, and museums which enshrine the accepted, often elite statements of influential intellectual individuals. Yanagita did not consider the written and material products of intellectuals as unimportant, on the other hand, but noted that these fine "visible" works of literature and art were vulnerable in a number of ways: they could be destroyed by fire or earthquake; they could be suppressed by the arbiters of culture; they could be mistaken—because of their brilliance and uniqueness—for typical by those who would romanticize their culture. Most important, the works of the visible culture are relatively few in number, and for this reason alone, they cannot give us a full and consistent picture of the whole ongoing culture. Vernacular expressions, even those which take the form of material objects, are not as subject to fire, suppression, and misuse, for they remain alive and recurrent in the culture. Thus, even though a boat or a house may burn down over here, or a proverb or belief may be misinterpreted or used for government propaganda over there, nonetheless, the long-range tendency of tradition is to continue articulating the values of the culture: the mountain cabin is not lost if even the best exemplar of the type burns down, for the plan is in the culture, not in the item.[1]

Among American scholars it was probably Fred Kniffen who most clearly articulated this idea with respect to folk housing; he held that "the study of the unique normally adds little to the sum of understanding of human behavior," and he urged his students to look at the most common items produced by the culture because it as in them that the researcher would find the most significant cultural meanings.[2] Following this trend, recent researchers have indeed come to important discoveries and positions by paying attention to the common denominators in vernacular expression; in addition to the well-known works of Henry Glassie, one thinks of Rhys Isaac's *The Transformation of Virginia, 1740-1790* and John Vlach's stunning demonstration of the multicultural background of the "shotgun" house—based on the analysis of vernacular sources, not on written records or formal histories.[3] Since it is the everyday people who make up and animate the bulk of any living culture, it is they and their expressions which are typical, common, and thus broadly meaningful; thus it is to their expressions we must turn for a consistent and "real" articulation of cultural values, for common sense would indicate that anything which can stay alive for a while in oral tradition must have *some* importance for those who pass it on, or it would not have survived. Vernacular records are not in short supply, and oral tradition shows no signs of dying out.

"The real world" in which a culture sees itself operating is seldom articulated in direct, intellectual terms; rather, reality seems to be a cultural construct governed by values we share with others in our culture. The whole culture (not just the literates or the philosophers) utilizes this construct to some extent, thus the whole expressive output of the culture—from the philosophical treatises of professional thinkers to the jokes of local garbage collectors—will speak to us, and eloquently, about the reality of the culture. This is not the same as claiming that everyone gets the "facts" straight, nor does it allow us to presume that literate people get their facts any straighter than anyone else.

Shared interests and values are given shape when they are articulated in a traditional form like a song or legend or house. That is, vernacular expressions work in at least two ways: they grow out of, and give voice to, a culture's abstract and generally unorganized (not *dis*organized) value system; and, when performed, they touch off other emotional responses which relate to the value system. We learn our culture by hearing its expressions, and we in turn express our culture whenever we engage in performing any of its vernacular genres. In this process, we are engaged in the cultural values somewhat more fully and emotionally than we are in the chiefly intellectual and analytical exercise of thinking *about* the culture—in the same way in which our use of spoken language requires our breath, muscles, and vocal cords, while reading does not.

In this view, the contemporary, active vernacular expressions (legends, jokes, rumors, tools, crafts) are more important to our understanding than are the written works of the Thoreaus, Coopers, Lewises, Marxes, Cronons—who, no matter how brilliant, are commentators *on* the culture more than they are vernacular participants in it by the time their works reach us. Although Henry Nash Smith's *Virgin Land*, published in 1950, is still used as a standard text in American Studies courses, it is safe to say that such a work, resting as it does almost exclusively on literary statements *about* the western experience, could not come forth in new print today pretending to provide insight on the nature of myth and symbol in the American West. It is not only because this work (and others like it) almost entirely avoids the vernacular record provided by folklore—although this in itself would be a substantial reason not to take the book seriously—but because the evidence provided by folklore resources often stands in direct contradiction to the intellectual observations of the distant scholar. Smith, for example, rhapsodizes about the positive aspects of the agrarian life in the West: "The hardy yeoman came out into the wilderness seeking land, and his search was rewarded: he acquired title to his farm and reared his numerous children amid the benign influences of forest and meadow. But the land was so fertile and the area under cultivation increased so rapidly that a surplus of grain and livestock quickly appeared." [4] While it would be pleasant to believe that at least some hardworking sodbusters experienced this fertile reward, it would nonetheless be more fair to note that in the songs sung by the next generation in the West—in other words, by those who had been born there or who were children while their parents were trying to homestead—there is a distinct note of irony, sarcasm, bitterness. Their parody of the idealistic hymn "Beulah Land" often contained the verse:

> Our neighbors are the rattlesnakes;
> They crawl up from the badlands' breaks;
> We do not live, we only stay,
> We are too poor to get away. [5]

Vernon L. Parrington discovered a frontier "bitterness" in the writings of later authors, but the general attitude was already available to anyone willing to look at vernacular sources. What? Take the word of an unknown South Dakota settler over the considered opinions of America's leading, known scholars? If we operate on the assumption that songs like this will not persist among the members of a group unless they somehow continue to dramatize or "speak for" shared values, then we must admit that the very anonymity of the song, along with its traditional persistence through time, along with its regional spread, indeed commend it to our attention as a verbal artifact of central importance.

What Yanagita Kunio felt about the veracity of customs, what Fred Kniffen felt about the reliability of vernacular architecture, can also be advanced as the compelling reasons for taking songs, legends, jokes, tales, and anecdotes as more than interesting entertainments. As Jan H. Brunvand has observed, a legend is not passed along because its factual content can be affirmed or disproved but because it satisfies and dramatizes a real set of attitudes which in and of themselves are seldom if ever scrutinized or verbalized.[6] Indeed, although tellers of legends usually assert that the content is true, or at least that the story is to be held up for consideration as likely to be true, they almost never attempt to corroborate their story and almost never claim to have been eyewitness to its central event. The legend, which purports in style and delivery to be truthful, may be impossible to verify, and this, of course, puts it in an inferior category of information for most historians. Yet, to the extent that a legend represents real beliefs and attitudes among the tellers and their audiences, it should be very interesting to us.

A widespread legend found in the Pacific Northwest (and spottily throughout the West generally) provides us an excellent example for the kind of reality treated here. Dubbed "Goldilocks on the Oregon Trail" by historian Francis Haines, who first published the story, it has been collected in the lore of more than a dozen Northwest families of pioneer descent.[7] Usually, the narration is triggered by mention of the pioneer era; then someone jokingly remarks, "Well, in our family we always say that Grandma was almost sold to the Indians!" The audience demands an explanation, and then follows the account, told as absolutely true, of an incident that occurred as the family made its way across the plains: a prominent Indian chief (sometimes Geronimo or Chief Joseph) comes into the pioneer camp to bargain for food or supplies; he sees the blond, blue-eyed six-year-old (our future grandma) and is so smitten by her beauty that he offers to buy her. In some versions he returns to the camp several times, each time with more horses to offer, in response to the girl's father's indecision about what price he would accept. Finally, the father puts an end to the joke by admitting that he will not sell his daughter for any price, at which point the chief sadly rides away. In a Utah version collected by Austin and Alta Fife, the girl's mother cuts off a golden ringlet or a braid from the girl's hair and offers it to the chief as a consolation, whereupon he presents the girl with a small thimble, which is still treasured among the family heirlooms.[8]

Everyone who tells this story asserts that it actually happened in his or her family, which brings up some interesting speculations on how often such an occurrence could have taken place on the frontier, or how busy the famous chieftains were (let alone how far from home they ranged looking for prepubescent blonds). Was the purchase or attempted purchase of young white girls by Indians fairly common on the frontier? Did it happen to all of these families, or only to two or three, or only to one (and in this case, how did the event get into the sober recollections of all the others)? Since there is absolutely no corroboration of the story in the otherwise meticulous diaries and journals of these same families (one would expect diarists who noted changes in temperature, isolated trees, miles progressed, and bison on the horizon to have at least made mention of an Indian coming into camp and trying to buy a small girl), we could decide to dismiss the anecdote as "only" a story and not consider it as a source of fact about life in the West. But this kind of response and the well-intentioned factual questions noted provisionally above are really irrelevant, for they do not address the more important question: why do so many honest people insist that the event occurred, that it occurred in their family, and that the narrative is worthy of being repeated? If we assume that the story is more like a "literary" expression than it is like a compendium of data, then we should ask the kinds of questions that produce literary insight: what kind of story is it, and what does it mean for those who tell it? What are its images and logical assumptions? What are its internal realities, seen from the standpoint of the culture that tells it?

Looking at this story even in a relatively cursory manner, we can easily notice the following:

1. The teller of the legend can claim an early family arrival in the West: "We got here when people were still coming by wagons and being threatened by the Indians." Among pioneer families, especially in the Northwest, early arrival provides an important pedigree, and attempts have been made to define a pioneer as someone who came before the railroad or who came by wagon, thus shutting out later arrivals from semisacred status.

2. The story illustrates the common white notion that Indians

find white women (especially with the marks of Nordic purity like blond hair and blue eyes) immensely attractive. Moreover, the narrative dramatizes the well-known racial theme of the dark-skinned, sexually mature male (member of a feared or denigrated minority group) pursuing the light-skinned, innocent female (member of our group)—racial fear of *them* projected as sexual threat to *us*.

3. The Indian in this story is the aggressive party, moving into the white camp and potentially intruding on the integrity of a white family, even though historically it was the whites moving into Indian territory and intruding on Indian social structure—intimations of guilt projected as blame.

4. The logic of the story is that of Euro-American social norms: men decide the fates of women; fathers make decisions for their daughters; men are the suitors (even when they are feared); family patriarchs may play a joke (pretending to sell a child), but their final role is to defend family propriety and cultural expectation. None of the versions has the mother urging the wisdom of a marriage with an Indian leader; none has the girl pleading to join the natives; none ends with the girl being sold at a tidy profit.

5. The Indian suitor is virtually always a chief, whether a famous one mentioned by name or not. This seems to be the inverse of the Indian princess syndrome: royalty is preferable to us in our interactions with "inferior" peoples. When we marry in with them, then it is at our volition; we play the male role and it is Grandma who is the Cherokee princess. When they threaten us, they take the aggressive male role, and our daughters and sisters are the presumed targets. Besides, interactions with chiefs and princesses provide more impressive family stories than do random anonymous encounters. Although human history seems to be made up more of the latter than of the former, stories of "how Grandma was almost sold to Chief Joseph" have a ring to them that would be lacking in "how some Indian guy got interested in my grandma."

This brief family legend dramatizes a meaningful constellation of real cultural concerns about family identity, racial fears, sex roles, and social norms; and it expresses the kind of guilt or ambivalence about moving onto someone else's land which one finds continually throughout pioneer accounts: by projection, the *Indian* is characterized as the aggressor, intruder, and predator. On a relatively superficial level, we refer today to the tendency to "blame the victim," and we realize that this attitude plays a serious and complicated role in our multicultural economics and politics. But on a deeper, more abiding cultural level, legends like "Goldilocks on the Oregon Trail," as well as other examples to be discussed below, provide ample proof that such abstractions have been dramatized over and over again in western vernacular tradition, so much so, in fact, that we may suspect that legends have had the effect of creating a sense of normalcy—of daily reality—which in turn has functioned to socialize people into their cultural value systems. Cultural assumptions, undergirded by legendary (that is, believable) illustrations, provide the contexts in which people choose where they will settle, how they will vote, whom they will marry, whom they are willing to shoot, how they define land ownership and water rights, and how they will distinguish between such delicate issues as *settlement* versus *land theft*. These are realities of life in the West, without a doubt.

- An interesting example of culturally created truth is the famous Almo Massacre, which was once thought to have been the biggest single Indian massacre in western history. The story came to light in the early 1900s that a train with 300 emigrants had been attacked near the present-day town of Almo, on the Utah-Idaho border. The emigrants were pinned down there for four days without water, and after several unsuccessful attempts to dig shallow wells, they were forced to turn their livestock loose. On the fourth night, five adults and a baby managed to escape, crawling on hands and knees (the baby's mother dragging the child by clutching its clothes in her teeth), and finally reached Brigham City, Utah. A party was sent out to the scene, but they could only bury the remains of the 295 murdered victims. In 1937, local citizens erected a memorial marker on the site to commemorate the tragedy.[9]

The most intriguing thing about this story is that there appears to be no objective corroboration of it at all: no accounts of the massacre in the daily journals and diaries of those who lived in the area at the time; no newspaper reports (especially striking, given the propensity of newspapers at that time to feature such items prominently); no archaeological evidence of bones, guns, tools, wagons; no agreement about the date (given variously as 1859, 1860, 1861). In other words, it now appears that the biggest massacre in the West never really happened. The historian Brigham Madsen concludes that the story grows out of lesser massacres and attacks which did indeed occur in the area and that the epic proportions of the narrative are testimony to "the hold such events have on people's minds." [10] While a historian might thus "demote" such a story because of its lack of verifiable detail, a folklorist would see its recurrence in both formal and vernacular circulation as a signal that, indeed, that "hold on people's minds" does not disappear in the light of factual analysis. I would go a step further and speculate on the possibility of a dramatization of racial fears, in addition to a tendency to project guilt, and a strong inclination to select and intensify topics which satisfy (or excite) cultural expectations as the driving forces behind such legendry.

Brigham Madsen and others report a considerable amount of evidence (diaries, pioneer recollections, court depositions, etc.) which suggests another, more macabre, subject which *never* shows up in the vernacular accounts of early life in the old West: it is the testimony that Indian raiders were accompanied and sometimes led by whites (with beards and blue eyes, speaking English and German). Still, we have yet to find family legends about how Grandpa rode and raped with his Shoshone buddies. It is as if, in spite of considerable data, such a thing never happened, while in spite of a lack of verification, the Almo Massacre did happen. This certainly represents not just a difference in opinion, but the construction of local reality.

This selective dramatization of cultural reality is nowhere more clearly visible, I think, than in Clyde Milner's recent work with Montana pioneer memoirs. In the early diaries of a Harriet Sanders—which are richly illustrated with detail, color, and event—there is a personal, eyewitness account of the trip west by wagon train, set down in the enthusiastic style of an excited young observer. Mrs. Sanders's memoirs, written in her old age, are full of wisdom, accumulated experience, and maturity, in addition to vivid accounts of how the family had to fight off the apparently daily attacks and provocations of the Indians. The day-to-day diaries, however, include only a single detailed reference to an Indian: a young woman in their traveling party fell into the water as they were crossing the Snake River, and an Indian man jumped in and saved her life. What can account for such a colossal discrepancy: was Mrs. Sanders a liar? Did she become senile? Milner suggests that she was taking on her culture's stories and sense of reality so thoroughly that (1) she could not separate her experiences from those talked about in her culture, (2) she felt because of their commonality that she had participated in them and could recollect them, (3) she could not construct a meaningful and true account without them, and (4) she would not and could not venture to cast herself as having lived in an *unreal* world, that is, a world in which Indians were helpful, retiring, or scarce. Milner concludes that while personal observation may control what one puts in a diary, memoirs are guided as much by the shared attitudes of the cultural audience as they are by the recollections of the authors.[11]

Lynwood Montell has shown how the legends and anecdotes about murders in the upland South are more accurate in their portrayal of local values about obligation to family, concepts of local folk law in contrast to outside formal law, and the frictions between insiders and outsiders, than they are about the "facts" of a given murder. But these are truths, nonetheless, which not only account for people's real actions but provide a local context in which those actions make local sense.[12] Barbara Allen has studied vernacular accounts of "heroic rides," episodes in which a young man rides for help or to carry a message or summon a doctor, and has found that the stories seem to be more about distance and the time needed to overcome it—perceived as the real factors of survival in the West—than about actual events.[13] Barry Lopez claims that there are few instances of wolves attacking humans in North America that cannot be explained by rabies; yet the folklore about wolves has certainly affected reality for both wolves and humans. They have become the predator-of-choice (replaced in some areas by the coyote), feared, hunted, almost exterminated in a frenzy which might easily be described as a paranoid counterattack on the untamable aspects of wilderness. When a rabid wolf wandered into Churchill, Manitoba, in 1926, the whole town apparently went berserk; by the time the wolf wandered back out of town (having bitten no one), it had been run over by a car, and six dogs and an Indian had been shot.[14] Such a scene would be hilarious in a movie; in life it testifies to a fear so real that it has to be shot at.

Less dramatic, perhaps, but equally interesting as a tableau scene of cultural value, is the story about the naming of Portland, Oregon. Even though it is mentioned in history books, this narrative functions more as a vernacular drama than as usable data, for it raises more questions than it answers, historically, while culturally it conveys a distillation of truth. In brief, two early settlers, both male, toss a coin to see if their community will be named after Boston, Massachusetts, or Portland, Maine. So much for data. The drama shows two *men* making the decision, *white* men at that, using possibilities drawn from their New England heritage and not from the new locale (their cousins in nearby Washington, after all, were naming cities after Indians and Indian tribes), and the decision is predicated on a *gamble*, not on democratic vote or opinion poll. A more compact and efficient cultural drama would be hard to find; it is a cameo of the forces behind Northwest history.

Historians of the Mormon West have dealt extensively with polygamy, but more often in sociological or genealogical terms than cultural. As we would expect, however, the topic of polygamy is not only emotionally loaded for many Mormons, it is inextricably bound up in family identity, ticklish questions about government suppression of religious freedom, and personal attitudes about female roles. Jokes and legends about polygamy thus function on a level deeper than that of mere oral history or personal recollection. A Swedish polygamist, on his way to court for a hearing about his citizenship, picnics in the shade of some cemetery trees with his three wives and leaves two of them there to wait in comfort. The judge asks about the other wives he is alleged to have; when he responds truthfully that they are in the graveyard, he gets his citizenship approved. Indeed, the problem of how to live one's religion and meet government requirements at the same time was a daily reality for a whole generation of Utah Mormons. Another family tells the story of a wife who—at an advanced age—was asked to accept a second, younger wife into the household. She went along with it; but according to the women in the family, even though her husband thoughtfully fixed up a room for her right above the master bedroom, she often "just got clumsy" and tipped over the chamber pot at night.

A Mormon friend from southern Utah recently told me that his grandfather had been hounded by his New England–born wife to provide a lawn for their desert ranch. He got so frustrated at the daily complaint that finally "he collected a bunch of the biggest lizards he could find. Then he made a little harness for each one, and every morning he'd herd them down to the river and fill 'em up on water. Then he'd just drive 'em back up into the yard, he said, and just beat the piss out of 'em." It is clear that the imagery of emotion is far more telling in stories like this than the data are verifiable (far more interesting, too). But the hyperbole in this story brings up another important genre of western expression which seems to have nothing at all to do with verifiable data at first blush. I refer to the tall tales, regional lies, artful exaggerations, and "blanket stretching" that typify much of western oral tradition.

In windy areas one hears that the cows have to be taught to stand on their hay, that the sand is blown out from around prairie dog holes (the animals fall and break their necks), that car lights are blown off the road, wells are blown over into the neighbor's yard, and that a hen was seen laying the same egg five times. In arid central Oregon, one hears a rancher say, "We measure the humidity by the amount of sand in the air," and "When it rains we keep the hired man in; we want all the water on the land," and "I got hit by one of them big rain drops and it knocked me out; they had to throw six buckets of sand in my face to bring me around." On the rainy Olympic Peninsula, a rain barrel tips over and the rain drives into the bunghole faster than it can flow out the open end; the farmer claims he watered his stock all summer on that one barrel of water.[15]

Folk lies, they are called, but anyone who has seen a tornado rip a house apart and leave the dresser sitting there with its photos intact or seen a two-by-four driven through a plate glass window without either being shattered does not have to go far to claim having seen a hen laying the same egg several times. The exasperation of ranching in dry or hot or flooded areas cannot be adequately expressed by, "My, it certainly gets hot here!" Hyperbole is the only viable language resource to articulate the extremes of experienced or perceived reality, whether that reality is constituted of weather or fear or frustration.

Of course, it is the local people, who share the local reality (as well as articulate its extremes), who know exactly where the hyperbole starts. When local temperature does go to extremes, when the rain does fall for fifty days without stopping, when the wind does blow a straw through a plank, then it is the local people who can best register the "reality" of it and express its effects on their lives and emotions. Indeed, in many areas, as Suzi Jones has shown, local people consciously use their local hyperbole to demarcate the difference between themselves and outsiders, who do not share enough information and attitude to know what is real.[16] When we remember that in some parts of the country "lies" may actually be told to strangers in such a way that the stranger has the sense of hearing the truth, we must realize how complicated the "objective" task of finding reality is. Reub Long, a rancher in central Oregon, was fond of telling a story about how a lost tourist interrupted him while he was whitewashing a desert rat. A neighbor had told him that the way to rid his place of unwanted rats was to catch a large one and whitewash it; the other rats would think it was a ghost and leave the place. Long and a large group of friends had caught a rat and had taken it out into the road so it could not escape; as they knelt on it, arguing about whether to paint it with the grain (to produce a smooth, shiny coat) or against the grain (more thorough, but not so attractive), a stranger drove down the road and stopped, asking what in the world they were doing out there. Reub Long's version in *The Oregon Desert* is a bit more polite than the one he often told friends; sharing the yarn with me once, he said: "Well, I got up and went up to this fella's car and I said, 'What's it to ya?' and he said, 'Well, what are you fellas doing there blocking the road?' and I says, 'Why, we're whitewashing a damn rat, what are you going to do about it?' and the first thing I knew, why this guy was backing up all the way down the road and out of sight, just as fast as he could go!"[17] Assuming that this incident actually occurred out in the lonely desert flats of central Oregon, there must be somewhere a tourist who still tells of being threatened by a group of crazy local buckaroos blocking the road. Whether anyone actually white-washed a rat and whether anyone actually believes that rats can be scared off by a whitewashed ghost are questions that are entirely off the subject compared with the dramatization of animosity and anxiety between insiders and outsiders.

The legends and lies I have referred to here are factually prob-lematic only on the most superficial level; seen more fully in their operational cultural contexts, they function the way good imagery and poetic diction do in literature generally: to convey and drama-tize more fully those abstract matters which cannot be well articu-lated and reexperienced in any other way. They need to be treated as expressions of shared value which are poetic in their formulation, cultural in their meaning, and historical in their impact upon peo-ple's actions. At the same time, we cannot overlook the fact that the intellectual or scholarly level of discourse is not immune to similar kinds of selection, interpretation, and foregrounding of shared attitudes about reality, for the poetic image of the West has had its effects on even the most "objective" thinkers. For many scholars, for example, the West is still very much the West of individual achievement, very much the West of cowboys and Indians, or of male occupations—mining, ranching, logging—seen as normal and central (while the most common female frontier occupations

are seen as marginal and exceptional). In spite of a general intellectual rejection of the Turner frontier thesis, the West is still usually
characterized by descriptions of frontier confrontations, east-to-
west geographical movement, and rural setting (all of which allow
us to overlook stable coastal settlements of eastern, urban, ethnically mixed populations). The West is presented as having fewer
class distinctions, so we often overlook the mass movements of
laborers by their virtual owners. The Indian is still the Vanishing
Redskin, even though some tribes are more numerous than ever
before; California, with more Indians and Indian reservations than
the rest of the country, with extremely rich—and early—ethnic
identity tying it together with the Hispanic Southwest, is often
described as if it were not a part of the West at all.

It seems quite clear that the realities of the West, as no doubt
those of other distinctive regions, are not to be fully perceived and
appreciated through the study of "objective" historical data alone;
for the "feel" of a region, its distinctive sense of place, is less a
function of fact than of accumulated human experience and response translated through the shared sets of values which animate
the culture. Since these values are demonstrably as well articulated
in vernacular forms as they are in intellectual publications, and
since the vernacular expressions are available to us in abundance, it
would seem folly to omit them in any serious consideration of
regional culture. It is my belief that any historical or cultural analysis which leaves out the vernacular material will simply provide an
inaccurate, incomplete account of cultural reality.

# Tornado Stories in the Breadbasket: Weather and Regional Identity

LARRY DANIELSON

*Environmental conditions in a region, as Barre Toelken suggests, can have a direct and profound impact, both physical and mental, on residents. That impact can be gauged from its treatment in regional folk expression. Along these lines, Larry Danielson examines the midwestern tornado stories to discover the role of tornadoes in regional consciousness. Drawing upon his lifelong experience as a midwesterner, Danielson identifies a characteristic feature of tornado stories—their emphasis on a bizarre image or visual detail of the everyday left undisturbed in the midst of chaos—as symbolizing the relationship between everyday life in the region and the threat of potential devastation.*

> "There's a cyclone coming, Em," [Henry] called to his wife; "I'll go look after the stock." Then he ran toward the sheds where the sows and horses were kept.
>
> Aunt Em dropped her work and came to the door. One glance told her of the danger close at hand.
>
> "Quick, Dorothy!" she screamed: "run for the cellar!" [1]

The rest is history. I've sometimes wondered how many children's imaginations, both through book and through film, have been informed by L. Frank Baum's description of the Kansas tornado that brought Dorothy to the Land of Oz. Other mass media narratives have also shaped our images of the midwestern tornado, for example, a vivid description in the popular "Little House" series by Laura Ingalls Wilder, the films *Country* and *Places in the Heart*, and the innumerable newspaper and television accounts of disaster aftermath, complete with dramatic photos and human-interest vignettes. [2]

I grew up in central Kansas with tornado stories, usually called forth by unsettled spring or summer weather or by newspaper coverage of twister strikes. In retrospect they seem to have expressed something significant about living on the prairie and about regional identity: the obvious importance of weather in agricultural life, providential intervention in human affairs, and the strength of Plains character in the face of natural disaster. The most forthright content pattern in the accounts familiar to me from everyday talk, however, concerns another matter: the incredible in the midst of the credible, the extraordinary consequence, the prairie baroque.

Tornado stories are commonplace in contemporary oral tradition of the central United States, and historical primary sources—diaries, letters, reminiscences, and newspaper accounts—suggest that such stories were compelling to the regional imagination in the past. Their content includes vivid descriptions of pretornado weather conditions, sighting the tornado funnel, its unpredictable path and behavior, its destructive consequences, remarkable survivals of human and animal life, and anomalous physical details noteworthy in the aftermath of the storm system. For example, in 1859 an observer in Iowa City, Iowa, wrote the *New York Daily Tribune:*

> Hastily, by the first mail, I inform you of one of the most fearful calamities that has ever happened hereabouts. Last evening, while yet it was light, there arose suddenly a violent wind, accompanied by strong indication of rain. In a few moments, the whole horizon became pitchy black, and the most vivid lightning darted athwart the sky. A terrible thunder-storm burst upon us. While yet it was raging fearfully, the sky suddenly appeared unclouded in the east for a space several degrees in width. Many of our citizens, who were watching from their windows the raging of the storm, discovered, instinctively at first, the rapid approach of an immense waterspout [tornado funnel]. The phenomenon was so unusual that the attention of hundreds was drawn to it. The appearance of the huge volume of water as it reached from earth to sky—swaying to and fro like a rope hung in the wind—was exceedingly grand. The water-spout [*sic*] remained in sight nearly fifteen minutes, when the sky became obscured, it was lost sight of. . . .
>
> The water-spout seems to have been from thirty to forty feet in diameter, and to have destroyed a large amount of property. Its extent was from seven to ten miles, and it is said to have traveled with great rapidity. In one instance, a

barn of Mr. Berry's was taken from its foundation, carried
some three hundred yards, thrown down and crushed into
a thousand fragments. A child of Mr. Walsh was taken up
and carried nearly 500 yards, thrown into a slough, but,
strange to say, escaped with its life. The spout appeared like
an immense funnel, and it seemed very near, for the whirl
and sparkle of the water could be plainly seen. But the mail
is already being made up, and you will probably learn from
other sources more concerning this great phenomenon.

P.S. As I am closing this letter I learn that eight are thus
far known to have been killed; but I have been unable to
ascertain any more names.[3]

More informal, less detailed stories are often shared in midwestern conversations, especially when spring and summer
weather becomes threatening. Narratives akin to the tall-tale tradition and an occasional ballad are to be found in the oral traditions of
twister country, but much more typical are brief accounts of the
eccentric incident, the freakish detail, the arresting artifact left in
the tornado's destructive path.[4] In time these stories become tradi-
tionalized in one's personal repertoire through their performance in
different storytelling situations. As they are told and retold, sometimes to the same audiences, their artistry is refined and their
treatment of selective details sharpened. Often they enter the
storm-story repertoire of captivated listeners, who may be family
members or friends. Their life is a vigorous one in midwestern talk.

My exploration of these materials has reminded me that we
should be cautious in ascribing too much significance to the dramatic narrative that meets our expectations of what "real folk narrative"
should be: extended, entertaining, elaborate, and classifiable
according to our conventional folk-narrative categories. Such stories about twisters exist, to be sure, and can be found in standard
collections, but I wonder whether or not they are to be trusted as
indexes to a regional identity shared by many people who live in the
same environment. Informal credible accounts that describe the
incredible are told more frequently. Everyday talk at home and at
work, in which such stories are freely exchanged, may provide a
more reliable index to regional identity than the remarkable narrator's entertaining and memorable performance. These kinds of
narratives seem to be an appropriate place to begin exploring the
relationship between traditional narrative theme and prairie identi-

ty. My research is based on surveys of primary and secondary historical documents concerning life in the Midwest and formal and informal interviews with midwesterners, very few of whom have experienced the catastrophic consequences of the tornado.[5]

Defining the region in question deserves some attention if we are to relate these narratives to a regional self-identification. A precise designation of the region fuses two discussions of the term separated by half a century. Walter Prescott Webb, in *The Great Plains*, divides the "Great Plains Environment" into three sub-regions: the High Plains, which contains the largely treeless, level, and semiarid areas running in a belt from North Dakota into Texas; the Prairie Plains, to the east, moving roughly from southeastern Minnesota, with intrusions into parts of Wisconsin and Illinois, into Texas, treeless and level; and the mountainous section to the west, treeless and arid.[6] Webb's Prairie Plains and High Plains boundaries neatly coincide with Joel Garreau's boundaries for the region he calls the "Breadbasket" in his study, *The Nine Nations of North America*. Garreau argues that the Breadbasket comprises a distinctive region because it, like the other eight "nations" of North America, is distinguished by a particular "web of power and influence," characteristic dialects and mannerisms, economy, and emotional allegiance from its citizens.[7] Both Webb and Garreau emphasize rough and changeable weather in their descriptions of this region. Writes Garreau: "Even the weather respects [these boundaries]. The Arctic winds that make Breadbasket winters so insufferable battle the high fronts off the Gulf of Mexico around these parts. Local meteorologists have been known to split their forecasts into two completely different sections to accommodate different conditions separated by only a few dozen miles. Not too surprisingly, the U.S. National Severe Storm Forecast Center is in Kansas City."[8]

This region also coincides with the "tornado belt" of the Great Plains, which runs north and slightly northeast from Texas through the flatlands into Canada.[9] The states of Texas, Oklahoma, Kansas, and Missouri, in fact, comprise the infamous "Tornado Alley," a designation that has been expanded to include states as far north as Minnesota.[10] The unstable weather systems created in the spring and summer by "cold air pushing in from across the Rocky Mountain summits [and riding] over the warm, moist Gulf air, while the entire weather system moves eastward," together with "a giant jet stream flowing in from the Pacific Ocean and racing eastward across the central plains," become a "vast weather cauldron," according to one authority. This radical climatic instability accounts for the proliferation of tornadoes in the region.[11] Tornadoes, then, are a fact of life in the Breadbasket, inextricably linked with topography and climate. It is no surprise that people in the region talk about them.

Their stories sometimes involve graphic descriptions of death and destruction, but other kinds of natural disasters effect larger numbers of human fatalities. Within the United States, only 2 percent of all tornadoes cause two-thirds of the deaths resulting from the storms, and the annual average of deaths due to tornadoes between 1924 and 1974 runs about 215 fatalities per year, somewhat fewer than deaths caused by lightning.[12] When a community or series of communities is hit, however, the grim consequences are dramatic. A tornado system rushing through Missouri, Illinois, and Indiana on March 18, 1925, took 689 lives.[13] It is cold comfort to the survivors of such a disaster to be told there are other phenomena more dangerous to human life. Nonetheless, the comparative statistics concerning the actual number of fatalities resulting from 20,886 tornadoes recorded in the United States between 1924 and 1974 may help account for the kinds of tornado narratives that circulate most frequently.[14]

Much more common than the death-and-destruction, or even remarkable deliverance-and-survival, narrative is the account that describes the bizarre consequences of the storm, uncolored by melodrama and tragedy. These may take the form of a relatively short narrative or a description in which narrative action is secondary. The tone of such accounts is largely unemotional, dramatic or incredible though the information may be. It is not unusual for these twister stories concerning the extraordinary to be told with some humor, although their purpose is not to ensnare the audience as with a lying tale. For example, one narrator in his forties recounted with delight the story of an air-borne police car caught in the path of a twister in central Kansas: "[The policeman] was sitting out on a hill somewhere watchin' for it to come and he . . . was supposed to come back to Lindsborg and tell everybody . . . and he claimed that he saw it coming and he decided to get goin' and put it in low gear and the wind came so fast that it lifted him up to where he could see out the window and see the fence outside of his window, which means that the car would've been four foot off the ground. . . . He just put it in second gear and came on into town."[15]

In a more prosaic vein, the same narrator described his cousin's curious discovery after another Kansas tornado had destroyed her school building, this time emphasizing the eccentric artifact: "when she came back [to the school] her desk was still sitting there, although the building had been obliterated, and her glasses were still sitting where she'd left them on top of the desk."[16]

A narrator in Illinois remembers a striking visual image from his Kansas childhood which struck him as both peculiar and provocative: "There was a Methodist church on Main Street that had a rather large iron cross . . . the cross was just balled up. Wasn't quite like a swastika, but it was bent so you couldn't recognize it as a cross. Some shingles missing on the roof of the church, and that was it, but it did take that cross and ball it up. I remember actually seeing that after it happened." A Kansan who had similarly experienced the power of a prairie tornado described another curiosity: "when I lived in Newton a tornado hit the outskirts of town and I fled for cover at that time. . . . the thing I remember about that was the filling station where . . . three walls were missing, one wall was remaining, and that was the wall that has the oil cans and everything. The shelves with the cans on it were still standing. There was a floor, and one wall, with things on the shelf."[17]

These narrative descriptions represent the tornado story in everyday exchange.[18] It is noteworthy and typical that in the case of the twisted cross and the extant service station wall in perfect order, the narrators said little about their own experience in the storm but focused primarily on its anomalous consequences. Such details also abound in printed narratives: photographs found remarkable distances from their frames, which remain undamaged on the living-room wall; straws and blades of grass blown into fence posts; two-by-fours driven through plate-glass windows without shattering the glass; vases of cut flowers left intact on a table in the midst of a disintegrated farm home; crates of eggs carried through the air five hundred yards without cracking a shell.[19]

Popular literature sources also emphasize the extraordinary. W.J. Humphreys in his chatty *Weather Rambles* writes:

So inconsiderate is the tornado that it has no respect for bird nor beast nor human being. It maims, kills and mangles any living thing. But, as already stated, the gruesome is here tabu. Returning, then, to the essentially curious: the "twister," without doing bodily harm, has pulled the wool from a sheep's back, stripped people of every stitch of clothing, and time and again left chickens with never a feather sticking in their skins. . . . On one occasion a tornado, on demolishing a particular railroad depot, laid one of its window sashes on a neighboring lawn and placed a heavy iron weight on it without breaking a single pane of glass. The same tornado smashed a dresser to kindling but left its mirror standing beside a fence some distance away entirely uninjured. On another occasion a house was torn to pieces and the kitchen cupboard, filled with dishes, carried off but set down so gently that not a single dish was broken.[20]

Laura Ingalls Wilder, drawing on her personal experiences of growing up in the Midwest, describes an occurrence similar to those described by Humphreys. As the narrator's father and her husband-to-be visit with a South Dakota homesteader and his family whose house, stable, farm implements, and animals have disappeared in the path of a tornado,

one of the children noticed a small dark object high in the clear sky overhead. It did not look like a bird, but it appeared to be growing larger. They all watched it. For some time it fell slowly toward them, and they saw that it was a door. It came gently down before them. It was the front door of this man's vanished claim shanty.

It was in perfect condition, not injured at all, not even scratched. The wonder was, where it had been all those hours, and that it had come slowly down from a clear sky, directly over the place where the claim shanty had been.

"I never saw a man more chirked up than he was," said Pa. "Now he doesn't have to buy a door for his new shanty. It even came back with the hinges on it."[21]

These accounts, both in oral tradition and in print, all seem to be verifiable as the historical consequences of tornado activity. Sober meteorologists, like the nonspecialist narrator, find them credible testimonies to the erratic behavior of the twister.[22]

John Steuart Curry, the twentieth-century regionalist painter born in Kansas, provides the last example of the extraordinary. Curry's work is not folk art, but the experience of growing up in rural Kansas influenced much of his painting. His second wife has reminisced about her husband's fascination with prairie storms: "There was always food in the [Kansas] storm cellar and they would go and stay in the cellar, though John really never encountered a tornado. When he went back at one period, there had been a twister and he went to the locale and saw the devastation. That's where he made the sketches of chickens rolled up in chicken wire. We have some drawings of cattle still in stanchions, but no barn around them. The buildings were all gone, still the cattle were there."[23]

One of Curry's well-known paintings is "The Tornado," executed in 1929. It depicts a rural Kansas family fleeing to the storm cellar as a malevolent twister races toward their farm.[24] The next year he visited his parents' home in Kansas, shortly after a tornado had swept through the area only a few miles from his parents' farm. About the same time his mother wrote a detailed account of the storm, and in addition to describing the resultant damage, injury, and deaths, she not surprisingly noted its bizarre consequences:

> At the Everett Pence's place the barn was completely swept away, but left the cows unharmed in the stanchions, although almost every other animal on the place was destroyed. When the cows were released, the stanchions fell over.
>
> The body of another house was completely wrecked and swept away. The floor of the kitchen was moved twenty feet from the foundation, stripped bare with the exception of part of the wall and the cupboard shelves, on which were kitchen utensils and two oil lamps with glass globes intact.[25]

Within the year Curry painted "After the Tornado," a visual statement that expresses directly the theme of anomaly in tornado lore. It depicts a cheerful doll, at ease in the corner of an overstuffed parlor chair which stands before a parlor rug—the undisturbed home furnishings and child's toy surrounded by twisted debris, the remains of a Kansas farm home.[26] The painting, a sophisticated creation by a professional artist intent on interpreting the region that shaped him, capsulizes the notion of the eccentric consequence found so often in oral traditions and vernacular print accounts about tornadoes in the Breadbasket.

Admittedly, some tornado stories are more dramatic. They bear the recognizable marks of traditionalization over time and may approach more closely our conventional expectations of the legend. In the course of my research on vernacular tornado stories, a friend told me of an acquaintance whose aunt had been sucked up the chimney by a tornado. I contacted the woman, a middle-aged high school teacher, and she provided me with a glimpse into the legend-making process. She had heard the family story about twenty years ago and remembered that it concerned her husband's aunt "drawn up the chimney and deposited in the yard." Once the prospective narrator knew I was interested in the story, she asked her husband about it, and found that she had unconsciously changed it over the years. She later had a conversation with her husband's aunt, who had survived the experience and revealed the nature of the historical event. The teacher then related it to me:

> She [the aunt of the narrator's husband] was in bed and the bed was picked up and put out in the yard. . . . She said, first of all, that she would believe any story she'd heard about tornadoes, because she's heard so many and it's such a preposterous thing that happened. . . . She was eight years old [in 1922] and she and her cousin or niece were in bed [during] this terrifically noisy storm. . . . So they'd gone downstairs with her mother and got in her mother's bed and the mother was standing beside the bed and when the wind came . . . she grasped the two little girls and held on, and, in fact they were all together then in the garden with the covers on and everything, and the bed was near by. She remembers that her father and brother had come down-stairs . . . saw a fiery ball coming at them across the fields. And they were hurt. They were blown about and the father had to go to the hospital. . . . And they had just bought the farm that they lived on and had a lot of buildings, barns and henhouses. . . . All of that . . . was reduced to kindling. When neighbors came to clean up they just came with wagons and rakes and picked up fragments from the fields. . . . The three of them, with their covers on, were deposited in the garden and the bed was near by. . . . I'm the only one [who ever got the chimney detail into the story]. . . . She says she remembers her mother having clutched them so tightly that her mother's hands were bruised.[27]

Such accounts are compelling both to narrator and to audience, but in my research experience they are unusual. Less dramatic narrative descriptions of bizarre consequences are shared more frequently. In the earlier versions of this story, which had been a part of the narrator's repertoire for some twenty years, she had unconsciously added the striking chimney detail. It became the narrative core, in fact, and when I first heard the story from the narrator's friend, it was that event which functioned as its central tableau scene.[28] The informant later realized that she had unknowingly revised the story through the years, noting that no other family member referred to the chimney in their accounts of the tornado. The significant change in the story, corrected and eliminated by the narrator's later discussion with her husband and his aunt, suggests the complex roles of time, creative imagination, and oral transmission in the transformation of first-person experience story into third-person family legend.

Nevertheless, even in this extended, dramatic account, we find the familiar anomaly—the juxtaposition of the commonplace with the idiosyncratic—and it is noted twice in the same story: the two children and woman wrapped in their bed covers in the midst of the family garden, the bed nearby. Are these stories told merely because they are interesting and make for good conversation when talk moves to tornadoes?

A number of folk-narrative scholars have pointed out the importance of the visual-image narrative, and these tornado stories illustrate its power, in both personal testimonial and third-person accounts.[29] I would like to suggest a possible interpretation of these eccentric visual images in everyday tornado stories, which in turn provide the raw content for the extended tall tales and legends about twisters.[30] The twisted cross on the undamaged church roof, the de-feathered chicken, the straw driven into the fence post, and all the other striking images encountered in oral and print literature about tornadoes in the Breadbasket perhaps function as something more than entertaining anomalies to be appreciated for their own sake.

Meteorologists affirm that the storm which creates such idiosyncrasies is itself unpredictable, eccentric, freakish. Its path can be erratic; it can touch ground, ascend suddenly, and descend as abruptly; it can speed up, slow down, or halt in one location; it can follow a straight or a looping path; it can double-back on its own path.[31] More generally, the weather systems on the Great Plains, which also affect contiguous areas to the east, develop quickly and forcefully. A regional proverb, in fact, argues, "Only a fool or a stranger forecasts weather on the Plains."[32] The region's range of temperatures and climatic extremities is dramatic and may involve high winds, tornadic activities, hailstorms, blizzards, drought, and deluges causing flash floods. The weather in the Breadbasket can change suddenly from one extreme to another in ways unbelievable to those living in more moderate or more predictable climates.[33] Such climatic drama not only makes good talk. More important, it affects human life in manifold and significant ways, even in today's age of technological wonders, and can destroy the Breadbasket crops that are essential to the economy of the region.

It is not surprising, then, that Breadbasket people talk a lot about the weather. The topic is used to open conversation and can provide its meat. Television and radio weather reports are followed closely. In traditional contexts, weather beliefs and sayings comprise a major component in the folklore of the region.[34] Regional vernacular art and artifact also reflect a preoccupation with the weather. For example, the Kansas State Network, a weather information service, published a calendar in 1981 devoted exclusively to Kansas weather. Its twelve illustrations dramatized the range of Kansas climate and were accompanied by captions citing remarkable climatic phenomena, three of them related to tornadic activities.[35]

If the weather can change suddenly, and if the weather plays an important role in the regional economy, it is to be expected that people in the region follow it closely. And it is to be expected that certain kinds of weather stories will be shared over and over again and invested with meanings particular to the region. Possibly, then, these iconographic accounts of twister consequences crystallize the more general idea of Great Plains and midwestern weather. The bizarre imagery testifies in efficient messages to its power, its unpredictability, its idiosyncrasy. The features of the weather also help to explain why the narratives so often focus on the extraordinary detail. The *threat* of a tornado and its destructive force is a fact of everyday life in the region even while its actual occurrence is rare. The very ordinariness of the objects described in the stories and newspaper accounts, and in Curry's paintings, as left undisturbed affirms that life can and does go on even under the extraordinary circumstances imposed on midwesterners by climatic conditions. Without self-aggrandizement, and with something that approaches self-effacement (a Breadbasket personality trait familiar to me as a native midwesterner), the nature of Breadbasket weather is capsulized in everyday talk. The accounts deal with the incredible, but their narrators testify credibly through such stories that the extraordinary meteorological event is a central reality in their lives.

The tornado is dangerous: it can destroy, maim, and kill, and its threatening presence lingers in the midwestern imagination from spring through early fall each year. Fortunately, however, twisters roar through comparatively few midwestern lives. Tornado stories, with their juxtaposition of the commonplace with the baroque, the familiar homely detail with violent idiosyncrasy, may be narrative expressions of midwestern character. Even though possible climatic disaster lingers just beyond the horizon, day-to-day life is lived confidently and without histrionics. By implication, such narratives also modestly imply a covert pride in coping with and surviving such an unpredictable and potentially dangerous climatic environment. They communicate without bluster and hyperbole: "I live in the midst of possible meteorological violence, capable of destroying human life and economy, and I endure." They are an effective, entertaining means of expressing a distinctive identification with one's regional home, accessible to all, whether a gifted storyteller or not.

In the mid-1960s, returning on a Greyhound bus from the East Coast to my home in central Kansas, my traveling companions and I watched boiling, greenish clouds roll in across the prairie. An urbane mother sitting in front of me, obviously from out-of-state, informed her wide-eyed young daughter, "We're in Kansas, the storm center of the nation." I felt proud.

# "One Reason God Made Trees": The Form and Ecology of the Barnegat Bay Sneakbox

## MARY HUFFORD

*In both Larry Danielson's essay and this one by Mary Hufford, the central issue is how the relationship between the natural environment of a region and the people who live there is articulated in folk cultural forms. Whereas Danielson focused on narrative, Hufford examines an article of material culture: a small boat made and used by duck hunters in the Pine Barrens region of southern New Jersey. Hufford offers a systematic analysis of the Barnegat Bay sneakbox as a resonant symbol of the connections that residents draw among themselves, the wetlands that serve as their hunting grounds, and the birds they stalk. Because the boat is carefully crafted for a peculiar set of local conditions, it becomes a unique marker of regional identity for the man who makes it, owns it, and uses it.*

Water is everywhere in southern New Jersey, its comings and goings engendering the rhythm of regional lifeways. In the Pine Barrens, rainfall gathers underground in the Cohansey Aquifer, surfaces in freshwater swamps and feeder streams, and is captured for a while in cranberry reservoirs before coursing its way into saltier waters. Some of it flows out through brackish tidal marshes to the east and south, where it is again detained by muskrat trappers and salt-hay farmers. The interplay of this water system with an ice-age legacy of varied soils and land forms yields a diversity of wetlands, and these wetlands support the region's complex of traditional lifeways.

While the Pine Barrens—with its cranberry plantations, blueberry farms, and logging operations—and Barnegat Bay—with its salt-hay meadows, fishing communities, and boatyards—look like two very different habitats, the forested region north of the Mullica River reaching eastward from the cranberry watershed around Chatsworth to the coast is best thought of as one cultural region,

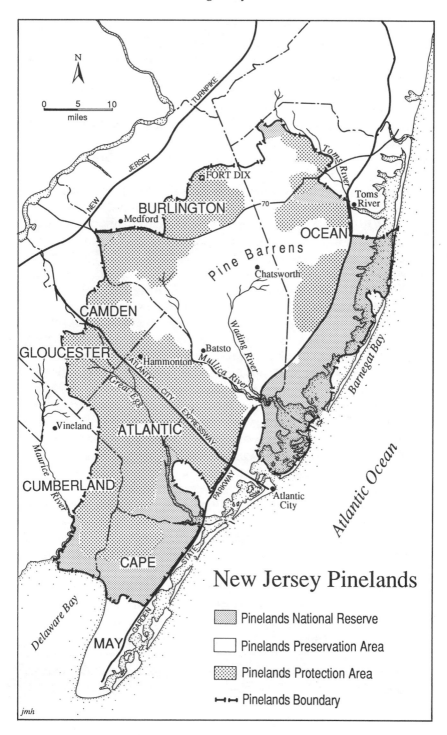

New Jersey Pinelands

Pinelands National Reserve

Pinelands Preservation Area

Pinelands Protection Area

⊢⊶⊣ Pinelands Boundary

comprising interdependent subregions. The tendency among natives to shift their attention from the bay to the upland forest or vice versa when resources in one area or another are depleted makes it a mistake to consider the subregions in isolation. The local maxim, "You can always make a buck in the woods or a dollar on the bay," celebrates the versatility that for woodsmen and baymen alike continues to be a matter of pride. Shared participation over the past two centuries in this geographically rooted ethos is related to a persisting self-awareness of membership in such subregional folk groups as Pineys and Baymen.[1]

Both Barnegat Bay and the Pine Barrens are located within the million-acre tract designated by Congress in 1978 as the Pinelands National Reserve. The term "pinelands" is a portmanteau word conflating "Pine Barrens" and "wetlands." In contrast to the Pinelands National Reserve, an "ad hoc" region, Barnegat Bay and the Pine Barrens are ontic regions, "owing their existence to certain geographical, social and cultural 'facts.'"[2] These geographical, social, and cultural facts combine to manifest what human ecologists call a "socionatural system."[3] Humans sharing in such a system, who in fact do much to shape it, are bound together and distinguished from outsiders by the intimate knowledge they have of the environment and its workings.[4] In South Jersey a sense of intimacy with the landscape is professed in sayings like "You can go away from the Pines but you can't get the sand out of your shoes" or "Let me die with the salt in my ears."

This intimacy with the landscape is also expressed in the range of tools, architectural forms, and artifacts devised for shaping, traversing, and harvesting the region, for dwelling in it, and returning to its pasts. Such artifacts, products of the kind of esoteric knowledge that helps to define regional folk groups, may be seen as indexes to that knowledge, compact means for storing and retrieving it. And these artifacts, which illuminate boundaries between insiders and outsiders, also serve as portals of entry through which outsiders may formally encounter regional culture. For natives they also serve as thresholds across other boundaries, entryways to alternative realms ongoingly constructed within the region.[5]

Throughout South Jersey, in backyards of woodland towns and coastal villages alike, one is likely to come upon an ingenious artifact, a regional hallmark that links the subregions. Looking over the assortment of vehicles, machine parts, woodpiles, bird houses, outbuildings, and dog pens marking many native yards, one's eye may fall upon an overturned cedar hull, shaped like a giant pump-kin seed, its hue a drab brownish green. It is obviously a boat, but a very odd-looking one, with no keel, stem, topsides, or chine. It may be in pristine condition or in an advanced state of disrepair, but in either case it could be more than fifty years old. Most local people, and duck hunters from other regions, recognize it instantly as a Barnegat Bay sneakbox.

The Barnegat Bay sneakbox, a small duck-hunting skiff that first appeared in South Jersey's backwaters in the mid-nineteenth cen-tury, offers a striking example of a form poised at the nexus of geography, society, and culture. Tradition holds that the first craft emerged in 1836 in the workshop of Hazelton Seaman of West Creek, New Jersey. According to Nathaniel Bishop, the eighteenth-century adventurer who first popularized the boat far beyond its native waters, Seaman was "a boatbuilder and expert shooter of wild-fowl [who] conceived the idea of constructing for his own use a low-decked boat, or gunning punt, in which when its deck was covered with sedge, he could secrete himself from the wildfowl while gunning on Barnegat and Little Egg Harbor Bays. . . . While secreted in his boat . . . hidden by a covering of grass or sedge, the gunner could approach within shooting distance of a flock of un-suspecting ducks: and this being done in a sneaking manner, the baymen gave her the sobriquet of sneakbox." [6] George Heinrichs, a third-generation sneakbox builder in New Gretna, attributes the form of the sneakbox to the meadows, the interstitial salt marshes where black ducks and other "puddlers" are found feeding on eel grass. It therefore has the draft for which it is celebrated, a draft shallow enough, as the saying goes, "to follow a mule as it sweats up a dusty road." Its spoon-shaped hull enables it to glide through areas marked as land on coastal maps, areas that are sometimes flooded and sometimes dry.

The traditional dimensions of the sneakbox (twelve feet long by four feet amidships) fits it to the social structure of independent yet sociable gunners. It is large enough to accommodate one man, or a man and his boy, together with scores of decoys, yet small enough for him to pull over the spits of land that riddle the meadows. A "V-notch," the width of a sneakbox cut into a spit between North Pond and Barnegat Bay, bears the name "Draggin' Cross Place" for that precise act. Tradition links the hollow decoys indigenous to Bar-negat Bay to the skiff's compact size. "Barnegat decoys are hollow," said John Holloway, a local carver. "They made 'em light for one

BARNEGAT BAY SNEAKBOX
Winter Sailing Rig · 1876

Fig. 2. The Barnegat Bay Sneakbox. *Drawing by Anthony Hillman, an artist and carver in Seaville, New Jersey. Copyright 1976.*

reason: all of 'em went on a Barnegat sneakbox, and they're carryin' about a hundred. If you're rowin' or sailin' this boat, you want 'em as light as possible, and as many as possible. They made 'em light and small."[7]

Made of cedar from the inland swamps to operate in places where fresh and salt waters converge, the craft represents wetland environments in constant flux. It synthesizes the observations that generations of Pineys and Baymen have compiled of water, air, land, wood, mud, man, ducks, and seasonal changes, anticipating and finely discriminating among a wide range of conditions. Its versatility and self-sufficiency remain a marvel to contemporary users who cherish these qualities in themselves.

Recently in Manahawkin a group of neighbors gathered in Ed Hazelton's "Bull Room," a home museum where he entertains visitors, many of whom have been growing old together all their lives. Hazelton, who claims common ancestry with Hazelton Seaman, is a retired carpenter in his seventies. Also in their seventies are Bill Cranmer, Eppie Falconburg, and Hurley Conklin. All have hunted ducks, carved decoys, and built small watercraft. Bill Oler, a man in his thirties, apprenticed himself for three winters to Hurley Conklin, the decoy carver he most wanted to "style off of." When asked what makes a sneakbox so good for duck hunting, the men responded with a collaborative, thickly textured description of the boat. Their discourse reenacts in a small way the collective imagination behind the making of regional artifacts.

"It doesn't draw any water really," began Bill Oler.

"It doesn't draw any water," Ed Hazelton agreed.

"It gets you around," said Bill.

"Easy to hide," Ed added.

"Well, a sneakbox," drawled Hurley Conklin, "it's easier to go and better for the weather, and you only got a little hole to get into, and you can keep dry into it and everything else. There's shelves along the sides—"

"You have your decks for your decoys," Ed pointed out.

"—you can carry everything right in that one boat," Hurley went on.

"Sure," said Bill Cranmer, "it's quite seaworthy for its size."

"Yeah!" Ed interjected. "God! Yeah!"

"Ice hook," Hurley remembered, "and our oars, you got everything right there in one place."

"You can tow it," said Bill Oler, launching into a litany of its locomotive possibilities. "You can pull it, you can push it, you can row it—"

"Sail it," prompted Ed.

"You can pole it, you can sail it," resumed Bill Oler.

"Outboard motor," supplied Ed.

"You can do just about anything," Bill Oler concluded.

"And go anywheres with it," Ed added.

"You can even pull it out on the ice," said Hurley. "You got an ice hook."

"Yup," said Ed.

"Yup," said Bill Oler.

"Carry an ice hook with you in the wintertime," Ed elaborated. "*There's* one on the wall." And he pointed.

"You can pull a sneakbox right out onto it," Hurley informed us.

Bill Oler thought of another means of propulsion. "You can also push your sneakbox with a pair of boots," he said. "One foot in, one foot out."

Fig. 3. Reminiscing in Ed Hazelton's "Bull Room," a home museum and local gathering place in Manahawkin. From left: Bill Oler, Hurley Conklin, Bill Cranmer, and Ed Hazelton. *Photo by Dennis McDonald, courtesy Smithsonian Institution Office of Folklife Programs.*

"You can do anything," said Ed. "Like a skateboard—sail 'em on the ice, they have runners on them."

"They have runners onto the bottom," reiterated Hurley. "You can pull 'em on the ice. And go along with the wind on top of the ice."[8]

The sneakbox is made to move, unhampered by anything it might encounter in marsh or bay. The classic boat is fitted with mast-hole, centerboard well, and rudder for sailing, and with oarlocks for rowing. In recent decades, a small mount for an outboard motor has been added. The sprit sails come in winter and summer versions, and a retractable centerboard keeps the boat from sideslipping under sail. This centerboard is angled so that obstacles in shallow waters push it up into the well rather than impede the boat's progress. Runners attached to the hull convert the boat to a sailing sled during icy weather, when gunners also use an accessory ice hook with two different attachments for pulling the boat through "porridge" (slushy) and "pane" (hard) ice. A canvas spray curtain, locally called a "breakwater" or "windbreaker," is traditionally made by the builder's wife. When fastened to the deck the spray curtain protects the gunner from wind and spray. The deck, rounded and planked-over, also deflects water, and its traditional tongue-and-groove joinery makes it watertight. A sloping transom helps in the often necessary task of rowing backward in channels too narrow to turn around in. The broad beam of the sneakbox keeps it from capsizing in rougher open waters.

"They are very seaworthy." said George Heinrichs. "My grandfather used to say that if you could cover the hatch up you could go to England in one of them."[9]

The boat is also made to stand still, to function as a hiding place. When the hunting season was longer, sneakboxes appeared in two different hues: dead-grass green for autumn, and winter white for snow. The centerboard well accepts a daggerboard for anchoring the boat in a V-notched piece of marsh, transforming it from a means of transportation into a stationary duck blind. The sprit sail can be taken down, mast and all, for storage inside the boat. The rudder is detachable. The hinged oarlocks, held upright by a movable stanchion when the gunner is rowing, can be folded down, and the decoy rack, held together with hooks and eyes when transporting decoys on the stern deck, may be removed to diminish the boat's profile.

The gunner further disguises the smooth, sleek lines of the stripped-down skiff with marsh vegetation, and then reclines in the boat with his rifle and duck call to await a migrating flock which he can lure within shooting range. Again the broad beam is pressed into service, keeping the boat stiff and steady when the gunner fires a shotgun with powerful recoil.

The boats are further fitted to meet gunners' needs for comfort. Some boats have two hatches, one for the gunner, the other for his dog or his boy. Some hatches are custom-made. "They used to build a boat special for a man," said Sam Hunt, a sneakbox builder in Waretown. "He used to lay down on the ground and they'd draw a circle around him and build a hatch so his belly could stick out."[10] Shelves on either side of the hatch are for storing provisions, such as food, beverages, duck calls, and cartridges. Small holes in the ribs keep water from collecting in one section of the boat, and a false bottom keeps the gunner dry. A hasp lock on the hatch cover turns the boat into a locker at dock or garage.

Insulating the insides with salt hay, hunting guides could spend a cold January night in such a "gunning bed," as the setup was called, in order to lay claim to a good spot, which varied from year to year with the weather conditions. "It all depended," said Ed Hazelton.

> It all depended where you would gun it. The bay and the shore and the islands are very irregular, and down through the years—goin' back a couple hundred years—the old timers, our ancestors gunnin' out there, they knew where the ducks were travelling, on what winds. So they passed the word on to me.
>
> They said, "Ed, when the wind's southeast you want to gun such-and-such a point. Now when the wind's northwest, you want to gun such-and-such a point. The ducks'll be travellin' there; the wind'll be pushin' 'em over; they won't fight it; they'll go easy; it's gonna pay 'em over; it'll make 'em pay over. You want to be there tomorrow."
>
> So you just learn from experience, and what our ancestors have told us, what point to gun and when, and what hours to gun, see?[11]

The sneakbox is built, as the artist, duck hunter, and connoisseur and miniaturizer of local boats Anthony Hillman put it, "in the spirit of flexibility."[12] It articulates the polar extremes of fluctuation encountered by gunners on South Jersey marshes and bays: stationary and mobile, solid and liquid, rough and smooth, windy and calm, deep and shallow, land and water, airborne and earthbound.

This flexibility promotes the use of the boat in other contexts. Though designed with duck hunting in mind, the sneakbox lends itself to a variety of other uses like tending traps, crabbing, harvesting "cut-outs" (mussels forced to the surface by frozen mud) in the winter meadows, and fishing on the bay in summer. According to Ed Hazelton, it was the perfect emergency vehicle for navigating flooded streets in Bayside, also known as "Mud City": "We had to get around the streets in sneakboxes and go from house to house and come all the way up to Hilliard Boulevard and come on up into town with your boat to get people's groceries and take 'em back down to 'em. A sneakbox is so low-slung, it's the perfect boat for that kind of thing." Other uses, from coffee tables to coffins, are reported on and contemplated. "Hell," wrote Henry Hegeman. "I'm seriously considering being buried in mine."[13]

The artifact relies to a high degree on traditional knowledge of inland as well as coastal environs, articulating the cultural links between woodland and shore communities. Traditionally, men who felled the cedar in freshwater swamps farther inland knew the needs of their coastal customers and could read beneath the shaggy bark the outlines of "settin' poles," stakes for fishnets and clamlots (territory in the Bay leased from the state for growing and harvesting clams), and boat boards for Jersey garveys and Barnegat sneakboxes. To supply such boards, which have to be "clear," or knot-free, a tree has to be at least eighty years old. Harry Shourds, a local decoy carver and hunter, gets his wood from the Great Cedar Swamp near Dennisville, where George Brewer has a logging operation. "Brewer really knows his wood," said Shourds. "He knows what's good for carving, for boats, and for shingles."[14]

"Jersey" cedar is widely touted as the best wood for fitting boats to the contours of meadows and bays at the region's edge and is celebrated for its capacity to withstand the stresses imposed by variable weather conditions. Recognizing this, Bishop wrote: "No wood used in boatbuilding can compare with the white cedar in resisting the changes from a wet to a dry state and vice versa. The tree grows tall and straight. The lower part of the trunk with the diverging roots furnish knee timbers and carlins for the sneakbox." Jersey cedar is also exalted by Barnegat baymen for its superiority over fiberglass. "Fiberglass doesn't handle itself in water the way that cedar does," said Joe Reid, a Waretown boatbuilder. "Cedar takes in just the right amount of water. When it's first put there, it tends to sit right on top of the water and settles down. Then it handles really well. You can't beat cedar for a boat." Fiberglass is too noisy. "A duck can hear it a mile away," said Heinrichs. To at least one enthusiast, sneakboxes are a raison d'être for trees. "Jersey sneakboxes must be one reason God made trees," wrote Pemberton Drinker. Boatbuilders maintain that only cedar can provide the compound curves that a classic sneakbox requires, where the bottom joins the top in a "feather edge." Pine is too heavy, and plywood cannot take the compound curves. "When I can't get cedar no more," said Heinrichs, "why, I'll just have to quit building sneakboxes."[15]

"The sneakbox," said Bill Oler, "is your number one tool." As a tool, the sneakbox lends itself not only to hunting ducks, but to the building of identity. "The tools of one's trade," wrote Mihaly Csikszentmihalyi and Eugene Rochberg-Halton, "perhaps more than any other set of objects, help to define who we are as individuals." [16] As a tool, the sneakbox enters into the shaping of individuals who are regionally distinctive.

Erving Goffman defines a region as "any place that is bounded to some degree by barriers to perception. Regions vary, of course, in the degree to which they are bounded and according to the media of communication in which the barriers to perception occur." [17] Though he is using "region" as an analytical concept for exploring the boundaries of social behavior in varied settings and not defining it as a cultural/geographic entity, there is a sense in which his definition is useful here. The sneakbox is a medium of communication that both traces and traverses barriers between insiders and outsiders.

The sneakbox slices between the worlds of the marsh and of everyday life; between the worlds of men and of women; between those who have inherited the right to build sneakboxes and those who simply figure out how; between the worlds of duck hunters and strangers to duck hunting; and between the worlds of waterfowl and men. The boat comprises a distinctive response to distinctively regional conditions, a tool whereby local men distinguish themselves as inhabitants of a singular region. "It's to this area," said Bill Oler. "Now down south they use bush boats or scullin' boats, and on the Delaware River their boat was totally different. North of here they had longer boats and they had higher-sided boats, 'cause I guess they had worse weather. So I guess everybody's got something built into their own area. Inland I guess they'll use a lot of canoes or john boats, little flat-bottom boats."

The production of sneakboxes is said to rely less on technical skill than on an ineffable relationship between their makers and their environment. In local tradition a mysterious charter makes it possible for some people to build sneakboxes while others fail, a charter related more to lifestyle and genealogy than to virtuosity with wood, as Bishop wrote: "The sneakbox requires a peculiar talent to build—the kind of talent which enables one man to cut out a perfect axehandle, while the master carpenter finds it difficult to accomplish the same thing. The best yacht-builders in Ocean County generally fail in modeling a sneak-box, while many second-rate mechanics along the shore, who could not possibly construct a yacht that would sail well, can make a perfect sneak-box." [18] The boat is notoriously difficult to build, and jigs and patterns are jealously guarded. Contemporary builders proudly report that their predecessors eschewed patterns. George Heinrichs points out that the fifty-year-old sneakbox awaiting repairs in his backyard was built by his grandfather, Gus Heinrichs, "by eye."

"Now my grandfather never had patterns," said Heinrichs. "If he did, nobody knows what he done with them. He built it from knowledge, and what he done, he handed down."[19]

According to Heinrichs, the fundamental secret of the Heinrichs sneakbox resides in the curve preserved by his grandfather's jig (a form that governs the shape of any sprung-timbered boat) to which the centerboard (or "set-up plank") is bolted during construction, to which in turn all ribs, transom, and adjacent bottom planks are attached. The profile of the entire boat is thus cued by the jig. Heinrich's father devised numbered patterns for the sawn-and-joined cedar ribs, no two of which were shaped identically.

The model on which the early boatbuilders relied was an idea about how humans and the environment interacted: their perception of the socionatural system. Contemporary boatbuilders now rely on patterns that crystallize those ideas, but they continue to distinguish between those individuals who are merely capable of building the boat and those who are entitled to do so. It is true that a skilled and canny woodworker could, by studying the construction of an old sneakbox, produce a replica. But those who see themselves as rightful heirs to the original process, bequeathed to them in tools and patterns, refuse legitimacy to the replica. Such builders conserve sneakbox building as a legacy, a process vital to the maintenance of regional and family identity, to be transmitted only to blood relatives. "I've been in the boat business all my life," said Heinrichs. "It's in the blood. My father and all of his family were boatbuilders. We're strictly a boatbuilding family."[20]

Heinrichs is under an oath he made to his dying father not to let the patterns out of the family. Said Heinrichs, "I made a promise to my father that if I didn't build boats, and my brother didn't, that I'd cut up the patterns and destroy them. Because it's his pattern, and no one has ever copied it. The Heinrichs sneakbox will die if I don't continue with it."[21] Thus sneakbox construction and membership in a regional folk group are made to be tightly interdependent.

Making the acquisition difficult seems in some cases to whet the appetite for it, both enhancing the value of the skill and distinguishing the man who owns it. John Chadwick, another builder in Barnegat, is heir to the J. Howard Perrine boatworks, which was in its heyday a leading manufacturer of sneakboxes and sails. He learned the craft from his father, who forbade him to take notes, ostensibly to keep the secret from leaking out. From memory then, in his room at night, John Chadwick jotted the plans down. Like Heinrichs, he shields the information from strangers: "There was a fellow come in here a few months ago, wanted to know everything about building this boat—wanted me to teach him how. And I said, you know, I couldn't do it. There's just something about it. It's all information that's been in the family, from my father, my grandfather, my uncle—you just can't go givin' it all away to strangers." [22]

Not only does the sneakbox play an important role in the task of self-definition, but it enhances the experience of losing oneself, an avowed function of the meadows for men in the region.

Related to the task of identity building is the work of "taking the other"—imagining the world from alternative vantage points. [23] Like the place requested by Archimedes, the sneakbox affords a place to stand outside of the world of everyday life and an opportunity to experience the world from the perspective of another species. Living along the flyways of migratory fowl, in other words, offers people a regionally distinctive way to define themselves as humans over and against other species. [24]

The boat is not only indexical, it is iconic, used in creating an appearance that "won't make the duck nervous," as John Holloway put it. Contrary to the boat's etymology, gunners do not sneak up on flocks of feeding ducks, but rather concentrate on the skies, crafting an illusion of animation on the water with inanimate objects to draw the interest of living birds. With its spoon-shaped belly the sneakbox lends ducklike contours to the human form, and with a little camouflaging, it is made to converge at its horizons with the surrounding water and marshes. The sneakbox, then, with its carefully fashioned rig of decoys, is a portable kit for crafting landscapes not only attractive to ducks but delightful to hunters who insert themselves into the ducks' milieu. "There's nothing like being out there," said Hurley Conklin, "in your nice little sneakbox, with a new gun, and your own well-made decoys all around you in the water." [25]

The sneakbox fits the duck hunter to the water almost as if he were himself a giant duck, the head of his own decoy rig, an alpha duck of sorts. From his vantage point in the sneakbox he manages the impression made by his floating rig of decoys on flocks flying overhead. The sight of a boat would make ducks nervous, especially the much-sought-after and intelligent black duck. "The black duck is popular," said Heinrichs, "because they're much harder and wiser to kill. That's the reason these boats come in handy. You can hide them. You have a big boat, you can't hide it."[26]

The sneakbox materializes an empathetic relationship between the hunter and his quarry. "There isn't a straight flat piece on it," said Hazelton. "Same as a duck. There's not really a flat part to a duck, Billy, is there?" The best duck hunter, according to Ed Hazelton, is one who "thinks like a duck," a cognitive style his brother-in-law, Paul Cramer, had thoroughly mastered:

> He was the type of fella that thought like a duck. He thought like a duck. He just knew every move they were gonna make. In other words, we'd sit there, gunning, and have the stools [i.e., decoys] out, and in would come some ducks. And they wouldn't come in just the way he wanted 'em. Just exactly right. You *could* kill 'em, but he says, "They gotta do better than that." And he would go out and he'd take this stool here and put it there, and this stool here and set it back there, and the next time they'd almost light in your lap. . . . He just thought like a duck all the time.[27]

The boat's nineteenth-century moniker, "devil's coffin," links the boat with the arch-deceiver, trickster, and crafter of the counterfeit. Duck hunters themselves are masters of illusion, voyagers in a skiff that articulates and resolves environmental oppositions. The boat becomes a tool for conjuring up the alternative reality inhabited by duck hunters. The container for the trickster who dupes ducks is itself a kind of culture hero, engendering confusion and reversals of the natural order, but ultimately enabling civilization to triumph over inchoate nature.

In decoy discourse we glimpse something of the marsh as an arena in which ducks and hunters may trick each other. The infusion of inanimate cedar with animacy emerges as a theme in anecdotes. "I used to carve decoys," said Robert Suralik, of Tuckerton. "But I stopped carvin'. I used to hunt over them. I used to paint 'em so precisely that they looked like real ducks. . . . And one day I was duck hunting, and when I got up to shoot they all flew away and they took my decoys with them!"[28] And vice versa: "I caught this one in my patch," said Eppie Falconburg, displaying a carved bird to those assembled in the Bull Room. "And I got my BB gun out and I stuffed it with wood."

The vessel is a means of transit into another kind of region, and a dwelling place in an otherwise uninhabitable zone that becomes for a time a world of men, a world apart from everyday life. In this world these men have richly developed the shared understandings that distinguish them. The sneakbox has helped them to transform the uninhabitable marshlands at the region's edge into a profusion of places, many of them marked by duck blinds, shanties, and gunning boxes (or "sink blinds"). These places, now managed by the Barnegat Wildlife Refuge, are minutes away as the crow flies but take hours to get to by sneakbox.[29]

"It's one of the last areas you can go and get away from everything," said Bill Oler.

"Yeah," said Ed Hazelton and Bill Cranmer.

"You can just forget traffic and you can forget other people and everything," Bill Oler explained. "You go out and get on the meadows—lose yourself for the day."

"I do, Billy," said Ed. "I go up the crick crabbin,' they don't push me around."

"I sit days with my decoys," Bill Oler said, "and just watch the birds fly in—don't even shoot 'em—just to get away from the house."

"Get up there to Turtle Cove," said Ed, "North Pond, Draggin' Cross Place—"

"Yup," Bill Oler confirmed.

"—Black Crick and anywhere," Ed continued, "Pettit's Point, you know."

This losing of the self is visually conveyed in the disappearance of the gunner into landscape, reclining in a gunning bed dressed with reeds and marsh elders. But knowledge of how to use a sneakbox keeps the negative aspect of losing oneself at bay, both literally and figuratively.

The marsh, an interstitial zone, is not only cultivated in the agricultural sense, but it is also used to cultivate stamina among hunters who undergo the sensual bombardment of cold and the stench of marsh mud. The pervasive odor of methane erects a perceptual barrier, dividing those who eventually come to enjoy it from those who remain disgusted by it. In time the odor itself becomes a threshold, cited by those gathered in the Bull Room as a powerful memory smell, one that plunges them into the realm of hunting.

"The mud, goin' over the bridge," laughed Bill Oler.

"Mud," agreed Ed.

"As soon as you smell the meadow grass and the mud," Bill Oler observed, "you know you're back huntin' somewhere."

"Or a sneakbox that's been damp inside," Ed said. "Take the hatch cover off."

"Cedar shavings," mused Bill Oler.

"That has a characteristic odor," agreed Bill Cranmer.

"I'll tell you the worst one, I think, of 'em all," said Bill Oler with waxing enthusiasm. "Pump out a box before gunning season. Hop in the hunting box when that mud's been sittin' there all summer long!"

"Oh yeah!" Bill Cranmer said, remembering, to a background chorus of "Whew!" and "Phew!"

"The first huntin' day you got all the smell in the world!" said Bill Oler.

"You get used to it though," Bill Cranmer defended it.

"Well," said Eppie Falconberg, "say, today we went over the big bridge to Pleasantville, and the tide's way up, and it stinks over there. My wife—she used to call it 'Lowtide.' Well, when it's low-tide it's worse. It's almost the same smell as the gunning box. Well, she didn't want me to go, but I just had to go. I don't know why. I've gone ever since I was old enough to have a gun."

"Always will," Ed predicted.

"Always will, I guess," said Eppie, resuming the story. "But she says, 'My God, Eppie, how can you go out on any meadow when it smells like this?!' And to me it's not bad, but to her it's sickening!"

"It is not altogether unpleasant," said Bill Cranmer.

"I *like* it, Bill!" exclaimed Ed. "I enjoy the meadows and the smell, and it's part of our way of life. We're brought up in it!"

"It might bother some other people," Bill Cranmer pointed out, "but not me. I'm like you. . . . It smells a lot better to me than following a diesel truck." The cultural group in this case defines itself by the shared affection of its members for marsh mud, a smell that conjures up vivid, emotionally laden memories.

In both broad and narrow senses, the sneakbox is also a tool for self-preservation. In the hostile ambience of the marshes, the sneakbox makes the difference between life and death, but only if one knows how to manage one, as another story by Eppie Falconburg illustrates:

"The days we spent there gunning for them brant [geese]," said Eppie. "I don't know how in God's name we ever lived."

"Right," said Ed.

"Oh, my gracious," Eppie continued, "and that man, I can't think of his name, we almost lost him one day when he stepped on the side of a sneakbox and slipped over in the goddam mud. And I remember gettin' down in that mud, gettin' my hand under his crotch, you know."

"Good shape," Ed observed.

"I wasn't muscular," said Eppie modestly. "But I was in pretty good shape. But that man was a little roly-poly fella, boy oh boy. He didn't want to lose his boots, so I took my huntin' knife and cut the straps, you know, on his boots. I had to cut 'em."

"Full of water," Ed commented.

"'You gotta come outa them boots!'" shouted Eppie, reenacting the scene. "'I can't get you back in the sneakbox!'"

"Full of water," again from Ed.

"He didn't know how to handle a sneakbox," explained Eppie, calming down. "It's like a canoe. Unless you step on it with your chewing gum just right, you're going overboard. And he went overboard."

In the broader sense, against the unsettling changes of urbanization and old age, the sneakbox has become, as an emblem of a whole way of life, a steadying factor: a prop snatched from a disappearing stage, a detachable part made to stand for the whole.

For the old men who see in the proliferation of fiberglass boats, housing developments, and environmental spoilage a way of life on the wane, the sneakbox enables journeys that keep sense of self and identity vivid. For such voyages, miniature sneakboxes are perhaps superior to life-sized ones. Within the past two decades a variety of miniature boats, including sneakboxes, have begun emerging in the workshops of local carvers and boatbuilders. The appearance of the miniature cedar boats at a time when small workboats are being built of fiberglass by larger companies is significant—arising like other historic examples of miniaturization, from a heightened awareness of change, in this case, changes wrought through the development of the region by outsiders.[30] When miniaturized and given to friends and descendants it becomes a metaphysical vessel, a means of transit into past worlds. The miniature sneakbox offers a way of "inscribing culture on the threshold of its disappearance."[31] It encapsulates the collective memory of a generation that knew well how to ply a vanishing landscape.

"It really I guess appeals to the fellows that know what it's about, you know," said Bill Oler, who makes miniature scenes of duck hunting in addition to carving decoys for gunners and collectors, "that have gone out on the bay and actually duck hunted that way."

We often find tools formerly used to ply the physical world transformed into tools that encapsulate it, a way of materializing what now only exists in memory. In miniatures, the encapsulating tools are diminished in size and amplified in significance, a means of transporting aging gunners mentally into the marshes, while transmitting regional identity to children and grandchildren.[32] For the men in the Bull Room the miniature sneakboxes offer a way to retain what is disappearing due to overdevelopment, wetlands preservation, and pollution.

As a showcase for local knowledge, a portal to native images of the environment, a threshold to other realms, the sneakbox holds implications for regional planners. It does what any good policy should: it anticipates and codifies the range of possibilities inherent in a given situation. Yet few of the management policies devised since the reserve's creation approach the sophistication and flexibility of the Barnegat Bay sneakbox.[33]

Hence there is an odd geometric dissonance between ad hoc and ontic regions in South Jersey. In its *Comprehensive Management Plan*, the Pinelands Commission has inscribed the region with a new center, deemed the locus of the purest natural and cultural resources.[34] Around this center the rest of the region is arranged like concentric rings around a bull's eye. The plan deflects most development to the outer "reserve," despite the complex relationship of fishing and farming communities to the core and their inherent status as cultural centers. Residents of coastal communities mourn the sacrifice of their towns to favor the interior. In recent years headlines lamenting the pollution of natural resources have given way to laments over vanishing lifeways: "Pinelands Preservation Threatens a Lifestyle"; "In Pinelands, A Way of Life Is in Peril"; "Pinelands Shellfishermen See Way of Life Fading Fast"; and "New Jersey Drives Pineys to Southern States."[35] In the midst of this the sneakbox emerges to stand for the vanishing ontic region, resolving as usual the problems it articulates. Not only does it sound an alarm for lifeways slipping over the horizon, but it offers a means of returning to them again and again.

"Everybody goes away always comes back," said Hurley Conklin.

"Get that mud between your toes," said Ed Hazelton.

"That's right," said Eppie Falconberg. "That's right."

# Mankind's Thumb on Nature's Scale: Trapping and Regional Identity in the Missouri Ozarks

## ERIKA BRADY

*In this essay, Erika Brady continues the theme of the relationship between residents of a region and the natural environment that surrounds them. Like Mary Hufford, Brady examines a regional hunting tradition, that of fur trappers in the Missouri Ozarks. She focuses on fur trapping as a traditional occupation with deep roots in regional history and as a potent source of regional identity. She describes how that esoteric identity is at the heart of a conflict between the trappers and the federal agency controlling part of the fur trappers' domain in the Ozark Scenic Waterways, and in so doing she explores the question of the relationship between a region and the larger political, economic, and cultural domain within which it exists.*

The Current River and its tributary, Jacks Fork, cut a winding path through the heart of the Missouri Ozarks, a region whose men and women have endured and flaunted an image as willful and free-flowing as the streams for the last two hundred years. Within this area of the Ozarks, the history and economy of the people have been bound up with the rivers from the earliest European exploration and settlement. When, in the mid-1980s, the National Park Service was instructed to enforce a ban on fur trapping on the portions of the rivers administered as the Ozark National Scenic Riverways, the result was a very public dispute over what had been heretofore a very private pursuit. Local response revealed multivalent, sometimes self-contradictory aspects of the regional cultural identity, including local perceptions of the area's history, attitudes toward wildlife and the land, intervention of outside authority, and the uses of cooperation and independent action.

Since 1964, 135 miles of these rivers have been designated the Ozark National Scenic Riverways, the first part of the system of

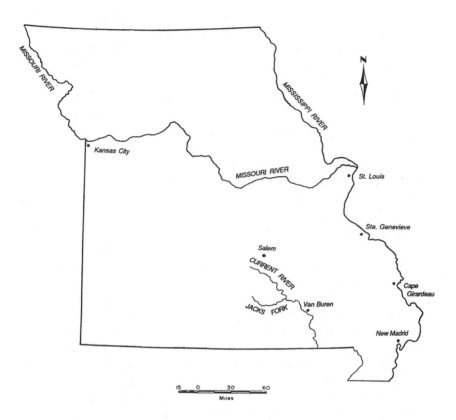

State of Missouri, showing Current River region.

federally protected rivers. From the beginning, the establishment of the Ozark National Scenic Riverways ignited dissension in the region. Considerable local concern centered on the continuation of hunting, fishing, and trapping. Congressman Richard Ichord, then representing Missouri's Eighth Congressional District, assured residents that their right to pursue these activities would be retained, and specific language was introduced into the enabling legislation to guarantee that "the Secretary [of the Interior] shall permit hunting and fishing on lands and waters under his jurisdiction within the Riverways area in accordance with applicable Federal and State laws."[1]

As it happened, this "specific language" was not specific enough. In 1983, the Department of the Interior instructed that regulations concerning activities in National Park Service units should be enforced strictly, excluding all pursuits not enumerated in the enabling legislation of each unit. Although when the Ozark National Scenic Riverways was established, "hunting" had been understood to include "trapping," the Riverways headquarters was ordered to ban that activity beginning with the 1986-87 season.[2]

The effect upon residents of the region was dramatic. Only about 130 individuals were known to be trapping in the area, some quite casually and none as a sole source of income.[3] Nevertheless, local sympathy for their situation ran high; meetings concerning the ban attracted two and three times the number of those actually affected, sometimes briefly doubling the population of the tiny towns in which they were held. If nontrappers were concerned, the trappers themselves were apoplectic: to a reporter from the *St. Louis Post-Dispatch*, octogenarian Jesse ("Buck") Asbridge exploded: "Big shots! All they want to do is step on you! The hell with the rest of us. *Damn* federal. *Damn* state. They just want to do something to aggravate you."[4]

Why this furor? In accounts of the heyday of trapping in the frontier West, when St. Louis was the hub of the nation's fur industry, Ozark trapping merits barely a footnote. The Current River and Jacks Fork today contain good habitat for furbearers—the relative warmth of their spring-fed waters is especially attractive to mink—but the area is by no means the most productive fur-producing region even within the state.[5] Although some buyers attribute a pleasing "bright" color to Ozark furs, the region does not have a particularly high profile in the fur industry nationwide. Neither historically nor currently is the Ozark upland a renowned trapping region. And although the regulation in question potentially affected at least twelve other NPS units in other regions, in none of these was the response so prompt, prolonged, and ultimately decisive.

Many local pundits attributed the vigorous counterattack on the ban to local economic reliance on trapping to supplement family income. In 1986, the year the ban was to take effect, the six counties affected included the two rated first and second in unemployment in the state. That same year the mean salary in these six counties averaged $6,293. A diligent trapper might clear up to $2,000 in a good season, working at a time of year when other sources of income are limited; the average annual income from fur sales in the Riverways areas was estimated at the time to be about $85,000.[6] Certainly, economic conditions in the region played a part in the response to the proposed ban.

Nevertheless, other regions affected by the ban also stood to suffer economically: trapping is common in rural areas where economic resources are scant. Furthermore, trappers in the Riverways region are drawn from all socioeconomic levels: some might hitch rides to the Missouri Trappers Association to save money on gas, but in the course of research in the area I was driven over the steep hills in every kind of vehicle from decrepit pickups held together with spit and baling wire to—on one memorable occasion—a gleaming Lincoln Town Car.

The energetic response to the trapping ban can be understood fully only in light of attitudes and conflicts in the region that reach deep in the area's long history, including but not limited to economic circumstances of the inhabitants. There is much in the Ozark past that lends a powerful local symbolic value to trapping, as well as much that leads to tension over intervention from the outside. An investigation of trapping and the attempted ban becomes an investigation of the factors that have defined the regional culture, past and present.

Unlike other regions of the southern uplands, the Ozarks of southeast Missouri early attracted the attention of the French and Spanish empire builders of the seventeenth and eighteenth centuries. Local historians still cling to the faint possibility that de Soto himself reached the upper Current in the 1550s seeking gold.[7] Gold there was not, but other valuable commodities were plentiful. In a letter to his superiors in 1688,the French priest-explorer Father Membre exclaimed that "our hunters, French and Indian, are delighted with the country," and shortly thereafter the French aristocrat Philippe Renault established several successful lead mines northeast of the headwaters of the Current.[8]

Although French and Spanish dreams of gold and silver were rapidly dispelled, the rich mineral and fur resources of the region provided incentive enough for settlements to be established on the eastern perimeter of the region at Ste. Genevieve, Cape Girardeau, and New Madrid, among others. Mercantile records of the eighteenth and nineteenth centuries from these settlements indicate that lead and pelts from the Ozark regions to the west were profitable commodities in national and international markets.[9] Today the most notable mark on the cultural landscape from this era is not the few buildings that survive but the names the French explorers gave the rivers and streams—hunters' names celebrating the useful creatures and materials that might be found along their banks, such as

Castor (beaver), Loutre (otter), and Saline (salt). The name of the
Current River itself alludes to its utility as a year-round highway
from the region to trading settlements beyond: seldom frozen, it
was named the "courant," or "running," river.

When Americans of English and Scots-Irish descent began to
arrive from Kentucky and Tennessee in the late 1700s and early
1800s, they found French and French-Indian settlers already established, with economic ties to Europe and Canada as well as the
United States, which acquired the region from France in the Louisiana Purchase of 1803. To the extent that early settlers aspired to
more than a barely adequate subsistence, they contended with
economic forces not only outside the region but outside the United
States itself.

Records of mercantile establishments in the counties adjoining
the Current River and Jacks Fork confirm that for settlers at all
economic levels, pelts and beeswax were the primary currency
exchanged for the few necessary items that could not be produced
on the homestead: coffee, sugar, calomel, and tobacco in the early
years of the nineteenth century; later, such luxuries as "made"
cloth, cow bells, shoes, rice, and ginger.[10] Even taxes were paid in
this manner; contemporary accounts tell of tax collectors whose
horses could barely be seen for the burden of furs.[11] The ambitious
young men on the Ozark frontier used the region as a base, under-
taking extensive trapping forays seasonally to the fur-rich upper
Mississippi and Missouri rivers and their tributaries.

Although documentation of the attitudes of nineteenth-century
trappers toward the animals themselves must be inferred from a
handful of published trapping manuals of the period, certain clear
patterns emerge. Discussions of the habits of individual species
read like field guides to animal morality: the greed of bears, rapacity
of weasels, cunning of raccoon, and lust of mink are all dwelt upon
to such an extent that these weaknesses of character not only appear
to bring about their capture but in a sense to justify it.[12] The
symbolic subduing of the frontier wilderness was a drama re-
enacted on a small scale in the allegorical triumph of the morally
and intellectually superior trapper over his animal adversaries—a
trope exploited almost identically in descriptions of the overcoming
of native human populations.

Despite a myth common among trappers of today that the
hunting activities of their ancestors were unrestricted, conflict between federal law and local practice in this domain is nothing new.

A letter survives from William H. McMurtrey, an Ozark trapper who owed money to relatives in southeast Missouri and hoped to pay them back by an expedition west into Indian Territory in 1831. He neglected to provide himself with a license, however—an oversight which proved costly:

> Thare was four of us atraping in partnership we ware a makeing from 20 to 30 dollars a night but it turned out as usual for whenever I am about to make a good try of it the pan is shore to turn over and spil the fat in the fire so it was with us for the indians came upon us and robed us of the fur traps and powder. . . .[Because he had no license, McMurtrey had no legal recourse. The federal agent of the region offered to return the ammunition and traps lost in the ambush, but McMurtrey, though "poor and neady," was not "lo spirited enough" to comply with this offer, which he suspected was at least a mockery and possibly a trick to arrest him.]
>
> My comrades seem to think of accepting the traps and so they may but as for me I can safely say that I will see General Campbell [the agent?] and all the Coosy Nation safely landed in hell and roasted in the blue curling flames of damnation and their [asses?] fiz and fry through the endless ages of aternity before I would take the traps after the yellow rascals has hunted the Beaver with them all the winter whilst I had to be bending my way homeward many times wet coald and hungary with my canoe only.
>
> . . . I pay tax and am subject to military Duty and am a subject of the general government tho not of common justus. If I go a hunting I am a vile offender of the laws of the land and a liable to be arested by a file of soldiers, caried to a garison, sent to the Little Rock lay in prison six months pay a large fine take a mess of lash layed on the naked back and if this is the fruits of the blood of our ancestors whoo faught for the common rights of man in the revolutionary war I _____ **** _____ **** _____ _____ [marks in letter indicate speechless rage] What I lack in dancing I will make up by turning around.[13]

This letter not only documents an early stage in the development of the distinctive Ozark accent, it also speaks with the authentic voice of the forebears of Buck Asbridge in condemning official meddlers in matters concerning sacred trapping and hunting rights to "fiz and fry through endless ages of aternity." Indeed, unconsciously echoing McMurtrey, local rhetoric concerning the legality of the ban included frequent references to service in the armed forces and the eroding of personal freedoms the veterans had fought to preserve. But in fact, in the course of the five decades preceding the trapping ban, Ozarkers of the Current River region had reached a remarkable accommodation of frontier attitudes toward wildlife to state regulation, an adaptation that McMurtrey would have surely regarded as "lo spirited" but which has proved profitable to trappers and wildlife alike.

By the 1930s, the threat to wildlife populations throughout Missouri was particularly acute in the once game-rich eastern Ozarks. Industrial use of the Current River during the preceding forty years of timber boom combined with poorly controlled trapping and hunting had severely depleted game populations in the region. Beaver and otter had completely disappeared. Through the state game department, wildlife biologists Rudolf Bennitt and Werner O. Nagel received federal emergency work funding in 1934 to survey Missouri game. Published in 1937, their study concluded that while the era of unrestricted pursuit of game was necessarily past, "the only possible hope lies not with more restrictive legislation but in increased natural production," in particular by improvement of habitat.[14] This landmark study remains an influential model in wildlife maintenance, forming the cornerstone of state wildlife policy with the establishment of the Missouri Department of Conservation that same year.

It was not an easy task to persuade Missouri trappers of the wisdom behind carefully controlled and enforced yearly seasons for furbearers. Not only did it require sacrifice of immediate gain for long-range benefits, it demanded a shift in attitude toward wildlife from the image of a vast, inexhaustible, God-given plenty to a more agrarian model in which the trapper functioned as a responsible husbander of a renewable but limited natural resource. This cognitive shift was particularly difficult in the Ozarks, where farming represented only one of many activities undertaken to make ends meet, and where farming techniques have been frequently rudimentary and tradition-bound.[15]

Nevertheless, such a shift has occurred and is relatively pervasive among trappers of this generation. Older men remember with bitterness the years in the early 1930s, when drought and poor management had cut into the animal population, and the depression years, when, as young boys, they brought in a few extra dollars for shoes and food selling pelts. Younger men carry a consciousness of the troubled regional past, as well. Kenneth Wells, a trapper in his late thirties, told me:

> I've kept a real close, accurate record of the Current River as far back as I could go, and it was always virgin pine. There was no brush—it wasn't in oak like it is now, it was virgin pine. . . . And [they] set up saw mill camps all over this area around here. And of course it gave people employment, but they went in there and they totally butchered the pine, the pine timber. And they were somewhat destructive, although I can understand their idea, because it was rough making a living. There was no programs that would help them in any way, and they had to make a living. It was either work or starve. And I'll never know how they felt. But I criticize them once in a while, and I even criticize the old trapper, when there was no season, and he went out there and he harvested more than the land would produce.[16]

The term "harvesting" in reference to hunting and trapping has become commonplace, even among older men, especially in the context of discussions of wildlife population. The sense of participation in a maintenance process is strong, especially among men active in the Missouri Trappers Association, which maintains close ties with the Department of Conservation. Wells continued:

> We're just harvesting the furbearers, and they've been harvesting furbearers ever since we came over here, white men, that's what built this country. . . . Now there's more people. If there was just Jim Bridger and Davy Crockett— you wouldn't need a season. But you need a season because there's more trappers. You harvest the animals to a healthy level, and you sell 'em. You might have to lengthen the season some years and you might have to shorten it some years. And I think that's up to trained experts. And of course I thank them for seeing where the years are. If I thought that fox were getting too close [few], I'd call Dave

Fig. 1. Department of Conservation biologist confers with trapper
Kenneth Wells concerning condition of mink habitat. Current River near
Cedargrove, Missouri, January 1988. *Photo by Erika Brady.*

Hamilton [Department of Conservation furbearer research specialist] immediately, and I'd say, 'Dave, you better get down here, because I think we've got a problem.' And I think I know Dave well enough to know that immediately, in less than a week he'd be here, and he'd be out there, and the next year we wouldn't have a fox season.[17]

In a striking image that conveys how completely the concept of the trapper has changed, Wells argues for the inevitability of the trappers' ecological role in controlling animal population, refuting antitrappers whose efforts would eliminate his participation in the natural system:

We've put our thumb on the scale of nature. And you can't just take it off and say things are gonna be like they were. Because they'll never be like they were—we haven't got the habitat. They call the Ozark National Scenic Riverways the way it was a hundred years ago—it's *not*. It's not and never will be again. . . .

I've got a small farm, and I raise cattle. And I can't put a hundred head of cattle on my farm because they'd run out of something to eat. So I have to keep my numbers down, in order to make any money on the cattle I have, because if you get a bunch of poor cattle they're not going to bring the quality price that they would if they're fat and slick and purty. And it's the same with wildlife.

Judged by their own objectives, the cooperation between the trappers and the Department of Conservation has been a major achievement in which both groups take justifiable satisfaction. Populations of most species are strong; beaver have been reintroduced with such success that they now represent a serious nuisance to landowners; and an otter reintroduction program is showing promise.

In light of the Ozark trapper's recently revised view of himself as a partner in wildlife maintenance, the prospect of a ban on trapping in the Ozark National Scenic Riverways was understood not only as a threat to personal pleasure and profit, but also as a threat to the well-being of the ecology within the region affected. In addition, it was seen as a direct betrayal of the always uneasy understanding that had grown between trappers and authorities at the state and federal level since the establishment of the Department of Conservation and the serious enforcement of game laws. Resentment was compounded by ongoing local feeling against the Ozark National Scenic Riverways as a tourist attraction: the economic benefits the unit promised never measured up to expectation, and visitors to the Riverways have been regarded with increasing suspicion and disgust by many, as inhabitants observe the unruly and indecent behavior of some "floaters" and canoeists.[18]

"History" has many symbolic levels in the Ozarks: the progress of wildlife management represents only one aspect of trapping in the local perception. The historian Robert Flanders has described the area as a "perpetuated frontier" in which older ways are not mere survivals but represent conscious choices maintained in a paradoxical process of vigorous and intentional cultural conservatism.[19] Trappers value and allude self-consciously to their sense of participation in a frontier activity: Wells refers to Jim Bridger and Davy Crockett, and the original name of the Missouri Trappers Association was the Missouri Mountain Men. (The women's auxiliary group is still called the Missouri Mountain Maids.) Ernest Gibbs remarks that they will divide trapping territory on the upper Current in "the old Indian way," and further explains: "A trapper, he's always looking. He's more or less like the Indian, they used to go by sign, going through the woods. That's what I like—I like to get out there to see the tracks, the sign. And you learn something every year."[20]

Along with the sense of participation in regional history evoked by trapping, the activity also represents an important component of personal and family history for many men. It is most commonly learned as a teenager or young adult, and because the teaching process is demanding and may take several seasons, an experienced trapper chooses his student carefully for qualities of stamina, patience, responsibility, and intelligence. Ralph Kelsick notes: "It would be hard to learn from scratch. You have to learn the animals. You have to learn the habits of the animals and how they travel. When I was a kid I would spend hours tracking an animal in the snow. You have to ask yourself "Why did the animal go this particular path, why didn't he go some ways else." You've got to figure out just where he's going to step. You have to have a little of the drive, you know, you can't be one of these guys who's kinda lazy."[21]

The relationship between master and apprentice often becomes almost familial. Indeed, there are genealogies of trappers in the

Ozarks within which personal style and technique have been shaped by the teaching process, and within a region most trappers can tell you the trapping "ancestry" of each of their fellow trappers. The activity is considered so suitable a socializing activity for young men that among trappers one hears it said almost proverbially, "I have never seen a boy get into trouble that held a valid trapping license."[22]

Beyond the regional and personal history that underlies each trapper's patterns and procedures lies the allure of the activity itself, an attraction described by many trappers in almost mystical terms. In *Trapping the Missouri Ozarks*, Doug Curtis describes this passion: "Trapping has always been to me a great mystery that I have not yet been able to solve. A mystery born out of sheer magic that quickens my heartbeat at the mere thought and more so when I smell fall in the air in mid-autumn. I don't think I could take all the words from the Webster dictionary and make a suitable definition of what trapping means to me. I don't think it's the act of outsmarting an animal but rather to have the ability to think like an animal."[23]

The nineteenth-century image of the animal outwitted by the superior human intellect is replaced by explicit identification with the fellow mammal: the ability not only to think like an animal but to interpret information in field and on riverbank through its eyes. For the Ozark trapper, whose geographic range and seasonal opportunity are far more restricted than those of the full-time trappers of the last century, this ability to "read sign" is perhaps his most important skill, enabling him to match wits with an individual animal, sometimes season after season, until a successful capture is accomplished. A veteran of fifty years of Missouri trapping, Ralph Kelsick describes the fine-tuned observation that provides the intellectual challenge of the activity: "You're always looking for something—sign, that kind of thing. You can go up on the riverbank, on the edge of a river or stream, and just look down, and it just tells you a story—it's just like reading a book. You can read the signs there and it just tells you a lot of things, what animals is using it, where. Course you got to have an experienced eye to notice it."[24] From his knowledge of the specific animal whose sign he reads, the trapper constructs a deceptive scenario—a "set" that will overcome the creature's natural caution and cause it to step just so. Not unlike a theatrical set, a trapper's set is an attempt to suppress distractions and to create an enticing web of olfactory and visual cues that challenge the onlooker to suspend native wariness and believe the constructed message. Kelsick remarks on this semiotic aspect of the activity: "You know you get out there among the animals, and you get to where, well, you can't *orally* communicate, but you can *communicate* through their signs. You see what I'm saying? You have to out-general the animals, and it's not easy. . . . You can learn a lot from them—they're smart little critters."[25]

Finally, for Ozark men of the Current River region trapping represents a satisfying solution to the strain between equally insistent cultural and personal urges. On one hand, there is a high value placed on independence, productivity, self-sufficiency; most recreational activities among men and women result in some item or product that is at least nominally useful, and trapping has the advantage of being a solitary, productive pursuit undertaken at the time of year when "cabin fever" attacks with greatest virulence. On the other hand, frontier patterns of hospitality and interdependence are carefully maintained. Most districts of the Missouri Trappers Association keep up social activities all year round, including rendezvous, fish fries, picnics, and business meetings, all featuring raffles and door prizes in which one might win anything from a valuable rifle to a gallon of coyote urine. Wives of trappers are most actively involved in this communal aspect of the pursuit and are often its most persuasive and informed advocates.

The most important social events connected with trapping are the fur auctions held during and just after the season. Once the pelts have been prepared for sale, the trapper can enjoy these get-togethers, where he and his wife can cast a competitive eye on others' "take" for the season, sample the food prepared by the Mountain Maids, and speculate on the results being tabulated on a portable computer by an industrious representative of the Department of Conservation. The quality of fur preparation is scrutinized with special care. Olan Yokum, president of the Missouri Trappers Association, writes: "When finally the pelts are placed on the auction block the accomplished trapper stands proud. He carefully displays his fur. He wants everyone to see his handiwork. His stature speaks, 'I am proud to display my skills, I have done the *complete* job, I have given the animal the respect due him, I have wasted nothing, I am proud.'"[26] At the auction, the actions undertaken in solitude in the fields, on the river, and in the fur shed become part of a public presentation, and the quality of the performance is judged according to the standards of his experienced peers.

Fig. 2. At a Missouri Trappers Association auction, fur buyers examine pelts and bid, as trappers and family members look on. In the background, Department of Conservation biologist Dave Hamilton computes the season's numbers and prices on a portable computer. Farmington, Missouri, January 1988. *Photo by Erika Brady.*

At the point of sale, the Ozark trapper participates in a larger economic world market that reiterates the very earliest patterns of trade in southeast Missouri. Much fur from the area is sold by dealers to the venerable Hudson's Bay Company of Canada, where it is purchased by European buyers. The destination of most of their fur will be the fashion centers of Europe; the story that begins with a solitary Ozark man thrusting a bare arm into an icy winter stream to place his set may end in the exclusive salons of Paris or Milan.

Like their ancestors, Ozark trappers are often astute concerning the social factors governing the market for their furs in the cosmopolitan world. Douglas Flannery, a trapper and fur buyer, informally analyzed the sociological significance of the world trade: "You take, like, Italy. Nobody owns any ground over there. In

America here, we look at what kind of vehicle we drive, how much ground we own, what kind of home we've got. Over there there's *no ground*. Everybody lives in a little bitty ol' apartment. The thing over there is diamonds and furs. . . . The clothes on your back is your prestige." [27] Ozark trappers take an interest in the trends illustrated in the advertisements in expensive magazines and Sunday supplements: they may provide the clue to a profitable season.

The men with chapped hands and mended waders, who start their rough beards in September so the growth by late November will warm them on the cold daily running of the traplines at dawn, and the glossy models who parade the sleek furs down the runways of European showrooms—the contrast is only the most conspicuous of many clusters of contradiction that lie at the heart of trapping in the Ozarks of southeast Missouri. It is a management strategy intended to benefit the wildlife of the region by reducing their numbers. It is a lonely sport that is the nexus of a social and economic network spreading beyond the region and the continent. It is a reflective intellectual and physical pursuit that demands intimate identification with and respect for an animal—like a bullfight, culminating in its death. Doug Curtis says:

> The act of trapping is a food that feeds the very soul of man. At times a man cannot explain why he traps with an intelligent answer, he only knows he is driven and almost powerless against it.
>
> There is no cure for the dreaded trapping disease that attacks a man in the fall of the year. Running a trapline is no cure, but it does ease the pain some. [28]

Trapping is done for money; it is done for pleasure; it is done because, for so very long in the Ozarks, it *has* been done; it is done, strangely but truly, for love.

Perhaps the culture of any region is best sought in such clusters of contradiction, rather than in simple enumeration of characteristics. The attitudes of Ozark trappers reveal contradictions which illuminate significant cultural tensions of the region: conservatism versus modernity, rural values opposed to but caught within urban-controlled power and economy, and ethical questions involving appropriate relations between men, animals, and the environment. These are issues of long standing in the Ozarks, dating back to the earliest days of European settlement. They are issues which defined and continue to define the regional character, without offering any promise of simple resolution.

Indeed, the trapping issue itself is concluded but unresolved in a circumstance that perfectly represents the tensions, paradoxes, and local truths that emerged from it. The local Park Service headquarters put the ban into effect as ordered for a little over a week in November of 1986, until a local court enjoined the Ozark National Scenic Riverways from enforcement pending further judicial action. In late May of 1987, United States District Judge H. Kenneth Wangelin decided the suit brought by the Missouri Trappers Association against the Secretary of the Interior in the trappers' favor, permanently enjoining the Park Service from enforcing the ban.[29] Meanwhile, Congressman Bill Emerson has made three attempts to pass a bill in Congress that would ensure the maintenance of trapping rights in the Ozark National Scenic Riverways by legislative enactment. The bills have never reached a final vote.[30] A symbolic contradiction remains embedded in the legal actuality: trapping is banned by law in the Ozark National Scenic Riverways; the United States District Court prohibits the enforcement of the ban.

# Regional Consciousness as a Shaper of Local History: Examples from the Eastern Shore

### POLLY STEWART

*The issue of regional autonomy versus interference by outsiders addressed by Erika Brady is the central theme in Polly Stewart's essay on historical legendry in Maryland's Eastern Shore. Stewart argues that Eastern Shoremen's regional consciousness has historically been shaped by the region's geographical isolation, and that regional identity is strongly marked by an "us versus them" mentality. Based on oral historical narratives describing a series of violent episodes in the region's past, Stewart suggests that the events were precipitated by regional outrage at perceived attempts by outsiders to interfere in the Eastern Shore's affairs.*

The simple principle that *a region's consciousness of itself defines the region* offers a sensible and effective means for interpreting local historical events. Regional consciousness bears no necessary relation to artificial administrative lines imposed by governments; for analytical purposes it is just as isolating as occupation, ethnic heritage, age, sex, or any of the factors that come into play when cultural groups identify themselves. It crosses all ethnic, class, and economic lines, and the highly educated are just as much imbued with it as are the unlettered. Regional consciousness is less a matter of geography than it is a state of mind. It is therefore possible to speak of "folk regions" as distinct from geographic or political regions.

The lands surrounding the Chesapeake Bay provide an unusually fertile field for examination of folk regional consciousness. The land immediately west of the bay is home to the nation's capital and to a portion of the megalopolis that sprawls between Richmond and Boston—the Eastern Seaboard. The largely rural peninsula situated east of the bay comprises the entire state of Delaware, nine counties of Maryland, and two counties of Virginia, and is called, from syllables in the three states' names, "Delmarva." (Border communities, by the same principle, are given names like Mardela, Delmar, Marydel). Residents often decry the carving up of Delmarva to meet various political demands, and for many decades there has been talk of merging the three political units into a new "State of Delmarva." But Delmarva includes an informal subregion known as the "Eastern Shore" or simply "the Shore." Its geographic boundaries are not obvious to the uninitiated, yet its cultural boundaries are deeply felt and passionately defended by its residents. An outsider who might innocently confuse the Eastern Shore with the Eastern Seaboard will not, in the presence of an Eastern Shoreman, make the same mistake twice. Such loyalty to a folk region makes it unlikely that Eastern Shoremen would be politically any happier in a State of Delmarva than they presently are in the State of Maryland.

Everything one can observe about the Shore validates it as a folk region. To begin with, in the minds of Shoremen the Shore encompasses only eight of the nine Maryland counties on Delmarva (the northernmost county is viewed as part of the megalopolis) and excludes all but the southern edge of Delaware. The portion of Virginia that extends south to the tip of the peninsula is called the "Eastern Shore of Virginia" and is regarded, for various political and economic and cultural reasons, as a different domain. The Maryland part of Delmarva divides itself into two Shores, Upper and Lower; the latter comprises four counties, Worcester, Wicomico, Somerset, and Dorchester. The county seats of the first three— Snow Hill, Salisbury, and Princess Anne—play a large role in the present study.

Originally settled by English colonists in the 1640s, the Shore existed for over three centuries in relative geographic isolation. Until 1952, when the Bay Bridge was opened, the only routes west were by ferry across the Chesapeake or overland across the head of the bay; a bridge-tunnel leading south to Norfolk was not opened until 1965. Today, ineluctably connected to the western mainland, the Eastern Shore is as easy to reach by automobile as Lane County, Kansas. But while the Shore is no longer geographically isolated, its people remain, on the whole, culturally isolated by choice. In saying this I do not wish to suggest in any way that Shoremen are not knowledgeable about the rest of the world, but rather that, whatever their level of education, Shoremen take an unusual degree of pride in setting themselves apart from the rest of the world.

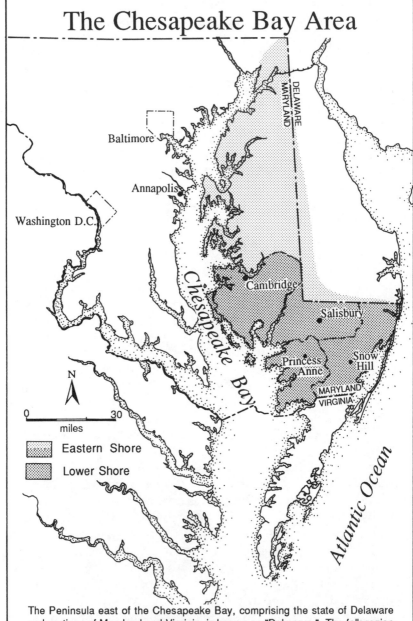

# The Chesapeake Bay Area

Baltimore

Annapolis

Washington D.C.

DELAWARE
MARYLAND

Cambridge

Salisbury

Princess
Anne

Snow
Hill

MARYLAND
VIRGINIA

Chesapeake Bay

Atlantic Ocean

N

0 ——— 30
miles

Eastern Shore

Lower Shore

The Peninsula east of the Chesapeake Bay, comprising the state of Delaware and portions of Maryland and Virginia, is known as "Delmarva." The folk region "Eastern Shore" excludes most of Delaware and the northernmost part of Maryland. The "Lower Shore" comprises four counties whose seats are Cambridge, Salisbury, Snow Hill, and Princess Anne. The folk designation "Western Shore" encompasses the urban corridor that includes Washington, Annapolis, and Baltimore and all of Maryland west of this corridor.

jmh

Membership in the group is rigidly determined: the only way one can be a Shoreman is to have been born in the Shore. (It should be pointed out that the term is generic, as in, "She's a Shoreman, but her husband isn't.") Those who find it necessary to secure employment away from the Shore yearn to come back, and many do come back upon retirement, because of the "sand between their toes."

The attitude of Shoremen toward outsiders is pervasive and unsubtle, though not necessarily unkind. Young people who come from the megalopolis to attend college in the Eastern Shore quickly learn that they are "Western Shoremen," a term they may never before have had applied to them. Shoremen are given to expressing their feeling about outsiders in a song, sung to the tune of "The Old Gray Mare," that states, "We don't give a damn about the whole state of Maryland, / . . . We're from the Eastern Shore." This song is performed annually at the close of the state legislative session in Annapolis by members of the Eastern Shore delegation—to the delight of the assembled throng—as a gesture of regional pride, but it can also be heard ardently sung in Eastern Shore taverns by men and women who have been discussing strategies for blowing up the Bay Bridge. Shoremen are inclined to exhibit more condescension toward Baltimoreans than to outsiders from other locales; the term "Baltimoron" is more or less good-naturedly bandied about, and one can hear many stories about "Baltimore hunters" who drive up to Shore game-checking stations with goats or cows strapped to their fenders.[1]

The principle of regional consciousness has great potential as an analytical tool. But when we add to it three others, two from the study of folklore and one from anthropology, the possibilities become especially powerful for interpreting local historical events in an unprecedented way. The first of these, invented by the late William Hugh Jansen, is known to folklorists as "the esoteric-exoteric factor"—a technical term for the "us-them" dichotomy that pervades the thinking of groups.[2] Sometimes exquisitely subtle, sometimes painfully overt, the esoteric-exoteric factor always operates as groups are perceiving themselves, perceiving other groups, and imagining how other groups perceive them. Because regional consciousness involves a sense of belonging to a place, it automatically posits an "other," a class of persons who do not belong. Jansen postulated that the more a group sees itself as beset by hostile outside forces, the stronger will be its esoteric, or in-group, identification and the stronger its need to construct defenses against those outside forces.

The second analytical tool—awareness of the importance of the number three in shaping Euro-American perception and behavior—has been examined by (among many others) folklorist Alan Dundes.[3] Citing Bronislaw Malinowski's observation that "Nothing is as difficult to see as the obvious," Dundes provides many examples of ways in which the number three pervades Western culture, even to the point of causing apparently objective students of natural and cultural phenomena to create analytical categories with three parts, whether warranted or not. (Witness the present analysis.) Everyday life is organized into patterns of threes, and people are likely to make sense of unusual or stressful events by noticing when such events occur in threes. As Dundes notes, "The child is conditioned by his folklore to expect three and his culture does not disappoint him."[4] The importance of the number three in the present study will be made plain.

The anthropologist Edward T. Hall has provided the third useful tool in interpreting regional historical events. He has argued persuasively that much of the experience of everyday life is processed so far below the level of consciousness ("out of awareness" is the term Hall uses) that many events cannot be subjected to rational analysis by even the most rational among us, that we respond instead, for good or for ill, according to deep-seated cultural predispositions that we do not recognize.[5] Such response, powerful enough in individuals, is likely to be even more powerful among groups acting under the esoteric-exoteric force mentioned above. In stressful circumstances entire populations, particularly in such strongly self-identified regions as the Shore, can be caught up in courses of thought and action that they might not otherwise follow. Regional consciousness can thus figure significantly in the playing out of historical events. More pointedly, historical events can actually be shaped by regional consciousness.

Some historical events are less pleasant to talk about than others. The three major events of the present discussion—a mass murder and two lynchings, which occurred in the Lower Shore between 1931 and 1933—are unpleasant in the extreme. My purpose in presenting them here is not merely to exhume, and certainly not to sensationalize, painful historical memories, but to illustrate the premises of regional consciousness mentioned at the opening of this essay. I offer the discussion in hopes not only of explaining these local events but also of showing that their causes differ markedly from the causes of apparently similar events that were occurring elsewhere in the United States during the same troubled period; many parts of the nation, during the late twenties and early thirties, were in the grip of lynchings and other violent outbreaks.[6]

The oral history of the Eastern Shore events is extremely guarded, though anyone from the Lower Shore is likely to know about them either through personal memory or through the oral narratives of others. I learned initially about the oral history through reading student folklore collections in the archives at Salisbury State University. I subsequently read a valuable unpublished manuscript by John R. Wennersten, a historian at the University of Maryland, Eastern Shore, in Princess Anne; in preparing his manuscript Wennersten had consulted newspaper accounts and transcripts of hearings and had also conducted oral interviews. Still later I conducted interviews of my own and studied printed accounts from the day in the three Lower Shore newspapers—the *Snow Hill Democratic Messenger*, the *Salisbury Daily Times*, and the *Princess Anne Marylander and Herald*—as well as in the *Baltimore Sun*. Because the Eastern Shore events attracted the attention of the American liberal press, I was also able to read outside observers' comments in the *Nation* and *New Republic*, which typically discussed the events in connection with others seemingly like it around the country.

As the various press accounts demonstrate, the violence in the Shore was explicitly and consistently interpreted by insiders as evidence of justified local reaction to outside interference, and by outsiders as evidence of backwardness and racism in the Shore. A clearer example of Jansen's esoteric-exoteric factor—"us against them"—could scarcely be found anywhere.

The first of the violent incidents was a multiple murder in Worcester County. On October 10, 1931, four members of a prominent and well-liked white farm family—father, mother, and two teenage daughters—were found shot in their beds. The only suspect in the crime was an employee of the family, an itinerant black laborer who had lived in the area for several weeks, named Euel (or Yuel) Lee. Items of clothing and jewelry identified as the property of murdered family members were found in the boardinghouse where Lee was staying. After several hours of questioning by local law-enforcement officers, Lee signed a confession and was jailed. There he was interviewed by Bernard Ades, a lawyer from the

International Labor Defense League (ILD), a communist organization that was waging an extensive labor, civil-rights, and antilynch-
ing campaign in the South at that time. Local sentiment against Lee
was exceptionally high because of the popularity of the murdered
family and, I believe, because of Lee's apparently unremorseful
presentation of self; he was described in the *Salisbury Times* as a
"cool, self-possessed man" who showed "little, if any, signs of
emotion" (October 16, 1931). Perhaps for these reasons the court-
appointed local defense lawyer had demonstrated little interest in
preparing a case on Lee's behalf, and Ades was soon granted
authority to take on the case. Lee subsequently changed his plea to
not guilty. Ades contended that a fair trial would be impossible for
Lee in the Eastern Shore and further charged that Lee was being
used as "an example to keep negroes in Eastern Shore counties in
their places." The ILD engineered Lee's extradition out of Worcester
County to Baltimore, and over the next two years, by the use of
various technicalities, it succeeded in keeping the Lee case in litiga-
tion (and Lee away from the gallows; there is little to suggest he was
not guilty of the murders).[7] Lee was eventually executed in Baltimore—exactly two years and two weeks after the murders—but
people throughout the Eastern Shore were outraged that the case
had been taken away from them by outsiders.

In the meantime, two months after the slayings in Worcester
County, when it had become apparent that the accused Lee was not
going to be brought swiftly to justice in the Shore, a second violent
incident occurred, this time in Salisbury. Daniel J. Elliott, a prominent and well-respected white lumber dealer, was shot and killed,
allegedly by a black employee named Matthew Williams. There
were no witnesses to the murder, but Williams himself somehow
sustained a gunshot wound and was taken to the local hospital. The
local papers later offered speculation that Williams had accidentally
or intentionally shot himself after shooting Elliott, but in the folk
memory the culprit in both shootings was Elliott's own son. The
following account from the Salisbury State University archives,
collected in 1973 from a sixty-two-year-old white woman, is typical
of about half of the several dozen narratives of the incident (in the
other half, Williams shoots Elliott):

> Everybody claimed the colored man had killed Dan Elliott at
> the lumber mill on Lake Street and had robbed him. But it
> ain't so because an old colored lady we had known for years

told us what happened. She said that the colored man had saved money from working at the mill and had asked Dan Elliott to keep it for him. So on that day the colored man went to get his money, but it was gone. It seems that Dan Elliott's son had stolen the money and when he was confronted by his father, he shot the father and then shot the colored man.[8]

Whether or not Williams actually had committed the murder will never be known, for within hours after Williams was hospitalized, a mob of about three hundred gathered at the hospital, got Williams out, dragged him several blocks to the county courthouse, hanged him from a tree on the courthouse lawn, and burned his body.

Local newspaper reports and editorials of the time indicate strongly a belief that this lynching would not have happened were it not for the pending Lee case. An editorial from the *Chestertown Enterprise*, reprinted in the *Salisbury Times* on December 11, 1931, typifies this position: "The Eastern Shore wants nothing more at this time than to be left alone in the settling of its problems. Outside interference which caused the delay in the case of the Worcester murderer of four was directly responsible for the deplorable lynching in Salisbury." In the oral record the message was blunter still: according to one account, collected in the early 1970s, "Well, you see, there was this other family that was murdered over [in Worcester County] and a black man had been accused of killing them but he got off. And so they decided, some people around town, that this man wasn't gonna get off."

Local news reports on the lynching suggest that outsiders were "responsible" in yet another way: it became known that the night before the Elliott shooting a meeting was held in Salisbury attended only by local blacks, during which outsiders identified as communists told the blacks they were being economically exploited by their white employers and exhorted them to take steps to end their oppression. Matthew Williams was reported to have been there, though no connection between the meeting and the shooting could be established once Williams was dead.

One day after the lynching, on December 5, 1931, the *Baltimore Sun* published an editorial, "Disgrace," which said, in part, "The lowest and least civilized elements [took] command; and that remains true whether or not men of position participated in the Salisbury lynching or tacitly approved it." Several letters to the editor followed, one of which, signed "A Reader," was captioned, "Very, Very Bold, But Not Enough So to Use His Name to This Letter"—an indication of the *Sun*'s negative attitude toward the writer (December 7, 1931). Though the letter was datelined Baltimore, it apparently was written by a Shoreman and I believe it represents the feelings of many Shoremen:

> It seems to me that you have taken only one side of the question, and also you condemn the whole Eastern Shore for this particular case. . . . The case of Yuel Lee hacking to death a complete white family was but a stimulus to the mob. . . . If this Negro had been promptly tried and hanged, there would not have been a lynching yesterday. . . . Negroes on the Eastern Shore are well-behaved. Where I come from the Negro steps aside and raises his hat. . . . I predict that there won't be any more white people shot down by Negroes for some time, for they know what is their due if they should.

Four days after the lynching a vitriolic new editorial, "The Eastern Shore Kultur," signed by H.L. Mencken, appeared in the *Baltimore Sun*. (It was reprinted in full on the front page of the *Salisbury Times* on the following day, December 8, 1931.) Well-known for his free use of immoderate language, Mencken here let out all the stops, attacking the Shore as a place "wherein there are no competent police, little save a simian self-seeking in public office, no apparent intelligence on the bench, and no courage and decency in the local press." He alleged that the lynching occurred in a milieu of social degeneration that had permitted "ninth-rate men" to come to power. And he argued for a concerted effort "to educate" the Eastern Shore: "The majority of people, even in Wicomico, are probably teachable." In his attack, Mencken did what many other outside observers did in writing about the lynching—he condemned the entire population for it, including those in high positions, not merely those who had actually participated in it. From the local perspective, outsiders were blaming the Shore for something that had been caused by outsiders.

The Wicomico County state's attorney conducted a grand-jury investigation to determine who had been responsible for the lynching, but witness after witness failed to identify any participant, saying the lynchers' faces were unfamiliar. It was reported in the local press that eyewitnesses thought the perpetrators had come from out of town, possibly from the Eastern Shore of Virginia. Fifty years later the state's attorney's son told me the same thing, stressing that people honestly did not know who the lynchers were. Oral accounts in the Salisbury State University folklore archives sustain this view as well; for example, a man who was in his teens when the lynching occurred said in 1972, "I right now could not tell you a single person I saw. . . . Amazing thing about a crowd—you don't see individuals, you just see a crowd."

No indictments were found in the grand-jury investigation, and in late January 1932 the Salisbury lynching case was closed. Outsiders were furious. Broadus Mitchell, a liberal professor of political science at Johns Hopkins University, conducted a brief survey of Salisbury for the Federal Council of the Churches of Christ in America and published a report critical of the town (and, by implication, the region). The *Salisbury Times* responded with a front-page editorial, "In Rebuttal to Prof. Broadus Mitchell," on January 30, 1932, which said, in part, "it is extremely difficult for any blue-blooded American to sit idly by and witness the spectacle of a wholesale indictment of the ideals and the institutions established by his progenitors. . . . The professor . . . concludes after interviewing a dozen persons during a three day visit here, that Salisbury is lacking in 'civic morality,' its residents are mentally deficient and they fail to 'apply religion to life,' and he tries to find an explanation for this in what he terms our 'isolation.'" The editorial then devotes considerable space to discrediting Mitchell as a commentator, citing his membership in the American Civil Liberties Union (a "communist organization") and connecting the ACLU with "the International Labor Defense, another known communist organization." But the real sentiment of the editorial is felt in the following: "The report may be worthy of a citation for the distinguished service its author has rendered to the cause of the Soviet government, but what about the humiliation it has brought a Christian, English speaking people here in Salisbury. . . . [W]e do not relish the injury Prof. Mitchell has inflicted upon us."

To recapitulate: the Salisbury lynching was not resolved to the satisfaction of outsiders and as events proceeded the collective feelings of the Eastern Shore had been battered; the Lee murder case had been usurped by outsiders and was to drag on in Baltimore for nearly two more years. Euel Lee eventually was found guilty of murder, but even after his conviction the lawyers from ILD kept staying his execution through a series of appeals to various state and federal courts. For two years, Eastern Shoremen had been reading of these trials and appeals, and it does not seem likely that the length of time it was taking to bring Lee to justice was doing anything to abate their resentment about the conduct of the case. After several last-ditch appeals, reported agonizingly in the daily papers, Lee was at last hanged in Baltimore on October 27, 1933.

The execution of Euel Lee, which presumably would have eased the anger and resentment of people in the Shore, came too late for George Armwood, a black man who died at the hands of a lynch mob in Princess Anne on October 18.

The events immediately prior to this second lynching are reported differently by blacks and whites. Were it not for the research efforts of John R. Wennersten, who conducted "ten confidential interviews of blacks resident at Princess Anne at the time of the lynching," we might never have a record of the black version.[9] According to this version, a white farmer in Somerset County, John Richardson, persuaded George Armwood, a farm worker, to help him rob an elderly white woman. The woman, who owned rental properties, was known to carry cash as she walked from property to property collecting rents. Richardson's plan for robbing her was preposterous, and Armwood, who was described by Wennersten's black informants as "slow-witted," would doubtless never have agreed to participate in it had he had all his faculties. The plan was this: Armwood would lurk in the forest waiting for the woman, Mrs. Denston, to come by. Disguised by a wool cap pulled down over his face, he would grab her money, take the money to Richardson, and split the proceeds with him. In the enactment of the crime, however, things did not work out as planned. Mrs. Denston struggled and Armwood succeeded only in disrobing her and having his pitiful disguise pulled off his face.

In the version published in newspapers (October 17-20, 1933), which we may take to be the white version, no mention was made of the Richardson-Armwood conspiracy; only the black man's attack on the elderly white woman was reported. Richardson's only reported role in the story was as an accessory after the fact, for Armwood had gone to him and asked for help in escaping, and Richardson had transported him several miles south to the farm of his brother, James Richardson, near the Maryland-Virginia border. It took only a few hours for the police to find and arrest Armwood, but in the meantime a rumor had gone abroad that Armwood had raped Mrs. Denston, who was variously reported as being seventy-two, eighty-two, and ninety-two years old.

Emotions in Princess Anne were therefore high, but they rose even higher when an officer of the State Police, fearing for Armwood's safety because of the Euel Lee case and the Salisbury lynching, telephoned the governor of Maryland and secured his permission (though the governor had no authority to grant it) to take Armwood to Baltimore under cover of night, which was done. The next day the Somerset County sheriff traveled to Baltimore with a writ of habeas corpus, properly issued by the Somerset County state's attorney, and brought Armwood back to Princess Anne. That night a mob of about two thousand people stormed the county jail, brought Armwood out, hanged him, and burned his body.

As a human being, I cannot help finding these facts appalling. As a folklorist I cannot help noticing that the Armwood lynching was the third in a series of nationally reported events, each contributing to the rage of Eastern Shoremen who, whatever their social standing or occupation, found themselves the object of ridicule and attack by outsiders. It seems that the power of the number to shape perception, the esoteric-exoteric factor that can foster "us against them" thinking, and the irrational way people can act upon cultural impulses below the level of consciousness all combined in the Armwood case. It is little wonder that Shore citizens, in editorials and letters to the editor over the 1931-33 period, claimed repeatedly that outside interference in the Lee case had been the root cause of the violence that followed. Matthew Williams and George Armwood were implicated in crimes at the wrong moment in history. Both became victims to misdirected anger against outsiders—a circumstance that, I believe, sets these two lynchings apart from others that happened elsewhere in the country during the same period.

The aftermath of the Princess Anne lynching constituted an exercise in ironic futility. As with the Salisbury lynching, a locally conducted grand-jury investigation found no indictments. This time, however, officials at the state level were determined to prosecute, and after a series of machinations that might be the stuff of comic opera were they not so grim, several Somerset County men were implicated in the lynching. At issue was whether the state or the county had authority to prosecute. Local feeling against the state's action was so great that the governor sent a detachment of three hundred National Guardsmen to the Shore in an effort to keep the peace as the men were being transported to Baltimore. Violence erupted at the Salisbury National Guard Armory, however; a crowd of two thousand was tear-gassed and shots were fired. The attorney general of Maryland, who was present at the incident, escaped with his life. (He later dropped his campaign to prosecute lynchers, and the Princess Anne case was closed early in 1934.) The anger generated in the Shore was so great that it contributed to the governor's losing his 1934 bid for reelection.

The anger of Shoremen was not directed solely at the governor, however; the *Baltimore Sun* was blamed locally for inflammatory reporting and for being prejudiced against the Shore. As one oral informant, a young woman at the time of the incident, said in 1971, "I still won't buy a *Baltimore Sun*. They were terrible about it—they called us everything in the book, said we were beating everyone with hoses, rakes, shovels—and if they hadn't exaggerated everything that happened it would have died down a lot quicker. The Baltimore papers sent reporters, and the militia was sent in to quiet us down. But the Eastern Shore people would have none of other people telling them what they should and should not do."

Even if the facts of the Eastern Shore events could be fully established and agreed upon (an unlikely eventuality, since the folk memory differs from the printed record and the black memory differs from the white), the interpretation of the facts would remain problematical. During the 1930s the Eastern Shore was racially segregated, but even the most thoughtful white Eastern Shoremen honestly did not see segregation as a valid issue and they earnestly and consistently denied that racism had anything to do with the violence reported in the news. Their position was, and continues to be, that the issue should be discussed in terms of local and county authority as opposed to the authority of the state (or, more broadly, to the putative authority of the Western Shore). Outsiders, by contrast, persisted in seeing the events in racial and cultural terms, and this profound difference in approach to interpretation of facts contributed heavily to the Shore's resentments.

That seems to be the real issue—resistance to and resentment of being meddled with by outsiders. I learned this myself several years ago, the hard way. The setting was the annual meeting of one of the Lower Shore county historical societies, a respected group of local white residents, many of whom hold high positions in the community. I was there because I had been invited to deliver the major address. I had been a Lower Shore resident for ten years at that time. Many members of the society were known to me through community service and through social contact, so I felt at ease with them both as individuals and as a group. I was excited by my topic, for I had been studying the Princess Anne lynching and was just starting to apply the theory of regional consciousness to it (I had not at that point connected it with the other two events). Knowing that everyone present would be familiar with the Princess Anne incident, I thought the annual meeting would be a perfect place to discuss the regional theory. Following my incisive and enlightening presentation, my well-educated and reasonable audience would see the historical event with new eyes and would come away with a new respect for themselves as tradition bearers.

That was my plan. What actually happened was that everybody in the audience stopped listening as soon as I said "Princess Anne lynching"—about halfway through the talk—and spent the rest of the time getting ready for assault. Years afterward it is still hard to write about this. I was hurt and mystified at the vehemence of their reaction, horrified at the irrationality of their anger. These people were my friends, and they were turning on me. Some responded with more anger than others, but it was clear that everyone there was really upset with me. Some of them still are.

Had I not ignored two key points in the theory of regional consciousness—that it applies universally in a region by crossing all class and educational lines, and that it operates without reference to reason—I could have avoided so egregious a blunder. But I misjudged my audience and became, in their eyes, yet another outsider telling local people what was what.

# Image and Identity in Oregon's Pioneer Cemeteries

## RICHARD E. MEYER

*The sources of regional identity and regional consciousness vary from one region to another. For residents of Maryland's Eastern Shore, according to Polly Stewart, geographical isolation seems to be the predominant factor. On the opposite side of the United States, Richard Meyer pinpoints the historical fact of westward migration as the wellspring of regional identity for residents of the heart of the old Oregon Territory. He concentrates on the grave-markers found in pioneer cemeteries in Oregon, finding in their motifs and epitaphs an emphasis on the rigors, dangers, and tragedies of pioneer life, experiences that are perceived by current residents as the bedrock of regional identity. (All photographs in this essay are by Richard E. Meyer.)*

Today's Pacific Northwest, an area encompassing the states of Oregon, Washington, and Idaho, in addition to portions of northern California, western Montana, and southern British Columbia, was, prior to the middle years of the nineteenth century, most often known simply as the "Oregon Country." This vast segment of the North American continent has a rich and varied history which has involved the fortunes of no less than half a dozen nations. Certainly a pivotal event in Pacific Northwest history, however, and the one which was eventually to bring a large portion of this territory under the permanent control of the United States, was the initial emigration of thousands of people from the southern, eastern, and mid-western sectors of the United States to the large and immensely fertile Willamette Valley region of the present state of Oregon. This process, which spanned nearly fifty years but saw its greatest concentration in the decades of the 1840s, 1850s, and 1860s, had always at its heart the lure of free and abundant agricultural land, though it was spurred considerably in the 1850s and 1860s by a series of rich gold strikes in southern and eastern Oregon, as well as in adjacent portions of Idaho, Washington, and California. The men, women, and children who took part in this vast enterprise (today usually referred to by the somewhat romanticized term "pioneers," though they most frequently called themselves "emigrants") were beyond question a most hardy and resourceful lot, and their deeds, real as well as imaginary, have become a significant part of the American mythology.[1]

For a variety of reasons, many of which seem quite justified in terms of both chronology and geography, Oregonians have traditionally considered their state to have been the physical and spiritual heart of Northwest pioneer settlement. Their pride in and ready identification with this phenomenon, manifested in a variety of expressive forms, ranging from frequent "Pioneer Days" festivals and reenactments of events in pioneer history to the recent statement by a political aspirant that "a new generation of pioneers" was needed to lead the state into the twenty-first century, reach almost obsessive levels at times and are quite apparent to any contemporary observer. What other state can claim an official, legislatively decreed Pioneer Mother, to take her place beside the usual state bird, flower, tree, and anthem? Perhaps even more striking are the many visual reminders, both permanent and ephemeral, of the pioneer experience which dot the cultural landscape. High atop the rotunda of the state capitol in Salem stands a huge gilded statue of the Oregon Pioneer, while eternally facing each other across a quadrangle at the University of Oregon in Eugene sit the stony-faced effigies of the Pioneer Mother and Pioneer Father. Cities and towns incorporate dramatic visual symbols of the pioneer experience into their signs, as do museums, historic sites, and buildings, but the phenomenon penetrates to other, more mundane levels as well (fig. 1), dominating names and logos of countless pizza parlors, motels, hair salons, and other small businesses.

These are largely contemporary artifacts, demonstrating the ongoing vitality of the pioneering metaphor in the imagination of today's Oregonians. But what of an earlier time, one in which the *actual* pioneer experience lived within the memories of those who participated in it? Did these early Oregonians also find avenues of material expression to proclaim the significance of their accomplishments, and are these artifacts still present and visible today? Fortunately, the answer in both cases is yes. Cemeteries, as more than one commentator has noted, are remarkable indicators of the dominant cultural values at work in the societies which produce them.[2] When I first became interested in Oregon's pioneer cemeteries

Fig. 1. Pioneer Motel, Pendleton, Oregon. Note image of covered wagon, oxen, pioneer.

several years ago, it was largely with the intention of testing the thesis that I would find mirrored within them a verbal and visual emphasis upon the pioneer experience which, almost from the beginning of the settlement period, was coalescing to form a significant part of the region's collective self-concept. The present essay, based upon fieldwork in some six hundred Oregon pioneer cemeteries, is an effort to validate not only this limited thesis, but also, by extension, the assertion made by folklorist Barre Toelken that "In Oregon, as in any other state . . . we should be able to find clusters of folk art that fairly represent the response of those folk groups to the life they lived and continue to live."[3]

Death was a dominant part of the Oregon pioneer experience from the onset. Vast numbers never survived the emigration process itself and received lonely burials at sea or, as was far more frequently the case, in unmarked graves along the Oregon Trail.[4] Hardships, danger, and disasters of every sort beset the emigrants, with disease the greatest terror of all. In 1852 alone, the so-called "cholera year" on the Oregon Trail, whole wagon trains were wiped out by the disease and left to rot along the way. The journal of the noted women's rights leader Abigail (Scott) Duniway, who as a child crossed the plains in 1852 with her family, grimly catalogs the number of new graves encountered with each day's passage, and Joaquin Miller, an early Oregon journalist and poet who made the overland crossing in that same year, would later remember the Oregon Trail as the place where "brown'd and russet grasses wave / Along a thousand leagues that lie one common grave."[5] A few who survived the greater part of the journey would, ironically, die within sight of their objective. Such was the case for forty-four-year-old William T. Hines, whose family, having come so far together, chose not to leave him along the trail but rather carried him onward to receive proper burial at their ultimate destination. His marker, which stands in the Pike Cemetery (also known as the "IOOF" cemetery), near Yamhill, Oregon, notes simply that he "Died at Emigrant Crossing, Snake River, Aug. 7, 1847."

The early years in the Oregon country were likewise ones of constant hardship, danger, and imminent death. Burials at first were often haphazard and isolated: certain of these sites are still identifiable, and there are a surprisingly large number of geographic features in the state bearing such descriptive names as Grave Creek, Deadman Canyon, and Tombstone Prairie.[6] But with the exception of the two Willamette Valley cemeteries established in the late 1830s in conjunction with Oregon's first missions—the Methodist (1834) near Salem and the Catholic (1839) at St. Paul—organized cemeteries as such do not begin to appear in the area comprising the present state of Oregon until the mid- to late 1840s, coincident with the increasing waves of emigration. Most of these early examples were private family cemeteries and many of them have remained such until the present day; others evolved into larger community cemeteries under the control of fraternal organizations, churches, or local governmental units. Typical in many respects of such evolution is the case of Salem's Pioneer Cemetery, one of the most beautiful and historically significant early cemeteries in the state. Originating as a private family plot in 1841 with the burial of the Reverend David Leslie's first wife, the site was expanded both spatially and functionally in 1854, when it was acquired by the local lodge of the Independent Order of Odd Fellows (IOOF). After some one hundred years of sporadic maintenance by the IOOF, it was eventually passed on to county and, finally, city control, where it remains today with the assistance of a dedicated and highly active Friends organization. Similar processes have resulted in the fortunate preservation of particularly important early cemeteries in Portland, Oregon City, Albany, and Jacksonville.

Not all pioneer cemeteries in Oregon have fared as well as these examples, however. Many lie in a state of virtual ruin, victims of the same diseases—neglect, vandalism, weathering, and airborne pollution—which seem to plague old burial grounds in all regions of the country. In a number of instances, one of these sites might be the last tangible reminder that a community once existed in a certain area, and, regrettably, sometimes even these have disappeared from the cultural landscape. Despite all this, well over one thousand of these pioneer cemeteries are known in Oregon today, ranging in size from very tiny to quite extensive and encompassing all geographic localities of the state.[7] Most important, they still contain an amazing array of artifacts which speak eloquently and forcefully of the hopes, fears, and values of those who created them.

If one were to attempt to summarize the essential character of Oregon's pioneer cemeteries, an immediate observation would be that they fall quite clearly within the general framework of the Victorian cemetery movement—a phenomenon distinguished by progressively elaborate treatment of both monumental and landscape features of cemeteries—as seen in the more settled eastern portions of the United States. This is demonstrated in a number of ways, including the frequent adoption of the more popular visual elements of Victorian gravestone iconography. Present everywhere are the ubiquitous clasped hands and weeping willow motifs. Readily apparent as well are numerous instances of ascending angels (fig. 2) and fingers pointing to heaven, two of the more obvious of the varied resurrection symbols popular during this period. Balancing these are the many equally popular variants of mortality symbolism—shattered pillars, severed chain links, and broken flower stems, all serving to denote a life cut off before its time—as well as repeated instances of those specialized motifs of child death—the dove and the lamb. A host of other symbolic devices complete the picture, including fraternal insignia of all sorts and, upon occasion, some striking examples of occupational imagery (fig. 3).

Epitaphs, at least the more elaborate, poetic types, tend to be those found in the popular sample books available to many marble carvers during this period; the most commonly observed are variants upon this favorite: "Shed not for me the bitter tear, / Nor give thy heart to vain regret; / 'Tis but the casket that lies here, / The gem

Fig. 2 (*left*). Ascending angel motif. Stone of Eliza Viola Smith (d. 1870). Masonic Cemetery, Albany, Oregon.

Fig. 3 (*right*). Marker for a pioneer blacksmith. Stone of John A. Buford (d. 1899). Emanuel Cemetery, near Cornelius, Oregon.

that filled it sparkles yet."Or this touching quatrain so often found on children's stones: "She was but as a smile / Which glistens in a tear; / Seen but a little while, / But, oh, how loved, how dear." Other shared elements of the Victorian cemetery movement include a trend toward increasingly elaborate monumentation as the century wears on and a growing emphasis upon the family plot as the primary spatial concept within the cemetery proper (fig. 4).

All of this emulation should come as no great surprise, however, for although Oregon during this period was definitely a frontier region, these recent settlers did not by any means relish the primitive conditions under which they were often forced to live. Rather, it was the fond desire of most of them to convert as quickly as possible this social as well as physical wilderness into a reasonable facsimile

Fig. 4. Ish family plot. Jacksonville Cemetery, Jacksonville, Oregon.

of the civilized portions of the country. Thus they were in many
instances eager to embrace the current fashions of mid- to late-
nineteenth-century America, including those pertaining to cemeteries and gravemarkers. This would explain, among other things,
the early appearance and rapid spread of stone-carving establishments in principal towns and cities—Eugene, Corvallis, Albany,
Salem, Oregon City, Portland—along the south-north flow of the
Willamette River.[8]

And yet, if in one sense Oregon's pioneer cemeteries reflect the
styles and customs of the Victorian cemetery movement in general,
in another they have their own unique flavor, stemming largely
from their insistent and highly visible emphasis upon the pioneer
experience itself. Nor is this the paradox it might at first appear, for
while longing for the secure and settled conditions of mainstream
America, these hardy settlers seem to have been acutely aware, as
indeed are many of their descendants today, of the great and enduring significance of their accomplishments.

There are two primary means by which the pioneering experience is manifested in Oregon's early cemeteries. The first of these
involves a careful chronicling of the hazards of daily life on the

Fig. 5. Hartless children stone (all d. 1854). Mount Union Cemetery, near Corvallis, Oregon.

frontier, which, as might well be imagined, took many forms in this frequently hostile environment. If disease was a scourge on the overland (or sea) journey, it certainly remained so once the settlers arrived in the Oregon country, and the progress of epidemics over space and time can often literally be charted by the evidence cited in the stone records of early burial grounds. Typhoid and smallpox are among the most frequently listed causes of death in all age groups, while the particularly devastating effects of such diseases as scarlet fever and diphtheria among children are grimly reflected in the numerous instances of multiple-child headstones found in pioneer cemeteries (fig. 5); on occasion as many as six children in one family are listed as dying within a period of several months. A particularly sobering reminder of the high incidence of child death during this period may be found in the old Sterlingville, Oregon, Cemetery: here, upon a single marble obelisk, are listed the dates of ten

children of Joseph B. and Mary E. Saltmarsh, all of whom died
before reaching their tenth birthday in a period stretching from 1856
to 1878.

The long and often bitter struggles between settlers and native
populations are prominently recorded upon white pioneer gravemarkers scattered throughout the state. Near the coastal town of
Gold Beach, a frequently-visited marker (now actually part of a state
park) proclaims that it is "Sacred to the memory of John Geisel / Also
his three sons, John, Henry, & Andrew / Who were massacred by
the Indians / Feb. 22, A.D. 1856." In the Jacksonville Cemetery in
southern Oregon a similar vein is struck in the memorial to
"William Boddy & Sons / Murdered by the Modoc Indians / November 29, 1872." This "Killed by Indians" theme is likewise echoed on
a number of markers erected in the Olney Cemetery, Pendleton,
Oregon, in memory of white settlers who died in eastern Oregon's
1878 Bannock-Paiute War.[9] And there are many more. By way of
contrast, however, it is perhaps worth noting that I have yet to see a
marker expressing sentiments of a similarly vituperative nature in
any of Oregon's Native American cemeteries dating from this same
period.

One of the most frequent causes of death cited on Oregon
pioneer gravemarkers is drowning, a reminder of the perils of
navigating the major rivers of this territory during the nineteenth
century. Two of the more spectacular examples—both testimonials
to the skills of certain stone carvers in early Oregon—actually
provide visual representations of the incidents in question. The
stone of Captain Robert B. Randall, located in the Pioneer Memorial
Cemetery in Umatilla, Oregon, not only tells us that he "Drowned
in the rapids near Umatilla, Ogn., March 7, 1875," but vividly
depicts him and his boat approaching this formerly dangerous
stretch of white water near the confluence of the Umatilla and
Columbia Rivers. And in Portland's historic Lone Fir Cemetery may
be found the unique stone of Frederic Roeder (fig. 6), whose death
by drowning on June 19, 1887 is dramatically represented by the
depiction of high waves, his boat, and his hands sinking below the
surface of the water.

The perils of certain occupations in a frontier region are amply
documented as well. This is particularly evident with regard to
those involved in various forms of transportation, as, for example,
the case of Captain Frederick K. Morse, whose marker in the old
Milwaukie Cemetery notes that he was "Killed on Christmas Day

Fig. 6. Drowning scene. Stone of Frederic Roeder (d. 1887). Lone Fir Cemetery, Portland, Oregon.

1850 by explosion of a cannon while celebrating the launching of the Lot Whitcomb at Milwaukie, Oregon, the first steam boat built on the Pacific Coast."[10] A marker for Asher F. Wall, a stagecoach driver, erected in Roseburg's pioneer cemetery by his fellow employees of the C.S.O. Stage Company, displays a handsome set of stage driver's whips along with the simple explanation that he "Died in the discharge of his duty, Dec. 17, 1974." Less decorative in design but more to the point descriptively is the stone located in the old Canyonville Cemetery which declares that it is "Sacred to the memory of Robert E. Lee Roberts, who died on duty as fireman in the wreck of the O. & C. R.R. Train in Rock Cut, Cow Creek Canyon, Or., Jan. 1, 1888." Other occupational hazards are recorded as well. What might well be the earliest extant marker for a logger in the Pacific Northwest, that of William F. Laymen in the Brownsville Pioneer Cemetery, utilizes language which almost seems to suggest a bizarre sort of antiadvertisement when it proclaims that he was "Killed by falling from a tree while working for J. Larkin, Nov. 3,

1880." A reminder that Oregon was indeed a part of the "Wild West" is provided by the stone in the IOOF Cemetery at The Dalles erected "In memory of Charles Keeler, born in Baden Gy, and murdered while in discharge of his duty as city marshal Sept. 5, 1867."

The sort of frontier violence captured on the Keeler stone is echoed on markers throughout the state. A quarrel with an acquaintance on the streets of frontier Scio led to twenty-nine-year-old James A. Young's burial in nearby Pleasant Grove Cemetery, where his inscription informs us that he "Died from the effects of wounds with a knife." A handsome double stone in the old Linkville Cemetery, Klamath Falls, tells the truncated story of Lee and Joe Laws, two young brothers who were "Murdered by masked assassins, June 24, 1882," while a simpler marker for William Moody in the Eagle Valley Cemetery, near the small eastern Oregon community of Richland, notes enigmatically that he was "Murdered by his pretended friends." In some instances families of victims were not adverse to naming names in a most extraordinarily permanent fashion, as evidenced by the gravestone for Isaiah Graham in Portland's Lone Fir Cemetery, which states unequivocally that he was "Assassinated by Thomas Ward, June 21, 1871." A smaller inscription at the base of the stone adds, "May the Lord forgive the evil doer."

Other causes of death listed on these early markers portray a wide variety of potential dangers consistent with a frontier environment: for example, "Was killed by a runaway team" (George Henderson, d. 1879, Henderson Pioneer Cemetery, near Dufur, Oregon); "Lost in mountains" (J.R. Bucknum, d. 1898, Alford-Workman Cemetery, near Harrisburg, Oregon); or "Killed by a grizzly bear" (B.H. Baird, d. 1864, Croxton Cemetery, Grants Pass, Oregon). A surprising number of stones, as, for example, that of fourteen-year-old Salem Dixon (d. 1853) in the Hobson-Whitney Pioneer Cemetery, near Sublimity, Oregon, record the cause of death as "accidental shooting." An occasional inscription teases the imagination by virtue of its understatement, so that one wonders, for instance, what fate befell young Thomas H. Judkins, whose marker in Laurel Hill Cemetery near Eugene simply tells us that he "Left camp twenty miles east of Eugene Mar. 6, 1881 / Remains was found 1 mi. from camp, May 12, 1881."

These stone records of pioneer hazards and death do not tell the entire story, of course. They may be supplemented, indeed vastly expanded, by examining municipal death records, newspaper accounts, and even the rather idiosyncratic records of cemetery sextons, wherein we sometimes find such fascinating entries as "Shot by her husband in a house of ill fame at the corner of Salmon and 3rd St." or "Killed by falling into sewer, suffocated in the mud."[11] But the cemeteries themselves speak quite clearly of a time in Oregon's history when life was lived in the shadow of sudden, and not infrequently violent, death.

The other primary manner in which markers in Oregon's pioneer cemeteries call attention to the pioneer experience is through inscriptions and visual symbols which emphasize the emigration and settlement processes themselves. An astounding number of these markers take great pains to highlight—often in letters enlarged for purposes of emphasis—the emigrant's state, or in some cases country, of origin in the inscriptional data found upon the stone. These artifacts provide the modern observer with a relatively clear notion of basic settlement patterns in the Oregon country; early markers in the Willamette Valley, for instance, show a heavy preponderance of New England and midwestern origin points in the northern portions of the valley, with the emphasis shifting to southern origins as one proceeds southward down the valley. The stones also emphasize clearly the inherent emotional dualism of the pioneering experience: the unwillingness to forgo entirely a link with a former time and place even while resting beneath the soil of what has become, indubitably, home.

Almost as prevalent are the numerous references, especially among those who arrived via the Oregon Trail, to specific dates of emigration (fig. 7). The year of emigration, or in some cases even the specific wagon train, became sources of pride and esoteric identification to settlers in the Oregon country.[12] In virtually any pioneer cemetery in the state the careful observer will find inscriptions which deliberately emphasize such data, often in conjunction with other elements of the pioneering experience (fig. 8).

In addition to these verbal inscriptions, however, one striking and pervasive visual image leaps out at visitors to many of the state's pioneer cemeteries—that of the covered overland wagon. This icon, which has come in many ways to sum up the entire pioneer experience to Oregonians, is, as I have previously noted, featured in a dazzling array of contemporary manifestations from the official state seal to business signs for taverns, banks, real estate offices, and pancake houses. That it is also present on gravestones from an early period onward should come, therefore, as no great

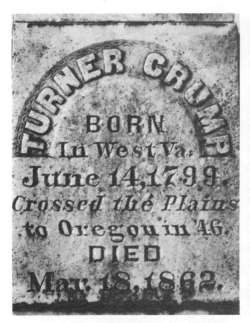

Fig. 7. Emigration date. Stone of Turner Crump (d. 1862). Salem Pioneer Cemetery, Salem, Oregon.

Fig. 8. Emigration date and other pioneer data. Stone of Samuel (d. 1891) and Huldah (d. 1907) Colver, "Pioneers of 1850 who located on this donation claim in 1851 amid hostile indians and who have seen the wilderness." Phoenix Cemetery, Phoenix, Oregon.

surprise. For high and low—from the impressive monument to David T. Lenox (d. 1873), captain of one of the first wagon trains to reach the old Oregon country, located in the West Union Baptist Church Cemetery, near West Union, Oregon, to the simple tablet which speaks to the life and deeds of Francis M. "Uncle Dan" Daniel (d. 1897) in Providence Cemetery, near the small mid-Willamette Valley community of Lacomb—this simple image conveys a unique shared bond of pride and historic significance. Speaking in a way for all of them is the lovely stone of Daniel Simons (fig. 9), which, though shattered by the hands of vandals, still manages to convey, through its detailed accounting of his journey to Oregon, its finely carved depiction of a pioneer covered wagon, and its declaration that "Men like this conquered the West," the awesome sense of accomplishment felt by these emigrants. Perhaps

Fig. 9. Covered wagon and other pioneer data. Stone of Daniel Simons (d. 1875). Pioneer (Old Lebanon) Cemetery, Lebanon, Oregon.

this is why, even today, it is not uncommon for the descendants of pioneer families to specify the depiction of covered wagons when replacing missing or damaged originals with newer, backdated markers (fig. 10).

In speaking of the intrinsic values of cemeteries, the cultural geographer Terry Jordan has written, "Nowhere else is it possible to look so deeply into our people's past."[13] How very true, for old cemeteries are unique and irreplaceable outdoor museums, full of words and images which reflect the worldviews and cultural values of bygone eras. In the case of Oregon's pioneer cemeteries, where site and artifact combine to produce such a diverse and beautiful element of the cultural landscape, past and present are intimately connected by an emphasis upon the pioneer experience which has come to form so important a part of the collective self-image, not only of Oregonians, but of Pacific Northwesterners in general.

Fig. 10. Covered wagon on contemporary, backdated marker. Stone of
Mary Jane King (d. ca. 1913) and Nathaniel C. (d. ca. 1909) Huntley.
Gold Beach Pioneer Cemetery, Gold Beach, Oregon.

# Carbon-Copy Towns?
# The Regionalization of Ethnic
# Folklife in Southern Illinois's Egypt

## JOHN M. COGGESHALL

*John M. Coggeshall also considers the role of settlement history in the development of a distinctive regional culture in southern Illinois's Egypt. He documents the complexity of Egypt's regional culture in the presence of ethnic folk traditions among groups drawn to the region by jobs in the local coal mines. By setting regional and ethnic identity side by side, Coggeshall offers the useful reminder that regional culture is multifaceted and that regional identity coexists with other forms and sources of consciousness.*

The place names of Cairo, Karnak, and Thebes evoke images of royal barges drifting past pyramids under a hot desert sun. But these names associated with the nation of Egypt are also known in the American region of Egypt, in extreme southern Illinois. From earliest Anglo-American settlement, America's Egypt has been recognized as a distinct region. Its uniqueness, enhanced by folklore, made of residents a regional folk group with an identity based on a shared history and expressed through distinct folklife traditions.[1] As Poles, Italians, and Slovakians entered the region in the nineteenth century to mine coal, they gradually adopted this identity as well, compelled by a common occupation, the pressures of assimilation, and the xenophobia of their neighbors to surrender many old-country customs.

Suzi Jones has described this process as regionalization; as groups continuously interact with one another, they modify or manipulate folklife traditions to reflect changing perceptions of themselves and their region.[2] Today, people in Egypt share a regional identity conveyed through specific folklife traditions.

Despite this shared identity, however, Egyptians also recognize differences among intraregional folk groups, since ethnic distinctions have persisted independently of regionalizing mechanisms.

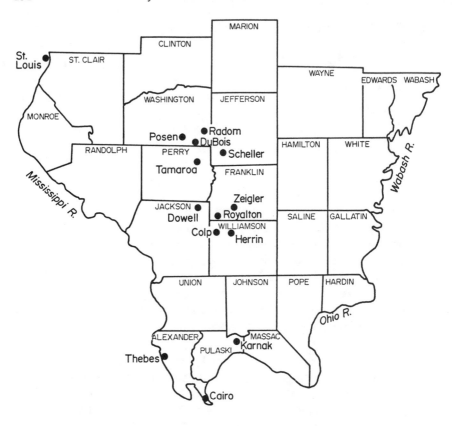

Communities investigated during summer 1986.

In effect, the combination of regional unity with diversity resembles a stained-glass window. Egypt serves as a frame, in which are suspended the multicolored panels of various ethnic traditions, delimited and interconnected by the lead of social interaction. Another layer of glass overlies the whole, a covering of historically evolved regional folklife expressions. In this essay I examine the stained-glass window of southern Illinois folklife traditions, first by discussing the outlines of regional folk themes and then by highlighting selected ethnic units whose uniqueness continues to shine. The pattern of light which emerges displays ethnic diversity within a unified regional identity.

The section of Illinois called Egypt is bounded on the west by the Mississippi River, the south by the Ohio, and on the east by the

Wabash. The northern boundary terminates in the glaciated prairies approximately at the latitude of St. Louis, Missouri.[3] The region contains several major physiographic forms, including the Shawnee Hills, constituting about the southern half; and the more northern Mount Vernon hill country, containing most of the coalfields and all of the towns mentioned here.[4]

The origin of the region's name is problematic. John Allen traced it to a legend about a severe crop shortage in Illinois in 1831. Farmers traveling south to obtain grain remarked that they were "'going down to Egypt for corn,'" comparing bountiful southern Illinois to the groaning grain coffers of biblical Egypt.[5]

The settlement history of southern Illinois established the independence of the region from the more northern counties. Aside from a few eighteenth-century French villages along the Mississippi River, most of the pioneers came from the southeastern states beginning in the late eighteenth century.[6] These uplanders chose the hilly areas of Egypt because of the resemblance to their former mountain homes, and because they possessed the technology to utilize the relatively rugged terrain. In contrast, Yankees settled the northern Illinois counties. The demographic contrast enhanced the regional separation, for the pioneers brought with them their "dialect, family traits, [fundamentalist] religion, and numerous folkways," creating "a region homogeneous with the western Appalachians and altogether unlike central and northern Illinois."[7]

From those beginnings Egypt became notorious. Legends arose of outlaws waylaying travelers. The southern sentiments of Egyptians created uneasiness for northern politicians during the Civil War, and Copperhead sympathizers patrolled the sandstone hills. The Ku Klux Klan briefly appeared during Reconstruction. Strongly Democratic and fiercely independent of the Republican counties to the north, southern Illinois retained its well-earned reputation as a rough frontier region into the late nineteenth century.

About that time Egypt entered a period of transition as huge deposits of coal began to be mined commercially on a large scale. Immigrants poured in, attracted by the promise of steady work at relatively good wages. Real estate values soared, towns were built or expanded, businesses boomed, and southern Illinois experienced a tremendous period of growth.[8]

The development of the coal mines and surrounding communities launched several influential forces which combined to regionalize the immigrants by merging diverse folklife traditions. Since most newcomers became miners, this occupation triggered the changes. Coal companies, fearing competition and unionization, isolated workers in company towns, inadvertently bringing diverse European cultural groups into close contact. Vernacular architectural styles faded as companies built shoddy houses for workers. Mine owners often paid in scrip, redeemable only at company stores, where goods were often relatively expensive.[9] Such monopolistic control created the potential for abuse.

Owner neglect and worker exploitation united immigrants under another regionalizing force: unionism. Initially the companies tried to prohibit unionization by breaking strikes. One method involved the importation of blacks from the Deep South "into a country, predominately Southern in its culture, classed as a no-man's land during much of the Civil War."[10] This importation heightened antiblack sentiment and increased union militarism even more.

The violent apogee came in 1922. During a national miners' strike, the Southern Illinois Coal Company hired strikebreakers, which infuriated the area's miners. In preparation for attack, the company had fortified their mine with earthworks, machine-gun nests, and watch towers; the miners besieged the fort with gun fire and dynamite bombs dropped from low-flying planes. Eventually the scabs surrendered and dozens were killed in the legendary "Herrin Massacre." The event electrified the nation and intensified Egypt's reputation as a "bloody" region.[11]

Unfortunately for Egypt, other forces enhanced that reputation further. Between 1890 and 1920 immigrant coal miners swelled the foreign-born population of the region tremendously. Native southern Illinoisans, having already established a regional identity, resented the newcomers.[12] By the 1920s fundamentalist nativists transformed this animosity into antiforeign and anti-Catholic enmity, enforced by a reborn Ku Klux Klan. Throughout southern Illinois, isolated immigrant communities were harassed and homes raided, largely under the guise of enforcing locally lenient Prohibition laws.[13]

For several years the region seethed with fear, hatred, and imminent violence. Several times the Ku Klux Klan patrolled the streets of area communities with armed guards, occasionally arresting hundreds of residents under pseudo-federal authority.[14] In many communities the Klan virtually controlled local government.

The xenophobia created by this reign of lawlessness erased many ethnic characteristics, further regionalizing the immigrants.

Exacerbating the reputation of Egypt as a dangerous area were the activities of the Birger and Shelton gangs. Having gained experience during the Klan raids of the mid-1920s, both gangs fought over the lucrative Prohibition trade in southern Illinois, lying between Chicago markets and the Gulf ports of entry. People would disappear and their bodies appear later. Eventually the Sheltons were imprisoned and Birger was hanged for murder, but regionalizing immigrants adopted their legends as part of the corpus of Egyptian folklife.

More recently the immigrant communities have been beset by other regionalizing pressures: unemployment and out-migration. After World War II coal companies shifted to the increased mechanization (and lower cost) of strip mining.[15] To the small immigrant towns this has meant the loss of jobs and the dissolution of ethnic communities as young adults depart forever for college or employment in more lucrative areas. Formerly prosperous stores have become largely vacant storefronts, and weeds grow in abandoned company mines.

These diverse forces form the basis of the regional identity of Egyptians today. Their sense of place is defined by a southern heritage and distinct dialect; legends detailing a violent frontier history, coal mining and union activism, Ku Klux Klan, and Roaring Twenties gangs; and underemployment. Despite these regionalizing influences, ethnic differences endure.

### POLISH-AMERICAN EGYPTIANS

Illinois in the 1870s was still largely a frontier, particularly in the central prairie counties. At this time the Illinois Central Railroad Company needed settlers to farm the lands near their tracks and to ship produce along the rail lines. To fill this need, the railroad hired agents who canvassed the nation's Polish communities to attract settlers.[16] These Poles founded Radom, DuBois, and Tamaroa, all directly on the Illinois Central tracks. Posen, about four miles east, and Scheller, on another line about four miles south, completed the small group of prosperous farming communities.

Polish immigrants settled the area for other reasons as well. Many were "pushed" from Europe by intolerable political and economic conditions. In the late nineteenth century, the Prussian

Fig. 1. Coal miners, DuBois. Adam Kuhn, mine owner, is seated at far left. *Photograph courtesy of Gene Waldman.*

and Russian empires had divided Poland between them, military service was mandatory, and poverty was rampant. Consequently, many Poles, bilingual in either German or Russian, left for the United States. Having heard of the developing Polish communities on the Illinois prairie, many chose Egypt.

Because the Polish settlers had been recruited primarily as farmers to populate an open countryside, coal mining had little initial impact on the group. Within several decades, however, mines had opened in the area, more immigrants arrived, and population soared.[17] Eventually mining triggered the regionalizing influences of company control, assimilation, and xenophobia.

An equally significant modifying force to the Polish communities has been their continuing social interaction with neighboring groups. Intermarriages occurred, for example, especially between German and Polish Catholics, many of whom already spoke German. And language use was itself changed. Starting sometime during the depression, "people felt ashamed" if they continued to speak Polish, one woman recalled, and schoolteachers forced pupils to speak only English on school grounds.[18] People also tried to disguise their heritage by changing their names: for example, Mydlarz became Mydler and Szramkowski became Sherman.

In contrast, ethnic antagonism helped preserve a sense of group identity. The earliest pioneers were Anglo-Americans, who disliked the Polish immigrants so intensely that they "refused to move into the same vicinity with them." Thus the Poles (and their German neighbors) tended to be "somewhat difficult to assimilate" due to native-born Americans' refusals to accept them.[19]

The presence of these unassimilated Poles, augmented by later coal miners, "gave rise to a series of bloody social conflicts" due to the xenophobia of the Ku Klux Klan.[20] While the Klan's depredations never directly touched the Polish farming communities, the potential of their doing so frightened schoolchildren of the area. As one woman recalled: "Sister [the parochial school teacher] used to ask us . . . 'what if they [the Klan] would come and ask you to spit on the Crucifix? Would you do it?' And we were so afraid . . . that maybe they'll come and . . . shoot us."[21] The ethnic antagonisms and (to a much greater extent) the general lack of assimilation between Polish- and Anglo-Americans have allowed numerous folklife traditions to persist in the Polish communities today.

One distinguishing ethnic characteristic is the Polish language. Many older residents speak Polish as a "native" language, having learned it from parents before entering school in the early twentieth century. Other informants learned Polish in special language classes in the DuBois parochial school. After World War II, though, Polish disappeared in public but remained in homes, largely as a concession to older relatives. Today, one woman noted, while she still speaks Polish with her children, "we mix it out" with English words.[22] The parish priest in Radom hears about 60 percent of his parishioners' confessions in Polish. Many older residents still have difficulty with English.

The existence of a Catholic church in four of the five Polish communities expresses the significance of that faith. Since nearly all Polish residents continue to practice Roman Catholicism, religious traditions remain a strong indicator of ethnic identity. In former times, parishioners brought baskets containing food for Easter Sunday meals to the church to be blessed by the priest. Covered by a clean white cloth, the baskets would contain ham, boiled eggs, butter, bread, and coffee cakes. Parishioners remembered the custom as widespread in the past; "there's just about six baskets nowadays on the altar railing," a woman lamented.[23] Still, by sponsoring parish festivals, offering an occasional Polish-language mass, and by permitting the continuity of old country customs, the Catholic churches help preserve a Polish identity.

Parish festivals and celebrations are also good places to taste traditional Polish foods, although such foods are also prepared at home. Many Polish cooks still make *pierogi*, fried pastries filled with cottage cheese, eggs, and cream. Another popular dish is *golumpki*, cabbage rolls filled with tomato sauce, hamburger, or rice. One less popular with non-Polish residents is *chanina*, a dark, sweet soup made with dried fruit and duck's blood.

Finally, the Polish-Americans preserve an identity through material culture.[24] For example, in the DuBois church several stained-glass windows depict Polish saints, and another illustrates a crucial historical event for Polish independence. The window also depicts the "Black Madonna," a national icon of Poland, under a double-headed falcon, both still powerful symbols. Several other churches have Polish-language inscriptions.

Even the area's place names preserve an ethnic identity. Unlike other groups who settled already-established towns, the Poles founded their own communities; thus they had relative freedom in the use of place names. Radom and Posen (from Poznen) recreated a familiar toponymy in an otherwise unfamiliar land, making home seem not so distant.

ITALIAN-AMERICAN EGYPTIANS

The Italians began arriving in the late nineteenth century, selecting the booming coalfields of southern Illinois as a general target and settling predominantly in the already-established town of Herrin.[25]

While the expanding coalfields were a strong pull factor, many Italians were pushed from northern Italy by oppressive poverty. One man's father had described the enormous gulf between rich and poor in the old country; the rich were "almost like God" and were treated with the utmost respect. In contrast, the man's parents, like most immigrants, were extremely poor, and left because they had heard the United States was "the land of plenty."[26] The Herrin-area coalfields seemed an appropriate place to test the limits of the American dream.

This dream seemed at times impossible to achieve, however. At first, the immigrants faced the overwhelming confusion of establishing new homes in a new land. Consequently, many fell prey to their new employers. As one narrator recalled, "Most of the people lived in company houses. . . . And we were under the domination of the miners' company; if you bought a company house the prices were twice higher than any place else."[27] Many Italians eventually escaped company control by forming separate corporations and separate neighborhoods. In turn, their self-reliance became branded by Anglo-Americans as "clannishness."

The mines also forced another form of collective cooperation on the Italians: unions. At first, unions were banned. One narrator's father met with other miners secretly in the woods to avoid company harassment. Violence increased as the Italians and other miners unionized, and collective power brought mass retaliation. After the "Herrin Massacre," one man (then a youth) witnessed the bodies of the scabs dumped in front of an Italian organization's meeting house because the local funeral home refused to embalm the corpses.

Another regionalizing force was the strong desire to assimilate into American culture; after all, most had specifically emigrated to become Americans. Some changed their names: Merlo became Marlow, and Pisoni became Payson, for example. Parents who spoke only Italian discovered that their children learned English in school and from playmates. As they became adults, narrators recalled switching from Italian to English, even in the same conversation, but with English used more frequently. Today one second-generation Italian-American felt that no differences separate Italian- from Anglo-Americans: "I think our children now are just like any other children." Her husband added, "We've all become Americanized, and proud of it."[28]

While much assimilation occurred easily and readily, the nativistic antagonism of the Ku Klux Klan had a direct impact on Herrin's Italians. One Italian recalled growing up in the 1920s: "We were Dagos. . . . We were foreigners. We were not wanted. We were Catholics. . . . I'd go to school a lot of times and a guy'd call me a 'Dago' and I'd come home with a bloody nose. 'Course he had a bloody nose too."[29] Italians and/or Catholics could not teach in the public schools. As the Klan gained influence, they often raided the homes of Italians because they were foreigners, Catholics, and wine makers. Current residents, then children, recalled the terror in parents' eyes as they poured out homemade wine, anticipating an imminent raid. The Klan even threatened the parish priest, one man noted, and his father and other men stood guard for protection.

This antagonism and resentment, along with the deliberate attempt to continue old-country ties, ironically increased Italian

self-reliance. "We became clannish," an Italian-American commented. "Everyone helped one another" with home repairs or child
care, his wife added.[30] Immigrants founded communal organizations, lending associations, and separate businesses, modeled after
similar ones in Italy; membership was often based on region of
origin. By the early twentieth century, a section of downtown
Herrin contained the Rome Club, Lombard Store, and the Christopher Columbus (C.C.) Club.

These organizations served numerous purposes. First, they
allowed immigrants to escape the repressive control of the company stores and company housing by supporting each other on
credit or by investing group money in entrepreneurial concerns.
Members of the Christopher Columbus Cooperative Association,
for example, paid a fee to join and then obtained annual benefits
from the club's investments in government bonds. Down the street
stood the Lombard Society store, which carried dry goods and
allowed members who had invested money to obtain goods on
credit. Italians opened a butcher shop and a grocery store nearby,
on the same terms. These stores also allowed immigrants to obtain
fresh and traditional foods without fear of being overcharged by
non-Italian or company clerks.[31]

Equally important, organizations like the C.C. Club and Rome
Club provided significant socializing places for Italians and, later,
Italian-Americans to congregate and to retain a sense of identity.
The president of the C.C. Club remembered that his father enjoyed
visiting friends, drinking beer, and playing cards as his forms of
entertainment. On Columbus Day the club held a huge celebration
and dance in the hall upstairs; the place was "wall to wall with
Italian people."[32] Today the C.C. Club still serves as a tavern, but
the forty-six remaining members of the association have sold the
building and paid the shareholders for the final time; the last
president has retired.

Herrin today presents a curious mixture of toleration of and
antagonism toward the Italian-Americans. While Italians now serve
as teachers and local politicians, some Anglo-Americans resent the
result. Italians "think they own the town," an Irish-American
said.[33] Herrin's Italian festival has become the less specific "Herrin
fest," due to concern by Protestant ministers about beer and wine
sales; Italians attribute this to the community's earlier disapproval
of alcohol. Non-Italians credit Herrin's notoriously violent and
corrupt past to Italian organized crime, whereas Italians blame the

Ku Klux Klan. According to an Anglo-American tavern patron, Italians make up the "bottom fourth" of Herrin's population today.[34]

The Italian language, formerly widely spoken in public, has now largely disappeared. Older informants recalled speaking English as a second language at school and using Italian to converse at home with parents. Italian playmates often used that language to separate themselves from their American friends. By the 1950s Italian started to fade. Despite attempts to teach Italian in continuing education classes in the Catholic grade school, only the oldest residents of Herrin today speak Italian.

Perhaps because Herrin is a much larger community than the rural Polish towns, perhaps because the former is less ethnically homogeneous, and perhaps because ethnic antagonism in Herrin has been much more prominent, few public holiday celebrations exist for the Italian-Americans. The Roman Catholic church, however, has always had a major parish festival, the "big day" for Italians, residents recalled. Formerly, the C.C. Club hosted a huge Columbus Day celebration, including a parade (later discontinued), patriotic songs like "God Bless America," and a family-oriented dance in the club, complete with "maybe half a dozen bottles of wine on each table" and traditional Italian foods, the former president remembered fondly.[35]

Italian foods, however, may still be found. Family-owned grocery stores, descendants from earlier cooperative ventures, process meat and prepare various kinds of sausages using traditional recipes and machinery. The Town Bakery, the only one still in operation, produces Italian bread and other delicacies on an early twentieth-century brick hearth "built like they built it in Italy," a retired baker noted.[36] Although more common in the past, family cooks still prepare *risotto* (a saffron-flavored rice dish) and *gnocchi* (potato dumplings). Traditionally, families also made their own wine, either from home-grown or imported California grapes. "We always had a bottle of wine on the table when we'd eat," a resident recalled.[37]

The old country also came alive for Herrin's Italians through the cultural interpretation of space. Unlike the Poles, the Italians had no opportunities to rename streets or cities after remembered towns. Nevertheless, the newcomers remodeled Herrin in several conspicuous ways. A specifically Italian business community developed around the clubs and stores on Herrin's north side, and Italian neighborhoods radiated from there. In these neighborhoods, "everybody had a grape arbor," one woman noted. Flower gardens also predominated, "but Grandpa used to say, 'if you can't eat it, don't put it out.' Grandma would have her rose bed, but . . . what he wanted was vegetables and stuff like that." As her husband noted, gardens became a depression necessity: "everybody and their uncle had their garden."[38]

## SLOVAKIAN-AMERICAN EGYPTIANS

The Slovakians entered Egypt in the early decades of the twentieth century, either directly from the eastern Carpathian Mountain region of central Europe or indirectly from other Slovakian communities in the United States. The primary force pulling them to southern Illinois was coal. The towns of Zeigler and Colp, for example, grew up around coal mines. Royalton, a few miles southwest of Zeigler, and Dowell, northwest of Colp, attracted many nationalities, including Slovakians. Having come from coal-mining regions in Europe or from similar areas in the eastern United States, the newcomers formed a sizable, already-trained corps of workers eagerly welcomed by the mining industry.

But other forces also pushed the Slovakians from their former homes. Since they lived in the rapidly disintegrating remnants of the Austro-Hungarian Empire, caught up in potential warfare, some emigrated to avoid compulsory military service. Most emigrated because of extreme poverty. For example, one woman's uncle had heard that in southern Illinois "the streets were paved with gold, and he was going to get rich." Another woman, an emigrant at four, remembered that in the old country, her mother had been a wet nurse for "the governor": "So they were rich, you know; they had all white bread, and good stuff they could eat. And they wanted to feed mother so she would have rich milk. So my mother would nurse my brother first and then those [wealthy] boys. And they would give her bread and she would hide it in different places, so she'd come home, bring it to my father—white bread!"[39] To such immigrants, conditions in southern Illinois seemed infinitely better.

While the coal towns offered new homes and better employment, the streets were likely not to be paved with gold but with coal cinders. "It was all coal mining. Every town you went to in southern Illinois, it was full of coal mines," a Colp resident noted. Many

Fig. 2. Company houses, Colp. *Photograph by Randy Tindall. Courtesy of the University Museum, Southern Illinois University, Carbondale.*

immigrants settled into booming, newly constructed towns like Zeigler and Royalton, towns with thousands of people, churches, banks, theaters, union halls, lumberyards (to support the new construction), and the ubiquitous taverns. Such communities also had other facilities, such as company stores, which accepted only scrip from the coal companies and provided the newcomers with "clothing, or food, whatever they wanted," a resident remembered.[40]

Coal communities quietly took on an appearance of homogeneity, dulling ethnic expression while enhancing poverty. The company houses "all looked alike," a resident recalled; another termed them "Sears and Roebuck houses," with plans purchased from the catalog. To save money and space, mining companies built houses as cheaply as possible, with few amenities such as wells. Similarly, a resident in Zeigler remembered apartment-like buildings she termed "the flats, . . . with about fifty families living in each flat." "They were built like sheds; that's what they looked like—sheds," her friend emphasized.[41]

The amalgamating forces of formulaic architecture symbolized the social assimilation of the Slovakians. First-generation Americans remembered playing with children from other ethnic groups, learning words from each other's parental language while playing new games, like baseball. In homes parents learned English from their children and sought an education for both genders, increasing their Americanization. Sisters attended school with their brothers for the first time, and both acquired novel values and ideas. Old-country customs consequently faded. For example, fathers had traditionally arranged marriages for their daughters; however, several women obstinately ignored their fathers' wishes and married men they had chosen themselves.

The immigrants were not always welcome, and assimilation did not always occur smoothly. As a woman recalled, the Slovakians "always stuck with their own people and they just didn't want to mingle with nobody else." As her neighbor reminded her, "Yeah, well, that's because when we were kids, . . . those from the other side of town used to call us 'Hunkies'; . . . I used to fight over that."[42] Such feelings were exacerbated by the nativism of the Ku Klux Klan, deeply feared then by residents, with a resentment still sensed today.

Despite regionalizing influences, a distinctively Slovakian-American ethnic community persists. The Slovakian language continues in use because the older immigrants arrived relatively recently and thus still recall their first language, and also because church services were conducted in Old Church Slavonic, a closely related language, until very recently. For many older people, English is still their second language, and some have difficulty with it. Slovakian was "all we spoke" at home, a recently retired teacher remembered; "my oldest brother, when he started the first grade, he couldn't speak English." One resident often hears Slovakian when older women gather to prepare food for church festivals. She can understand Slovakian but she "can't think fast enough to carry on a conversation." One man confessed that he telephones an older woman "every once in awhile . . . just to have a conversation [in Slovakian] with her; and she calls me once in awhile. I do that so I won't forget."[43]

Because of the distinctiveness of their Orthodox Christian faith, Slovakians see religious customs as playing a significant role in their lives. For example, many parishioners celebrate Easter with traditional practices, such as the blessing of the Easter meal. Common Easter Sunday foods include decorated hard-boiled eggs (*pesanki*), egg cheese (*hrutka*), ham, kielbasa, butter, green onion, and *pascha*, a grapefruit-sized bread loaf with a braided cross on top. Parishioners bring these foods to church in baskets covered with cloths embroidered with Slovakian sayings. To end the Easter season, a few parishioners decorate their houses on Pentecost Sunday with greenery.

Another significant Christian holiday is Christmas, but many older practices have disappeared. Today, Christmas trees (an "American" custom) are commonplace, and even the date has been moved by church decree from January 7 to December 25 to coincide with other Christian denominations. Many families found the transition difficult to manage, though, and compromise by leaving Christmas decorations up through early January.

Food traditions of the Slovakians show potential borrowings from other European groups. For example, Slovakians claimed to have learned to make *helupki* (cabbage rolls) and *kolachi* (a pastry with fruit fillings) in local communities. Whether originally shared with Polish neighbors across the Carpathian Mountains or later learned in the mining communities in southern Illinois, these foods today appear prominently as ethnic markers at Slovakian festivals.

Narrators hinted at a rich tradition of customary beliefs and tales, both from the old country and from southern Illinois, most of which have not been passed down. Two sisters remembered their mother as "gifted," able to effect cures. In Royalton, one woman noted, everyone had cows, "and as soon as the cow stopped giving milk, they always accused somebody of witchcraft." "They were very superstitious," her friend added. As these informants noted, much of these traditions will soon be lost. "I guess we weren't that interested in it. . . . We wouldn't pay no attention a lot of times," one woman sighed.[44]

During the discussion of such traditions, three women noted the male chauvinistic sentiments in many of the earlier beliefs. "Poor women. Isn't that awful? Poor us!" one exclaimed.[45] These women had also been of the first generation to challenge paternal authority by choosing their own husbands. Not all narrators lamented the loss of old-country traditions; many welcomed social advancements as assimilation introduced a new value system.

While traces of an ethnic heritage exist in various expressions of material culture among Slovakian-Americans, their ethnic identity is most vividly expressed in the organization of space.[46] The Orthodox church in Royalton, with its distinctive Russian Byzantine onion-shaped dome and three-bar cross, stands proudly in the old neighborhood of company houses in "Russian Row," within sight of the abandoned mine. Whether by accident or design, a nearby cemetery recapitulates this arrangement, with Roman Catholic graves to the west and Orthodox Christian to the east, divided by a roadway. In the church itself, four hand-painted icons of saints illustrate several of importance to Eastern Christians. One of Saint Demetrios Megalomartyr, popular in Greece, is dedicated to the memory of several Greek parishioners killed in a mine disaster in 1914.

Residents of Slovakian neighborhoods rather sheepishly noted the usual disorder of their yards in the past, which inevitably contained various sheds, farm animals, and a large vegetable garden. In addition, a resident noted: "Each yard had a fence around it. . . . A long time ago, you could tell foreign people because they always had fences around their yards. . . . Our kind of people always have a fence around their yard. Privacy, I guess." Another woman in a nearby town confessed that her home "just wouldn't look right" without a fence around it.[47]

The incomplete process of the regionalization of ethnic folklife traditions provides research suggestions for other areas. Many regions are unified not only by geography but by ethnicity; thus a shared folklife tradition becomes easier to establish and maintain. But, where ethnic diversity occurs in the same region, can traditions thrive? Which, if either, is the stronger force: regionalization or ethnicity? Can both processes occur simultaneously, as in Egypt, or is this example unique?

Unlike their fellow Europeans who had emigrated to large American cities, the Poles, Italians, and Slovakians of southern Illinois did not develop a large cohesive community around which to coalesce. Residents in isolated rural towns or in small ethnic neighborhoods faced almost overwhelming regionalizing pressures. Since most immigrants became coal miners or were associated with related industries, that occupation unified diverse groups. Men spoke their native languages at home but discussed wage increases and shop conditions with their fellow workers in English in union halls and mine shafts. Company stores and company housing projects integrated mining neighborhoods into carbon-copy homes, often burying vernacular architectural preferences or cultural perspectives on spatial arrangements. Regionalization increased further as the third generation came to share a common Egyptian identity, expressed by stories of gangland violence, union activism, or Ku Klux Klan vigilantism. Today, residents of the towns discussed above describe themselves first as southern Illinoisans, linked by shared folklife traditions into a common regional identity.

A deeper examination of the unified traditions of Egypt, however, reveals an underlying diversity of ethnic folklife. In southern Illinois, the carbon-copy mining company towns did not create a completely unified Egyptian folk group. Shared traditions have established a strong basis for regional identity, but ethnic diversity persists.

# A Regional Musical Style:
# The Legacy of Arnold Shultz

## WILLIAM E. LIGHTFOOT

*The complexity of factors that comprise regional culture in Illinois's Egypt also exists across the Ohio River in western Kentucky. In this essay, William E. Lightfoot describes how the artistry of a single individual—the musician Arnold Shultz—was shaped by the regional context within which he learned music, and goes on to demonstrate how Shultz's personal musical style in turn influenced the region's folk musical tradition, which itself became a crucial factor in American country music.*

While the cultural geographer George Carney's recent complaint that we know "little or nothing about the stylistic variations of American music" may be well-founded, we know nevertheless that American music is an amalgam of numerous regional styles.[1] Jazz, for example, developed from regional stylistic patterns established in New Orleans, Kansas City, Chicago, the West Coast, and the neighborhood around Fifty-second Street in New York. Stylistic blues regions include the Delta, the East Coast, Chicago, Detroit, and East Texas. Distinctive types of rock-and-roll are associated with Memphis, Detroit, southern California, and Miami. And country-western music calls to mind Appalachia, middle Tennessee, "the Austin Scene," "the Nashville Sound," and the Texas-Oklahoma-Hollywood connection. Individual musicians are quite often associated with many of these regional styles—Robert Johnson with Delta blues, Louis Armstrong with New Orleans jazz, Bob Wills with western swing, Brian Wilson with southern California surf music, Bill Monroe with bluegrass, Muddy Waters with Chicago blues, and Blind Boy Fuller with East Coast blues. When dominant musicians such as these are linked strongly with regional styles an interesting question arises: do performers inherit regional styles or do they shape them? Or as the eminent blues scholar Paul Oliver puts it, "Is a 'style' a manner of playing and singing which is characteristic of a region, or is the dominance of a single musician over his fellows the conditioning factor in the formation of a regional style?" Oliver leans toward the latter explanation, citing the influence of Waters, Johnson, Fuller, and Lightnin' Hopkins on "a whole retinue of imitators," suggesting that the ability of dominant musicians to influence others is perhaps "the basis, then, of the regional style, whether it is in the Mississippi Delta or North Carolina."[2] An exploration of the profound influence of the western Kentucky folk musician Arnold Shultz on the regional style known as Travis picking, however, yields an alternative answer to Oliver's question: that regional forces help shape a performer who, in turn, informs a regional style.

For some thirty years scholars have acknowledged the importance of Travis picking. Referring to what D.K. Wilgus in 1961 called "the western Kentucky variant of the 'thumb-picking' or 'country-ragtime' guitar style," Charles Wolfe, for example, has written that Travis picking was "a style that came out of the western Kentucky coal fields [in the 1930s] and within the span of two decades was the dominant picking style in country music everywhere, thanks to the skill of its two most famous practitioners, Merle Travis and Chet Atkins."[3] Atkins learned the style from Travis, who had absorbed it a few years earlier through a regional "tradition of artistry" developed by dozens of coal miners who had been touched, directly or indirectly, by the extraordinary musicianship of Arnold Shultz. Although this chain of transmission has been alluded to frequently during the past few years it has yet to be adequately documented. But through a thorough examination of the regional folklore surrounding Arnold Shultz and his disciples we can come to a better understanding of how this regional tradition developed and how it became a part of our national culture. It is first necessary, however, to examine the qualities of Travis picking as well as its regional context.

Although Merle Travis did not invent Travis picking, it is appropriate that it bears his name, as Travis not only perfected the paradigm established by Arnold Shultz but also popularized it to the extent that, as Wolfe and many others have suggested, it has become an important part of American music. (Travis, a modest man, never referred to the tradition as the "Travis style" or "Travis picking," using instead the term "thumb style," occasionally even suggesting that it should be called "Rager picking" after his primary mentor, Mose Rager.)

The tradition experienced a complex maturation and is itself complex. Travis picking is a method of playing a guitar in which a single musician performs simultaneously four major musical elements: melody, harmony, rhythm, and bass. It is of course a finger-picking technique, but it has about it a markedly distinct flavor that sets it apart from the performance styles of such other master finger pickers as Blind Blake, Etta Baker, John Hurt, Doc Watson, Elizabeth Cotten, Mance Lipscomb, and even Chet Atkins. Travis picking synthesizes widespread technical qualities with purely regional ones, creating a unique stylistic "feel" that has six main characteristics:

1. A pulsating alternating bass line, played with a thumb pick (the only pick used), which emphasizes a strong, metronomic one-three rhythm (i.e., the thumb accents the first and third beats of a ¼ cut-time measure).

2. A steady but lighter afterbeat, played also with the thumb, that accents the second and fourth beats, resulting in a bright, bouncy dancelike rhythm. Rather than simply striking a single note, however, the thumb brushes a four-or-five string chord that provides a harmonic foundation for the song. These chords are invariably complex and sophisticated, rarely played in first position, but, rather, high on the guitar neck, using not the barre technique of classical musicians but unorthodox thumb-oriented positions formed by grabbing the guitar neck, as Travis put it, "like a hoe handle."

3. A soft, playful, syncopated melody line that darts in and out of where it should be, played with the fleshy part (sometimes the fingernail) of the index finger.

4. What may be called the Travis "texture" or "touch," expressed by the soft melody dancing over an emphatic but muffled bass, created by the heel of the right hand resting lightly on (and thus dampening) the three bass strings. Further, on the second and fourth beats the left hand's grip on the full chord is lightened, creating a "choke" or "sock" effect.

5. A repertoire of such regional "licks" as ornamental figures played with the little finger; walking bass runs; and smooth, silky rolls, Möbius strips of sound that flow on at times for several choruses and that occasionally utilize the middle finger.

6. An application of the techniques to a wide range of musical genres—rags, blues, breakdowns, ballads, hymns, Tin Pan Alley

tunes, and sentimental and parlor songs. Among Travis pickers it has always been customary to attempt to apply the style to as many seemingly inapplicable songs as possible.[4]

When the first five elements above are put together, the music becomes complete in itself; one hears a melody along with harmonic, rhythmic, and bass support. In fact, it sounds like several guitars:

> A fellow by the name of Red Phillips . . . played with Curly Fox at the time I did. Ol' Red was tellin' me a story about guitar playin':
>
> He said he went out and cut him some kindlin' one morning real early. And he turned his radio on when he come back through the livin' room. Said, "There's some guitar players on the radio." Said it was the prettiest music he ever heard. Said he just throwed his kindlin' right down on the floor and set there and listened to the guitars, guitars pickin'. And he said, "Man!—" said he never heard such guitar players in his life [laughs]. Said it sounded like four or five guitars. Then he said he's just a-wonderin' if they were going to tell their names.
>
> And so when they got through playin', he [the announcer] said, "That was Merle Travis and his guitar." He said, "Man, I ain't never heard nothin' like that!" He said, "Merle Travis and his *guitar*? That sounded like four or *five* guitars [laughs]!"[5]

Travis first recorded under his own name in mid-1945, although Red Phillips could possibly have heard him in a live performance (as did Chet Atkins) on the Cincinnati radio station WLW in the late thirties or early forties. At any rate, Phillips's response was similar to those of innumerable others upon first hearing Travis picking. It was also the response of those who first heard Arnold Shultz perform in the region as early as 1918.

The "culture" region formed by Shultz and his followers lies directly in the center of one of Kentucky's five physiographic regions, the Western Coal Field, which is surrounded by the Ohio River, and the Jackson Purchase and Pennyroyal regions.[6] The node of the Shultz-Travis region is the point where Pond Creek flows into Green River on the Muhlenberg-Ohio County line, between Cen-

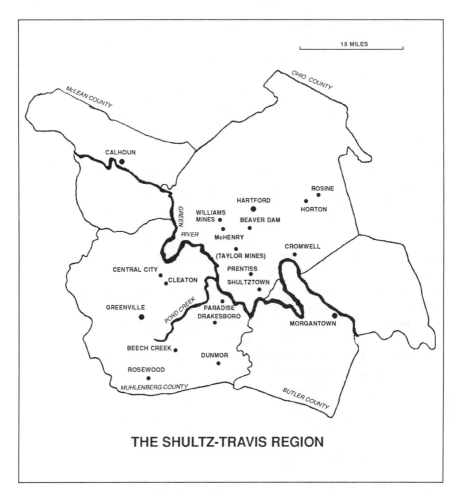

**THE SHULTZ-TRAVIS REGION**

tral City and Cromwell. The radius of the region is about seventeen miles, circumscribing an area that includes most of Ohio and Muhlenberg and parts of Butler and McLean counties. This region is defined primarily by the wanderings (and subsequent influence) of Arnold Shultz, much in the manner of the demigods of mythology who established the perimeter of their kingdoms by executing enormous steps.

The lower Green River valley's settlement began in the 1780s when Revolutionary War veterans were awarded sizable land grants in the area. Mostly from Virginia and North Carolina, many of these pioneers brought slaves with them, usually three or four per family. In 1800 there were 125 slaves in Muhlenberg County, and by 1860 there were 1,584; Greenville, in fact, became the site of a fairly active slave market. Similarly, Ohio County had 1,292 slaves in 1860.[7]

Although used infrequently for commercial purposes during the early years, the Green River became a source of cultural unity for inhabitants of the valley. As Helen Bartter Crocker puts it, "strong ties of local tradition developed, increasingly held together by the people's common relationship with the river."[8] But prodded by the "steamboat fever" of the early 1800s, which saw steamers traveling the Ohio River from Pittsburgh to New Orleans, valley residents demanded that the state make the Green River more navigable; in January, 1828, the first steamer, the *United States*, cruised all the way to Bowling Green.[9] In addition to commercial packets, steam-operated showboats began tying up at cities along the Green River, bringing such forms of "outside" entertainment as melodramas and Dixieland music to an otherwise isolated back-country region. Katie Dee Johnson, who grew up on the Green at Rumsey, has fond memories of the showboats: "When it came around the bend up there they would start playing the calliope and everybody would start gathering around. . . ; they'd be real excited to see it coming around the bend and hearing the calliope play. . . . And the shows that they had were really melodramas, you know. But between acts they would have sort of a vaudeville-type thing—a little bit of comedy. . . . I think they would do some banjo pickin'." Mrs. Johnson's husband, Sherrill, remembers that the showboats "had something like a four-piece band: sax, cornet, maybe a drummer and of course the piano . . . jazzsters."[10]

According to local tradition, a man named McLean discovered in 1820 that the "black rock" on his farm would burn, and by 1830 a few barges of coal were being mined at the McLean bank, near Paradise in Muhlenberg County.[11] As the river became more navigable the commercial mining of coal increased; by 1850 there was quite a bit of coal traffic on the Green, and in 1870 the newly chartered Green and Barren River Navigation Company began using steamers to tow barges of coal from the region's mines to Evansville.[12] By 1911 the coal output of Muhlenberg County alone was two and a quarter million tons. The region's coal supply is apparently inexhaustible; Rothert estimated that two veins alone, No. 9 and No. 11, could produce three million tons a year until the year 2500.[13]

These historic, physiographic, and socioeconomic forces—slavery, the Green River, and the mining of coal—are crucial to an understanding of the development of Travis picking.

In early 1833 Washington Irving interviewed William P. Duvall, who had been a member of the Kentucky legislature from 1813 to 1815 and who had been appointed governor of the Florida Territory in 1822. Before becoming a lawyer Duvall had experienced an exciting life as a frontiersman during the latter years of the eighteenth century in what was later to become Ohio County, Kentucky. Irving published these anecdotes of Duvall's "early and eccentric career in . . . the very words in which he related them" as "The Early Experiences of Ralph Ringwood" in 1840 in *Knickerbocker Magazine*, and in 1855 as a sketch in *Wolfert's Roost*.[14] This sketch gives us a clear picture of frontier life in the region as well as a portrait of the white man ultimately responsible for Arnold Shultz's surname.

In the sketch Ringwood attends "a grand frolic" at the home of the fiddler Bob Mosely, which was "on the Pigeon Roost Fork of the Muddy, which is a branch of Rough Creek, which is a branch of Green River."[15] Polly and Patty, the two "strapping" daughters of old Simon Schultz, a generous but huffy local landowner, disrupt the frolic by displaying their dollar-sized looking-glasses given to them by a peddler whom Simon had helped. Local historians believe that either Duvall or Irving confused "Simon" with "Matthias," as both are "apostolic names," and that the Schultz in the sketch was in reality Matthias Shultz (the *c* was dropped by the family early on), indeed, one of the very first settlers in the lower Green River valley.[16]

Local records indicate that Matthias Shultz was born in 1756 near Winchester, Virginia, and at the age of sixteen joined the Continental Army's Virginia Militia as a private; he was a member of Washington's Army at Trenton and served under Lafayette at Brandywine, where he was wounded.[17] After the war he migrated to the lower Green River valley as early perhaps as 1785. The 1799 Ohio County tax list shows "Mathias Shults" as owning six hundred acres on Muddy Creek, ten horses, and no slaves. But by 1820 Shultz owned five slaves, and by 1830 he had twelve.[18] He is shown to have owned no slaves in 1840, but his son Joseph owned six during that year. Joseph's son Nathaniel was also a slave owner, and about 1845, when he was in his early twenties, he purchased a five-year-old boy named Jack. Jack's daughter Ella Shultz Griffin, who was a "cousin" of Arnold Shultz, tells the following story:

> My father [H.J. ("Jack")] got the name [Shultz] in slave times. There was an old white man raised him; he was Shultz, Nat Shultz. . . . He stayed with him till he got grown. And when he got grown he give him that little piece of ground that he lived on, just give it to him; he didn't have to buy it. For him and his family. 'Course wasn't any family then, until he married. His mother. He just stayed there. Never did buy no ground.
>
> Nat Shultz was my father's slave father. He had him when he was a little boy—taken him from his mother when he was little. Uncle Nat Shultz taken Jack away from his mother when he was small and he kept him till he was a grown man.
>
> Somebody had him (I don't know the man's name), and Uncle Nat taken him. They sold him. They put him up on a stump or table and sold him, just like they did the horses or anything else. Just a little boy. . . .
>
> And when he turned him loose, why, he give him that little spot of ground there in Prentiss where we lived. . . .
>
> When my daddy died he [Nat] came out just hollerin' and cryin', sayin', "I want to go with Jack! I want to go with Jack! Let me go with Jack." Just cried like a baby.[19]

Jack's "cousin" David Shultz, who was about the same age as Jack, and David's brother Lou Ransey were probably owned by other sons of Matthias Shultz—John, Nicholas, Charles—or perhaps Joseph himself; an 1894 article in the *Hartford Herald* celebrating Joseph's ninety-fourth birthday said that "he can sit in his door and look over the graves of fifty-two slaves."[20]

Both Lou Ransey and Jack Shultz became fiddlers, and many of Jack's children also took up music: Luther, banjo; Hardin, fiddle and banjo; Rastus, guitar; and Ella, fiddle, guitar, and banjo. Hiriam Rogers remembers that "Jack Shultz and Luther and them . . . used to have big dances about every Saturday night—barbeques. . . . Down at Uncle Jack Shultz's every *one* of 'em played; everyone in the family played."[21] Other occasions for music making in the black communities in the region were brush dances and taffy pulls:

Well, they would go out mostly in a field, and they'd cut down bushes and all that kind of stuff, and they'd put down sawdust, and they'd make seats out there, and they'd have lanterns hanging up, and then they'd go out, you know, and they'd have a dance out there. They'd square dance a lot and, you know, just different kinds of dances.

They had a lot of house parties and taffy pullings. They'd have a big taffy pull, and then they'd get up with the old string instruments and so forth, and they'd start to makin' music and dancin', and they'd have a *good* time. . . . They did this practically every Saturday night.[22]

Consequently, David and Elizabeth Shultz's son Arnold, who was born in February 1886, grew up in a highly musical extended family in the heart of a musically active community, absorbing traditions from those around him. "He learned [music] at home. He just picked it up himself," said Ella Griffin. "It just runs in the family."[23]

Although some accounts place Shultz's birth at Cromwell, many are quite positive that he was born in Taylor Mines, a defunct mining camp some two miles southwest of Beaver Dam, which is only a few miles from the homes of other Shultzes in Prentiss and Shultztown.[24] While he is known to have played fiddle, banjo, mandolin, and piano, Shultz obtained his main instrument, the guitar, when he was about fourteen:

Now I know that [Arnold's] [half-]brother, who was older than him, worked on riverboats and bought Arnold his first guitar. Ed Shultz used to work on riverboats, and he's the one who bought his brother his first guitar. . . . Ed said that back when Arnold was young, he had come back home and he was going off on another riverboat trip, and he asked Arnold what did he want or something, and he told him he wanted a guitar. And he did get him a guitar when he come off one of his trips. He left, and when he came back again, Arnold, he was almost a pro with it. He just picked it up naturally. . . . I guess he was around fourteen, fifteen [1900-1901], something like that.[25]

Mose Rager reported that a man named Paul Landrum showed sixteen-year-old Shultz some chords when Arnold worked as a porter in a Beaver Dam hotel: "What I think, [Arnold] just kindly started playin' a guitar along about that time, and he probably knowed maybe two or three chords. And Paul, I think he played a guitar a pretty good while, with a string band. . . . And that's what Paul was tellin' me: he used to show him a few chords. . . . Paul said he used these chords and said Arnold caught 'em just like that."[26]

That the white string-band musician Paul Landrum exchanged traditions with Arnold Shultz about the turn of the century is symbolic of widespread black-white cultural exchange in the region. When slavery was abolished blacks had turned either to subsistence farming or working as roustabouts on the steamboats, but when large-scale steamboat activity evaporated on the Green in the late 1920s, many black men became coal miners, working and making music with their white neighbors. Mose Rager characterized the situation like this: "Man, we always got along in this part of the country with black people . . . played music together, and, oh, have *big* gatherings."[27] The irregular schedule of mine operations helped to charge black-white interaction:

> The mines, back then . . . would run, sometimes, would get down to one day a week. And that's when we'd get together and get out and have parties. And have guitars and fiddles and mandolins . . . , bass fiddles . . . , five-string banjos. . . .
>
> You see, you couldn't get out of town; there weren't any roads . . . , had dirt roads just about everywhere. . . . People would walk up the railroad—it never was muddy, you know, on the railroad. . . . And me and, oh, several of the ol' guitar players . . . [would] get a guitar and go up to the railroad, you know, come up to a railroad crossin' and stop. And, boy, I'm telling you: there'd be people goin' each way, you know, and the first thing you'd know you'd have a big crowd listenin' to you. Guitar pickers'd come along, go along the railroad and play guitar, stop on railroad crossin's and play.[28]

Mose regretted that he never had the chance to hear him play, but he knew that Shultz participated in these kinds of gatherings. "Arnold would come down the railroad from Morgantown, he'd come over from Rochester . . . , he'd come through Browder . . . , walk down the railroad with his guitar. Come down around Cleaton . . . and ol' Kennedy Jones, you know, he'd get him to play." Paul

Arnold Schultz (*left*) and Clarence Wilson, ca. 1930. *Photograph courtesy of Charles Wolfe.*

Landrum and Kennedy Jones were only two of several white musicians with whom Shultz played music; he also played with Clarence Wilson, Pendleton "Uncle Pen" Vandiver, and the "Father of Bluegrass" himself, Bill Monroe.[29] In fact, the first music Arnold played was probably "old-time" country music; Ella Griffin said that the Shultz family band, which included Arnold, played such old tunes as "Waggoner" and "Old Hen Cackle": "It was called hillbilly music then and it was hillbilly too. . . . But it was all I knew, all I ever heard."[30]

But Shultz also absorbed black folk musical traditions: blues, rags, breakdowns, gospel tunes, and songs suited to open guitar tunings. Almost everyone who remembers Shultz reports that he performed blues exceptionally well; Raymond Kessinger, for example, recalls that Arnold used the common blues technique of "pulling" strings: "When he was chordin' he'd twist his strings, bend 'em, make 'em *cry*, you know. . . . And he looked to me like he'd *push* 'em 'bout half-way 'cross the neck."[31] Malcolm Walker, Arnold's nephew, plays a blues that he believes was his uncle's favorite tune; Walker does not remember what Shultz called the song, but Mose Rager played it as the "Joe Turner Blues," a classic blues tune. Walker's version of the song, which is "just like Uncle Arnold played it," bears a slight resemblance to Big Bill Broonzy's performance of "Joe Turner No. 1 (Blues of 1890)" (Folkways Records FG 3586); in both versions the thumb plays a monotonic (nonalternating) bass line while the index finger up-picks melody notes and riffs (a style known generally as "Texas area").

Malcolm Walker and several others remember that Shultz frequently open-tuned his guitar, and fretted with either a knife or bottleneck: "Also, he'd tune his guitar in what he called a 'Bastapool' [almost surely "Sebastopol," from the late-nineteenth-century "The Siege of Sebastopol," an open-tuned favorite among rural black musicians]. . . . And he'd lay it down, like this [places guitar horizontally in lap], and he'd play it with a [steel] bar."[32] Again, this method usually calls for finger picking, with the thumb striking alternating bass notes. John Walker, Malcolm's brother, recalled that Shultz played the hymn "Nearer My God to Thee" in this manner, with a knife.[33] An open-tuned "parlor" song that Arnold evidently played rather well was "The Drum Piece"; Ike Everly's father, Meford, once paid Shultz five dollars to teach the "extremely intricate" tune to Ike's sister Hattie.[34]

Ike Everly himself, however, was apparently more interested in Shultz's performances of ragtime music than in set parlor pieces; it is fairly certain, in fact, that Ike learned the famous "Cannonball Rag," the anthem of Travis pickers, from Shultz, who wrote the song.[35] Nolin Baize's statement that Shultz "could come nearer to making [a guitar] sound like a piano than anybody I ever heard" in all likelihood refers to Shultz's ability to play rags on a guitar, which once again involves the technique of finger picking; the thumb imitates the left hand of a ragtime pianist, which plays an alternating stride bass part, while the index finger assumes the syncopated treble part of the right hand.[36] It was almost certainly Shultz's performances of rags that laid the foundation of Travis picking. Tex Atchison, who later became a member of the influential string band the Prairie Ramblers, was greatly impressed with Shultz picking: "I watched him play quite a bit. I was very interested in Arnold's pickin' because it was something I had never heard. . . . He played his *own* rhythm. He was the first that had ever done that, to play the lead and his own rhythm at the same time. He didn't need another guitar—it just got in the way."[37] In 1922 Tex replaced Shultz in a Hartford swing band called Faught's Entertainers. Forrest ("Boots") Faught, the leader of the band, had hired Arnold about 1918 and was also amazed at Shultz's ability to play both "lead" (melody) and "second" (accompaniment: rhythm, bass) simultaneously. When asked if Shultz was the first musician he had encountered that played guitar in this manner Faught replied: "Yessir! Arnold was the *only* man I ever saw do it back in them days [1918]. And people thought that was *something*, you know; it was something unusual. And he was *good!* He absolutely played the first lead guitar that I ever heard played. I heard 'em second, chord it, but he'd pick it out. . . . And people were amazed: 'Looky there—that man's *lead-in'* that music on that guitar and playin' his own accompaniment!' "[38]

Another of Faught's stories serves to illustrate Shultz's mastery of both popular music and advanced chords, which also became characteristic of Travis picking:

> Arnold Shultz showed a bunch of us one night—we were sittin' under a coal tipple—and we was playin' "I'll See You in My Dreams," but we was usin' the three chords—back then three chords was about all you heard a musician play; if he was playin' in C he'd be usin' F and G; they didn't make these accidental chords—and Arnold Shultz says, "Throw that A in there!" And we'd start puttin' that A in, and he'd say, "See how much better it sounded?" That A *belonged* in there, that A chord. . . . He played mostly up on the neck.

Other folks in the region tell similar stories about Shultz's wide knowledge of sophisticated chords and the popular music of the day.

So by at least 1918 Shultz's music contained four of the six qualities of Travis picking: an alternating bass played under a syncopated melody, supported by rich, rhythmic chords, and applied to a wide range of music. And given Shultz's connection to "Cannonball Rag," we may assume that some of the regional licks—little-finger doo-dads, bass runs, rolls—came from his playing as well. The "choke" effect was later added to the style by Mose Rager, who had learned it from the black musician Jim Mason.[39] But if it were not for

Shultz's extensive roamings around the region the style would probably not have been disseminated to the point of becoming a "regional" style.

Arnold Shultz's presence in the region from 1918 to 1931 is well documented in local oral history. Raymond Kessinger provided a clue as to Arnold's whereabouts from 1905, when Paul Landrum showed him some chords, to 1918, when he joined Faught's Entertainers in Hartford:

> And Arnold Shultz played the riverboats up and down Green River. . . . That would've been about 1915, 'cause we still lived in High View, near Cromwell. . . .
>
> I know a showboat there, one time, set up at Cromwell and there were so many *on* there that the thing almost sunk. And so they told them that the film was broke—they had a show and then they would have, later, music, you know.
>
> But, anyhow, Arnold Shultz was to play that night, I remember hearin' my mother say, because my mother was raised up near them [the Shultzes] too, see.
>
> The boat would come up and then it would go down and then it would come back up, and he'd take off a week and come stay with his sister [Minnie].
>
> Anyhow, they'd play all up and down the river—Green River, Ohio River, Mississippi.
>
> He played guitar in these bands on the boats; he played jazz and he played blues.[40]

One imagines that Shultz assimilated a great deal of music during these voyages to such culturally active cities as Evansville, Louisville, Cincinnati, St. Louis (the center, then, of ragtime), and perhaps even New Orleans. When he returned from these trips Arnold would visit his relatives in the region—his sister Minnie in McHenry (Malcolm and John Walker's mother), Ella Griffin in Prentiss, another sister in Cleaton, others in the Horton-Rosine area. Many of these folks report that Arnold would drift in unexpectedly, hang around a few days, then disappear without a word. Malcolm Walker's account is typical:

> He traveled a whole lot. He would leave, and we wouldn't know where he was. He didn't write or anything. But, somehow or another, we'd all be around the house there

and the first thing you knew, you'd hear that guitar. And
you *knew* it the minute you heard it. A lot of times he'd come
in, probably be twelve, one, or two o'clock in the morning,
or three—maybe we wouldn't have heard from him for
several years—and he'd come in, lay down on top of us—
we'd be in bed —he'd come in and lay down on all of us, roll
on us, you know.

And then he'd stay around there for awhile. And then,
the first thing you know, he'd get himself together and he'd
take his guitar, and he'd go out in front of the house and sit
there and play a song. Then the first thing you know he'd
get up and walk a little farther, and the first thing you know,
why, he'd be completely out of sight; we'd just barely hear
that guitar. And we wouldn't hear from him for several
years after that.

"He'd play as he walked away?" I asked.
"That's right; that's the way he was."
"And wander off?"
"He'd just kind of ease on away."[41]

And, like a medieval minstrel, he spread his music wherever he
went: "All he wanted to do was just travel around all over the
country and play, play the guitar, and play the violin. . . . He went
everywhere. Everywhere he could go, that's where he went; played
that music."[42]

During the last thirteen years of his life Shultz apparently
remained in the region. He played off and on in Boots Faught's band
from 1918 to 1922, and oral history places him in the Horton-Rosine
community during the mid-1920s. From the late 1920s until his
death in early 1931 he lived in Morgantown, in Butler County (still
only twelve miles or so from Shultztown and Prentiss), boarding
with the Beecher Carson family.[43] Shultz of course continued playing music during these years, and his musical prowess began to
become legendary; indeed, Arnold Shultz became a folk hero.
There are many stories in circulation in the region about Shultz's
remarkable musicianship; the following is one of the best:

There's a fella came out of Nashville one time—one of them
hotshots—and was playin' a violin down there in a crowd
down around Drakesboro somewhere, and he wanted
somebody to follow him [to play accompaniment on the

guitar]. And said that there's two or three people there, and this guy'd *lose* 'em real quick, you know; he'd just run off and leave 'em. There wasn't anybody around there to play with him; they couldn't follow, you know. And said that this guy said, "Can you get somebody to play *with* me?"

And said some man walked up there and said, "I know a man that can follow you," said, "if you'll just wait while I go get him." Said, "There ain't *no* man around here that can follow me." He said, "Oh yes there is."

Said he went—Arnold lived up there, his mother lived up there on a switch up there on the railroad tracks—said he went up there and Arnold was down on the railroad tracks a-pickin' up coal. And this man asked Arnold, said, "Would you come down there and play with this guy? He said he'd play if he could get somebody to follow him."

Arnold said, "Yeah; let me clean up a little bit." He was dirty, you know. So he changed clothes and went up there, and said he put this old guitar around his neck.

And so this guy started out on one, and Arnold listened to him play. And the guy said, "Now do you think you can play?" Arnold said, "I think I can, yessir; play one for us." And the man said, "Well, what do you wanna play?" He said, "Anything *you* want to play."

And said he struck down on one, thought he'd lose Arnold, but Arnold stayed right with him. And said that Arnold put some stuff in there that *that* man didn't even know [laughs].

Said the man played two or three tunes and *quit*! Said he never lost Arnold. Said when he just changed into them minor chords, Arnold went right in there after him too. Said he put some more in there that *he* didn't know.[44]

The bridge between Shultz picking and Travis picking was built in 1918 when the teenaged Kennedy Jones moved from Dunmor to Cleaton and heard Arnold play in a Central City tavern: "Oh, boy! Arnold Shultz was an *awful* nice guitar player. He went around in the clubs . . . [and would] sit down and play. And he'd throw his hat over here on the bar, you know, and they'd throw him the money in."[45] Jones became obsessed with Shultz's picking technique, and in 1920 purchased a whole box of thumb picks, which he distributed freely in the region. The tradition then began to spread like wildfire, passing from Shultz and Jones to Ike Everly in Brownie, Mose Rager in Weir, Lester "Plucker" English in Five Spot, Orval and Howard Raymer in Luzerne, Pip Stevens in Browder, Raymond McClellan in Cleaton, Arnie Miller in Graham, Bob and Cundiff Durham in Drakesboro, and such other Muhlenberg Countians as Howard Evitts, Robby Hogan, and B.W. Johnson, all of whom influenced young Merle Travis of Ebeneezer, thus helping to shape, collectively, the Travis style.[46] In 1936 Travis took the tradition from the region to Evansville and, subsequently, the world.[47] Arnold Shultz's part in the process, however, was over; he died on April 14, 1931, officially of heart disease, unofficially in regional lore of either "bad" whiskey or poison administered by white musicians jealous of his musicianship.[48]

As well as being a preternaturally talented performer, Arnold Shultz was a walking anthology of early-twentieth-century southern folk music. As he didn't sing, he was not a "songster"; Shultz was, rather, a "musicianer," one who concentrates on instrumental work, "drawing broadly on all aspects of Negro song and music traditions within the folk culture."[49] The regional contexts in which he performed were wide and varied: on company store porches, at railroad crossings, at house parties, and in both schools and taverns. Shultz played for dancers—square dancers, toddle dancers, and buck dancers; a bouncy, cut-time rhythm was therefore in much of his music. As he often played alone, and being unable to rely upon vocals to take up musical slack, he was forced to develop an instrumental technique in which his guitar became a band in itself, expressing melody, bass, harmony, and rhythm simultaneously. Keeping the bass going at all times necessitated the development of upper-neck thumb chords; using many different chords for variety also kept the music interesting, both for Shultz and his audiences. And as he had to be heard, he played hard, which was easier to do with a thumb pick.

As a highly accomplished finger-picking musicianer, Arnold Shultz became a model for numerous landlocked coal miners who found in his music a way in which to escape the drabness of their depression-weary lives. Learning to thumb pick became the thing to do; it became an engaging, highly functional diversion. Mose Rager, for example, said that when he first heard Kennedy Jones play in Cleaton in 1925, it "was the greatest thing that had ever happened to me in my life," then added, "as far as music is concerned."[50]

And were it not for the unique set of regional circumstances that surrounded the birth and distribution of the tradition, Travis picking may not have been brought into being. Indeed, strong regional forces—historic, physiographic, cultural, socioeconomic—helped to shape Shultz and his music. Slavery led to the large population of blacks in the region and to the subsequent formation of tightly knit black families and communities. The Green River facilitated the introduction to the region of a wide variety of musical styles and helped in both the assimilation and dissemination of Shultz's music. The coal mines enhanced cultural exchange between blacks and whites and, by not operating, provided numerous opportunities for musical interaction. Travis picking is truly a "regional" tradition.

The Travis style is being kept alive and flourishing by an extensive circle of Travis pickers—engineers, surgeons, morticians, professional musicians, insurance salespersons—many of whom gather annually at such ritual-like gatherings as the Thumb Pickers Tribute Show in Daysville, Kentucky, and the Ozark Folk Center's Tribute to Merle Travis in Mountain View, Arkansas. And while some of these pickers may have a dim notion of who Shultz was, they probably have yet to realize his influence on the music that they make. Folks in the region do, though: "A lot of people play the guitar, you know, but, really, the style of thumb pickin' came from Arnold Shultz, even though they never heard of Arnold Shultz, they never did know him. But somebody else had learned somethin' from him, and he learned from them, and they—it all goes back to Arnold Shultz."[51]

# Creative Constraints in the Folk Arts of Appalachia

## CHARLES E. MARTIN

*Like William Lightfoot, Charles Martin is interested in the relationship between the individual artist and the cultural context within which the artist operates. Focusing on the southern Appalachians, Martin argues that folk artists in that region are constrained not only by traditional aesthetic judgments of form and style, but by a regional ethos that emphasizes an individual's role within the social structure. Martin argues persuasively that for the traditional artist in Appalachia, this aspect of regional culture creates a tension between personal expression and social responsibility.*

John Kouwenhoven, in the *Arts in Modern American Civilization*, interprets American design as evolving from the experience of surviving in a receding frontier during an age of expanding technology and democracy; that American design leaned toward innovation and utilitarianism was inevitable given these circumstances.[1] Americans who lived without surplus, whose survival was always precarious in an uncertain environment, would seek to combine the artistic with the useful, expressing an economy of time and effort which reinforced an agrarian worldview. Yet folk artists and artisans found themselves bound by other mitigating and unbreakable forces, limited by the vision of those they lived and worked with.

In contemporary Appalachia, still serving as a model for earlier rural, national behavior, utilitarian creation continues to be common. But the decision to satisfy artistic impulses in workable objects has been largely determined by the special laws under which creative people in the area have had to exist. I use the perfect tense because in Appalachia the process of shifting from the agrarian ideal to an industrial one, from few industrial and professional opportunities to many, has already peaked. Since the mid-1980s, for example, Music Television and Home Box Office have begun broadcasting in the region, national fast-food restaurants have opened, and shopping malls are under construction. The images of mass culture have taken hold in Appalachia, yet creative forms remain restrained, a vestige of the older cultural system through which social stability was maintained by way of historical continuity and the appearance of egalitarianism. (The restraints described here, however, lessen even as I write this. One man recently said to me, "If you want to study this [he swept the horizon with his hand, indicating the totality of Appalachian culture], you better do it now because it's going fast"—a plea heard throughout this century, yet it was not the disappearance of specific folkways he was alluding to but the fading of the social structure which determines the retention of folkways.)

Many social practices have changed. It is no longer obligatory, for example, to demonstrate kinship respect by naming a child after a revered relative: girls are being named Heather, Nicole, and Danielle, and boys Jeff, Troy, and Kevin. But other practices show more strength. Art is still conservative and examples of the eclectic still rare. A painting tradition does not exist, nor one of sculpture.[2] Yet creativity must exist, since art is an innate human characteristic and need.[3] In Appalachia, observable individualistic activity is still discouraged, since the activities of the individual can frequently come in conflict with the concerns of the family group. Human nature dictates that individuals create in order to define themselves in relation to those around them, but in Appalachia, the culture demands that they be discreet about it, that they hide the overt intent of their art in utilitarian forms, or what is more commonly referred to as folk art. Folk art is not merely the result of provincial isolation from elite urban art centers. What helps determine folk art's form is the cultural context within which the artist must work: in Appalachia's case, the dominant context is the one that the family provides.

For example, Manton Cornett was a local postmaster, justice of the peace, and schoolteacher along the Kentucky-Virginia border toward the end of the nineteenth century. When he married, he built a one-and-one-half-story, single-room-and-loft log house, but found it necessary to add on to the structure as his family grew. The innovations he used in building more rooms, although not unique in the eastern United States, were rare enough to suggest that Manton sought to express his own abilities rather than simply adhere to traditional logic. Sometime between 1880 and 1894, Manton first removed the board roof and then the upper one-half story, substituting a full second story. Since the lower room was considered too cool in winter, the upper floor was lowered about one foot in an effort to retain the wood fire's heat better in the room below. Rather than box notching the new floor joists into the wall logs, however, Manton installed a joist suspension system whereby the joists were held up by a board which was pegged into the log under each joist.

In August of 1894 a rear log room was added. This new room, separated from the main structure by a covered breezeway, was divided into a smoke room and loom room. Because Manton's wife Julia feared smoke permeating her fabric, Manton extended the center vertical plank partition up to form the roof's ridge board. This continuous wall was then sealed with newspaper held in place with a flour-based glue; entrance to each half-room was through a separate doorway.

In 1900 another two-story, two-room structure was added alongside the original, separated by upper and lower dogtrots (breezeways). The logs in this addition, rather than being hewn and stacked in the traditional manner, were split down the center and hewn on the remaining three sides. The split side facing into the room was smoothed for appearances. Reminiscent of Scandinavian folk architecture, the top and bottom edges were straightened with bladed tools until they fit one onto the other, allowing no perceptible space between them.

As Manton constructed the new rooms he must have felt no real temporal urgency; the manner in which he patterned nails into horizontal door braces suggests someone intent on creating something singularly unique with little regard for the time it took. Manton's granddaughter, Ann Cornett Holliday, observed, "of course she [the new rooms] was done as the family grew up and he [Manton] had more time. He had more help and could afford to spend a little more time on it."[4]

Another example: Howard Acree's chimney contained four fireboxes venting into a central chimney, and sat directly in the center of a one-story, four-room frame house built in 1935. The central location of the fireplace meant each room had a firebox angled in the interior corner of its respective room rather than standing against the center of a short wall, as was the overwhelming architectural preference in the area. Although constructed by Howard's brother-in-law, Jones Martin, a professional builder, the chimney's unique form resulted solely from Howard's particular preferences. For

Howard, it was a journey into the uncertainty of what, by mental calculation, should work, rather than what, by imitating tradition, would work. A four-firebox fireplace was not the simple duplication of a fireplace with two openings; here each duplication had to meet the next duplication at perpendicular angles, causing a nightmare of conceptual refiguring in order to maintain structural strength.

While his idea of tightly compressing four chimneys into a single unit was a seemingly utilitarian effort aimed at heating his house while saving the space conventional fireplaces would have taken up, it was also an act of creation which placed his ideas against the customary solutions of those surrounding him. Howard probably had never seen a fireplace like the one he imagined, but applying his own geometry without the certain knowledge of success based on previously observed models failed to daunt him.[5]

Cody Jacobs built his two-thirds double-crib barn in 1936, cantilevering the top level to keep the lower exterior walls dry and to give him the storage space in the loft that he did not need in the stalls, "nine square feet being enough for a horse or mule." Larger stalls would have meant longer logs and more work. Winter's cold winds, however, moved up the hollow from the northeast causing much discomfort to his stock. Cody dropped board walls down from the overhangs, creating narrow hallways along the north and east sides which he filled with "insulation," fodder which his stock fed on through openings cut into the stall walls. By the time his stock had exhausted the fodder, warmer weather had returned.

Sliding gates are used on both sides of the barn's driveway. According to Cody, "sliding gates stay put, the wind can't shut them."[6] Cody's gates run on homemade tracks consisting of wooden-spool pulley wheels moving along one-and-a-half-inch pipe. The stall doors are fastened with forty-five-degree slide bars, which gravity locks automatically, preventing the doors from being left open due to forgetfulness. What does Cody attribute forty-five-degree door latches, pulley wheels, and insulated barn walls to? "Inspiration."

Cody's brother Otis also prides himself on his ability to innovate. His rat-proof corncrib, for example, sits four feet above ground atop square pieces of sandstone cut larger than the blocks making up the piers. Blacksnakes, squirrels, and rats cannot climb up around these larger blocks. Otis says he arrived at this particular design principle after experimenting with lard cans turned upside down through which log piers were fitted. Rats found themselves blocked by the walls and bottom of the tin container; tin, though, quickly rusted. When asked where such ideas come from, Otis replied, "I don't know. I just take it in my head."[7]

Many of Cody and Otis's innovations, however, have antecedents outside the area, so can they be truly considered innovations? Probably, since these ideas are rare within their immediate cultural context, qualifying these ideas as singular choices rather than borrowings on the cutting edge of cultural diffusion. Otis's notion of design forms appearing in his head is a generalized response, frequently given when a form has been freely adopted.[8] Other common explanations are: "I just studied awhile on that," or "It's the only one in these parts like it." Perhaps this is self-delusion, but it's also an indication of how important it is for these builders to have a sense of individuality. Otis elaborately shapes horseshoe door hinges, Rudell Thomas uses a vine-choked tree for a stair railing, Boss Slone rounds the top of his chimney "'cause it's prettier that way." This need for self-definition is the common thread these individuals share. Lech Watson, a family patriarch, "took it in his mind" in the 1930s to build a four-stall barn with aisles between each stall. His son Crafus says there were no others around like that and that his father "just wanted something different."[9]

Creativity in gardening becomes a striving for visual order and color balancing; there should be few weeds and the rows must be uniform and neat. One gardener planted a grape arbor around her garden and each year plants flowers and herbs between rows of vegetables. Rather than planting all the green vegetables together, she prefers to intersperse them with radish plants, yellow squash, carrots, and asparagus. Aside from the inexpensive production of food, the garden becomes a large color montage which can be continually fussed over. Another gardener prefers her patch plowed from side to side and then planted from front to back, improving, so she believes, its appearance when the vegetables begin to sprout. She also likes to mix her colors and textures while planting. She plants the potatoes at the bottom of her hillside plot, followed by green onions ("which grow straight and tall"), peas ("a lighter green than let's say the beans"), beets ("a mixture of red and green"), turnips, radishes, lettuce, and green beans (preferring dark green at the top). The visual condition of one's garden is a common summertime topic of conversation, and it is a high compliment to be known as keeping a "pretty" garden.

I asked one fellow who plays and sings mountain music, and

who has hosted the music segments of an annual folk festival for the last eight years, to recall those times when someone performed a piece in a particular style that may have surprised him in its originality, in its unexpected individualization. Since he tapes all performances, I thought this would be a good opportunity to hear what he considered original, rather than what I might. "I don't recall anyone ever doing that," he replied.

How is creativity expressed, then, in "old-time" Appalachian music? It appears that rather than through instrumentation or phrasing, it lies in the voice. The singer must show "feeling" and "soul" to be considered good, and it is through feeling that personal style is achieved. But what is "feeling?" Benny Moore couldn't define it, except to recall a story about Ricky Skaggs: when Ricky heard Carter Stanley perform and saw the tears running down Carter's cheek onto his guitar, Ricky knew then what feeling was.[10]

Cooking also is an area of personal creativity, with each customary dish varied slightly to accent what is thought to be individuality. One woman cooks fryers with carrots, green beans, potatoes, and cabbage wedges on top. Not at all uncommon, but she feels it is, thus separating her from what she considers the commonplace. She also bakes five-layer fruit cakes with apple butter between the layers. The last step is to put the stacked and layered cake back into the oven to "brown." This gives the cake added texture, one that is particularly appreciated by her family. "I'm the only person that I know of that does this," she claims.

Are all forms of creativity in eastern Kentucky intended for use, sale, or live performance? Not exactly. Quilting, for example, is decorative at the same time that it is utilitarian; indeed, the liberty some quilters take with designs makes this medium border on the overtly expressive.

One local quilter is renowned for her skill at traditional design, perhaps giving her the confidence to experiment with visually disordered patterns which seem to mock the idea of traditional design. Many quilters pride themselves on making quilts out of available materials, yet she appears to strive for the discordant pattern, mixing plaids, floral prints, and stripes. Since she has stacks of pieced tops she says she plans to quilt one day, one wonders if these tops are not actually a form of "painting," quickly assembled in a dash of inspiration in the medium she feels best able to control, the one in which she has established her reputation. She, like any artist who feels a sense of control and familiarity over a chosen medium, tries to redefine and test the rules of her art. If repetitive squares are the structural components of a quilt pattern, then her quilts (in a legal sense) satisfy these rules. But, like the modern artist, she incorporates artistic avoidance of common and predictable shapes. By testing the rules of her art she examines the power she has over the medium she is most associated with, echoing Ernst Kris's contention that creativity enables one to communicate an internal image to the outside world under the protection of an aesthetic illusion.[11]

Other area quilters occasionally produce quilts with disconcerting shapes and colors, perhaps also to achieve a private sense of individualism. The daughter of one quilter surmises that her mother has on occasion made "ugly" quilts (her term, by which she means the use of only blacks and browns) simply because she was bored with quilting, bored with the exacting precision expected of quilters, and somewhat bored with life. Shortly after producing the last black and brown quilt, her mother entered the work force and seemed much happier.

At least two customs among quilters in eastern Kentucky promote artistic privacy. Their latest works, instead of being prominently displayed, are hidden under cheap bedspreads, ostensibly to keep them clean. The quilters also refuse to sell them, instead giving them as gifts to members of the immediate family.

Although regional personalized creation seems generally hidden away in utilitarian forms or under the bedspread, the work of a few artists apparently has existed entirely outside the pale of tradition, utilitarianism, and commerce. Willie Owsley made baskets for a living toward the end of his life. He also decorated the exterior of his house in an intensely personal manner, covering the front with stones from all fifty states and cementing into these walls a variety of objects: dolls, marbles, horseshoes, statues, shells, a pistol, bottles, broken glass, and toy cars—objects which for him alone had significance.

At the midpoint of his career Chester Cornett, one of the area's more famous craftsmen, moved from manufacturing common chairs (functional, comfortable, attractive, and predictable) toward personalized sculpture. Chester's four-rocker chairs are not very comfortable, since the middle two rockers extend up under the knees. His early chairs were very comfortable, but he had his customers in mind then. His later creations, according to Chester, were built because "you meet somebody who just wants something different."[12] The only one who wanted something different was Chester, who, by redefining the client-craftsman relationship, allowed himself to transcend the definition of craftsman and what we think a chair to be.

Aside from personalities like Willie and Chester, there seems a reluctance in the area to produce a visible art devoid of functionalism. Since art is recognized as a visual necessity, why is personal expression so often hidden in the utilitarian? It appears that the family, in its regional form, may have much to do with it.

Although in Appalachia basic familial structure is nuclear, the majority of nuclear units form affiliations based on blood ties, marriage, geographic proximity, and common outlook for the purposes of social and financial security.[13] This security is achieved primarily by the group banding together to support political candidates who will later be expected to be helpful to the family group by extending political patronage to it. Before election day, candidates attempt to establish blood ties with as many voters as possible in the hope that kinship loyalty will override all other obligations. After election day, the voters begin establishing ties to the winners (when in fact many did not vote for the winner) in the hope of securing similar kinship loyalty. Political advertising for most candidates includes little mention of what are considered the standard qualifications for office: educational record, military record, former political offices and appointments; instead, principal qualifications are the personal character of the office seeker, established with a genealogical record extending back two and three generations.

Family status also plays an important role in the group's social and financial security, since key members of one highly regarded family group can often play an influential role in the political choices of key members of other groups. A winning candidate will reward the man (and this does appear to be a male ritual) who can deliver not only his group's vote but also another's. Since eastern Kentucky's largest single employer is the county public school systems (an intensely political organization), a large and respectable family group who can agree on a winning school-board candidate might be rewarded with employment for many of its members.[14] Supporting the right county judge and magistrate can mean getting the road and bridges leading out of the hollow repaired after spring rains. A family's disunity and its inability to influence key members of other families because of low status usually results in the family's roads remaining lined with ruts and other families' sons being chosen over theirs for available employment—a crucial consideration in an area where the unemployment rate consistently ranges between 18 and 40 percent.

A family group's security, then, is immeasurably tied to its ability to be well thought of. To achieve this, the family group must in part be willing to monitor the behavior of its members in order to maintain its good name. Since family traits affect the reputations of members, and the reputation of an entire family can be impugned by the behavior of one errant member, such monitoring becomes accepted. Erratic behavior can result in gossip, which can mean a loss of family status, a loss of influence over others, a loss of an election, the loss of jobs and financial security. When a political candidate lists his family tree, he is reasonably certain that the behavior of his ancestors will reflect favorably on him, but he must also be aware that his behavior today will reflect on his descendants tomorrow. Such continuity assures family loyalty and an adherence to the behavioral values of the society.

As gossip can be so costly, members are reluctant to embarrass the family group. As one informant stated: "One of us can shame all the others. If I am shamed and a relative walks down the street, people will say, 'I know who that is, that's ____'s kin.' And how they feel about me determines their attitude toward her. If my reputation is good, they're going to love her; if it's bad, they're going to hate her from across the street." [15] Accordingly, the demands of conformity impinge on the individual from three directions: inwardly (sensing the individual risks of controversy), from the family (which must protect its position in the local hierarchy), and from nonfamily members (who are on the lookout for odd behavior in other groups potentially to improve their own family's position). Many informants have expressed the belief that their own behavior is monitored constantly by both people within their group and outside of it. This is not to suggest that an aura of paranoia surrounds eastern Kentucky's residents. People are no more watched by their neighbors than they would be in a metropolitan suburb—folks are always interested in the doings of others; however, the stakes are higher in eastern Kentucky and Appalachia.

Since the family group is often considered responsible for the behavior of members, individualism is not considered as positive an attribute as it is in the mythology of mass culture. The maintenance of all culture depends to some extent on the subjugation of the personal desires of its members. In eastern Kentucky, though, individualism in conflict with the needs of the group is to be avoided. Getting along with each other is the primary obligation of family members, since it suggests unity to the outsider and helps maintain internal stability. Although harmony is frequently broken as members vie for status within the group, argumentative tendencies are thought best kept in check, with gossip directed at outsiders and at members not present.

Rather than individual members being expected to make choices which best meet their particular needs, they are expected to defer decision-making power to the group. The group is concerned not only with how a member will be affected by an action but with how the group will be affected by the outsider's perception of this action. If outsider perceptions might be gauged as negative and hence detrimental to the reputation of the group, the proposed action will either be abandoned or modified.

When asked to describe home and family, people present images of emotional security and the absence of individual responsibility. But they also describe an atmosphere where personal privacy is not encouraged, since it implies rejection of the group. Loyalty to family means being concerned enough with the group to want to take part in continual house-to-house visits and to avoid the eccentricity of seclusion.

Creativity naturally enters into this behavioral scheme. If a major purpose of creativity is to allow artists to define themselves in relation to their emotional and physical environment, what social rules apply? For modern artists very few, since their role is to expand our notions of reality beyond what culture teaches us. For some nationally known artists purported to be folk, like Simon Rodia, Creek Charlie, and Edgar Tolson, there are again few rules, since these are true eccentrics whose visions appear so singular as to exist outside of what could be considered folk culture.[16] The traditional artist uses conscious or unconscious symbols shared by the group; his or her vision is an extension of the group's vision. For the eastern Kentuckian, creativity must be weighed alongside social realities. To be expressive and personal is to invite comment and analysis, since both qualities are considered prideful and indicative of assumed self worth and the willingness to intervene in the lives of others. As one informant noted,

> To publicly display is to brag and to assume that because you think an object has worth, the audience will too. In fact, the

audience is offended because the object is offered when you didn't ask for it. What's implied by the offering is that what you [the viewer] has is not enough, and the artist will supplement what's missing in your life. When you show yourself like that, you're asking for others to make decisions on you. It's all right to be talented and to be discovered, but it's not all right to be talented and to look to be noticed for it.[17]

The life of any contemporary artist in the most favorable of circumstances is precarious in terms of financial rewards and acceptance, but when the group can suffer for the inventiveness of one of its members, this intensifies creative risk.

Some examples of unappreciated creativity in the area: a married couple painted their window facings blue and neglected to hang curtains, saying that they thought the glass panes inside the blue facings were particularly attractive. Neighbors and family disagreed.

A woman, newly married and unable to afford a cabinet for her dishes and canned goods, made one of heavy cardboard boxes. While she was particularly proud of her ingenuity and her ability to fashion furniture from generally overlooked items, her family was embarrassed by her efforts. Pressure finally caused her to replace the cardboard cabinet with a manufactured one.

A man, recently returned to eastern Kentucky after living a number of years outside of Appalachia, built a cinderblock house which, rather than facing the road as was the custom in the area, faced—front porch and all—toward the back hillside. He also painted the house an uncustomary color, perhaps satisfying his personal tastes while declaring his independence from community conservatism. His neighbors laughed at his house and actually asked him what he was attempting to accomplish (face-to-face questioning a sign in itself of his questionable status). Friends began to avoid him, relatives pleaded with him to change his house, since it threatened all their reputations. Society finally imposed its will, and he remodeled, opening a front door facing onto the road, ripping down and moving the porch to the opposite side of the dwelling, and altering some interior walls. He has subsequently been known as "the fellow with the house," and it has taken his family some time to rebuild its reputation. The best way to reach this man, it turned out, was by the unarticulated threat to the social position of the family group.

These people made decisions based foremost on personal preference without considering the effect of their respective acts on the group. What most area artists do under similar conditions is to play it safe. Creativity is best hidden in utilitarian objects or in objects for sale at flea markets and festivals. The woman who makes and sells doll pillows, for example, protects herself. She sells what she makes and what she makes requires little interpretation from the audience. Perhaps she would like to test the limits of her ability, but if she does, her work would require a different type of evaluation with wider ranging implications than the counting up of sales provides.

But how do the Willie Owsleys and Chester Cornetts get by with such overt expression without similar ramifications? In Willie's case, the reputation of his family had long been based on producing handmade items; Willie's father, Bird, for example, was a basketmaker of legendary skill. Inasmuch as the family group was expected to be "handy," the status of the group could not be as damaged from the idiosyncratic inventions of one or a few of its members. The status of the family might have even been enhanced by a member's public creativity. It appears, however, that such craft-oriented families had diminished political and social power. The reputation for collective creativity may have allowed for more community acceptance than was normal, but that same reputation denied them positions of real influence. Their talents may have been appreciated, but they were relegated to standing apart.

Chester Cornett, according to his neighbors, had little extended family. His father moved to Oregon early on and Chester was raised "twixt both" Kentucky's Letcher and Harlan counties. If Chester had had extended family whom he lived near, associated with, and felt responsibility toward, he might have been somewhat more reluctant to test the artistic rules of his craft. Having little family and hence little power, Chester derived a degree of creative freedom denied others, since there were few relatives his activities could jeopardize.

Chester's neighbors considered his behavior quite eccentric until he began receiving national exposure. Interestingly, his neighbors then began reinventing his history to cast his behavior in a more positive and even patriotic light. Chester, stationed on the Aleutian Islands during World War II, was said to have been badly shell shocked during combat; it was also rumored that he was a survivor of the Bataan Death March.

For the vast majority of local artisans, however, creativity is a limited activity. Even though a primary function of their work is contextual self-definition, the population sample they place themselves against is small, mostly the folks up and down the creek. Compare this, for example, to the urban subway graffiti artist who derives self-definition from dealing with a larger group. The train-long signature that rolls through four boroughs is a form of billboard immortality, making one's presence known to literally millions of people in an environment where a large population accentuates anonymity. Among eastern Kentucky residents, the search for definition is more circumspect: the audience is more geographically contained, often personally known to the artist, and more critical. If local artists are blatant in their quest for self-definition, they risk rejection. And, since they cannot afford rejection from an audience known to both them and their families, creativity is normally displayed in workable objects, the obvious functions of which obscure their quest for singularity. The chairmaker will personalize his chair with minor design embellishments or with seemingly novel construction techniques; the quilter will make innovative searches to avoid the predictable, but she will hide the results of these forays in anticipatory geometric patterns; the gardener hides behind the rows of carefully placed vegetables; the cook in the steamy aroma of food. The musician accepts the criterion by which the emotional rendering of a song is considered more creative than the altering of its structure. The builder constructs a joist suspension system; he builds a chimney comprising a labyrinth of angles deep inside his house and mind; he builds a four-stall barn because no one near him has one—all meet a utilitarian need while confirming a psychic one. "Art," as defined by a local quilter, "is making something work." The advantage of utilitarian form (aside from its usefulness) is its ability to hide the intent of its creator.

Restraints on individual activity, the lack of privacy, decision making through consensus, and the need to maintain the appearance of group unity do not necessarily mean an atmosphere that is in conflict with all types of creativity. But for the artist to create a sound ordering of society through artistry he or she must, as Erich Neumann states, be "at liberty to realize his own inner creative freedom," more freedom than the family group has been safely willing to grant.[18] For an Appalachian to create modern art might require the rejection of family values and supervision, as well as personal rejection by the family, particularly since personal creativity is frequently seen by the family group as an attempt to address family problems under the guise of art.

There may be many people in eastern Kentucky and Appalachia desiring overt expression but avoiding it; we should consider their circumstances, though recognizing that this particular society has placed utilitarian expression over the fine arts, not because of a preoccupation with work and a lack of appreciation for beauty, but because the family maintains much of its position and power through the predictable behavior of its members. When economic security exists independently of family unity and behavior, the reins which limit individualization can be loosened. As more industry moves into the area, employment security will be maintained other than through family ties and anticipatory behavior. The probable cost of this new creative freedom will be the diminished impact of the family: as an atmosphere of artistic liberty increases, it does so at the expense of the emotional security the family group provides. Artists will no longer be able to share the responsibility of their vision; they will have no choice but to stand alone. For the present, though, creativity is tied to a family's total sense of well-being. These are the circumstances under which the artist works.

# The Genealogical Landscape and the Southern Sense of Place

## BARBARA ALLEN

*As Charles Martin points out, kinship patterns are an intrinsic part of the way people in southern Appalachia conceive of their home region. Farther west, in the upper Cumberland region of Kentucky and Tennessee, ties both to family members and to the land serve as a field of reference for residents of a rural neighborhood. In this essay, I show how conversational patterns in this subregional culture of the upland South reveal residents' sense of place and identity.*

Southerners' attachment to home—their sense of place—is perhaps the hallmark of their regional identity. It is attested to in literature and popular culture, from William Faulkner's focus on his "postage stamp of native soil" to the southern migrant's musical cry "I wanna go home." And it manifests itself as well in folk culture, from refusing to sell the old homeplace, even though it stands empty, to having one's body returned home for burial.[1]

In part, the southern sense of place is constructed, maintained, and articulated in a distinctively regional conversational pattern that emphasizes placing people within a social and geographical frame.[2] While this pattern can be found throughout the South, it is perhaps most apparent in the rural neighborhoods that have historically been the seedbeds of southern folk culture.[3] In the conversations I've listened to in one such neighborhood in south central Kentucky, residents reveal their conceptions of place, as well as personal and social identity, in talk revolving around the relationships between people and the land they live on. That talk is grounded in personal and generational memories and the accretion of myriad concrete details about the lives of their neighbors, both past and present, gained in lifetimes of observations, interactions, and conversations. In these conversations, the landscape becomes a symbolic one, with historical and social as well as physical dimensions, a complex structure of both kinship networks and land-ownership patterns. The sense of place evoked in conversation then becomes a filter through which people perceive the landscape around them, indeed, which structures their very thinking about the land and the social relations carried out on it.

I first encountered this conversational pattern and the sense of place it expresses in 1979 when I moved from Los Angeles to Bowling Green, Kentucky, and discovered a world utterly different from my own peripatetic suburban California background. Having lived in seven different houses and four towns before I was eighteen years old, I was astonished to discover that people in that part of the South often lived in houses or on land that had been in their families for four, five, or six generations; the family I had married into, for instance, still owns the land taken up by their forebears in the 1790s. Accustomed to the sprawl of southern California, where one municipality blends into another with little more than city-limit signs to mark the boundaries between them, I was intrigued with the cultural landscape in Kentucky where settlements are widely separated by miles of rolling, apparently empty, countryside. What I didn't realize at first was that the rural landscape is as much a patchwork of interconnected communities as the Los Angeles Basin, and that the boundaries between rural neighborhoods are as plain to residents there as the line between Santa Monica and West Los Angeles was to me—although both are invisible to outsiders. Once I recognized this hidden dimension of the landscape, I began to look for the principles by which the residents render order out of local landscapes that appear to outsiders like me to be both literally and figuratively chaotic.

The division of the rural landscape into distinct neighborhoods and the strong identity that residents feel with their home communities were first brought home to me in a conversation with my husband, Lynwood, within a few weeks of my arrival. Searching for some commonality between my western experience and his southern life, I asked him if he had ever seen any rattlesnakes around where he grew up. "Oh, no," he said. "We never saw a poisonous snake in Rock Bridge [his home community], but down on Meshack Creek [three miles away], now they had snakes over there." My first impulse was to laugh because his conception of "where he grew up" was so at odds with mine. I had meant the phrase to refer to south central Kentucky in general (just as I thought of "where I grew up" as southern California), but he understood it to mean the immediate neighborhood in which he had spent his childhood. That neighborhood was centered around the Rock Bridge store and post office and encompassed the surrounding area within a radius of roughly three miles.

Lynwood was eager to take me there, to show me where he had grown up, to visit the site of his family's old homeplace, to see the graveyard where many of his ancestors were buried and where he planned to be laid to rest himself one day, to stand on the hill from which he had photographed his childhood environs before leaving home for the first time. He wanted me to see the place which had shaped his identity. So we set off on what was for me truly a voyage of discovery. To my eyes, acclimated to the subdued tones of an arid region, the green Kentucky landscape seemed lush, almost tropical. With euphonious but impenetrable Spanish place names fresh in my memory, the clear imagery of names like Summer Shade, Persimmon, and Bugtussle delighted me. My western sense of direction, oriented to roads that were for the most part straight and usually crossed each other at right angles, was thoroughly and permanently skewed as we drove along twisting, hilly roads where a straight, level stretch of more than a couple of hundred yards was a novelty.

Sixty miles from Bowling Green, Lynwood proudly announced, "Here we are!" I looked around expectantly. "Where?" I asked somewhat stupidly. I meant "Where *is* it?" because while Lynwood saw his home community, all I saw was more of the same landscape we had been traveling through for the past hour—woods, fields, and low rolling hills, with houses and barns scattered apparently at random over the countryside.

When we arrived at his mother's house, the first thing she wanted to know was, "Well, which way did you come?"

"We turned off on the right just before Eighty-Eight," Lynwood told her. "You know, the road that goes through Nobob and makes a T down by the Oak Grove Church."

"You mean down there by the old Tudor place?" she asked.

"Yeah, you know the road that goes by the Lewis Williams place. Then we turned just before we got to Lemon's store there in Sulphur Lick and came by the old Jesse Bowman place," he continued.

"Well, Lynwood, is that old place still standing?" she wanted to know.

"No," he said. "Whoever bought it just took a bulldozer in there and tore everything down. All there is left is a big pile of lumber back in the corner of the field."

"Oh, that was Dale Stevenson bought that place," she said. "He's come into this country from Mount Poland [about a dozen miles away] and bought up everything he could, for the timber, you know."[4]

If the landscape had been a visual enigma to me, this bewildering jumble of so-and-so's place and such-and-such a road added a new dimension to my confusion and made me long momentarily for the comforting familiarity of the corner of Westwood and Wilshire. Ten years of similar conversations have followed, between Lynwood and his mother, with other family members, with their friends and neighbors. Sometimes the conversation begins with the mention of someone's name.

"Lynwood," Hazel (his mother) says, "did you ever know Willie Page?"

"Was that Calvin's boy?" he asks.

"No, Calvin was his uncle. Clarence was Willie's daddy," she explains. "They lived out on the Forkton road, out past the Robert MacPherson place."

"I didn't know there was a house up that far."

"Why, Lynwood, don't you remember that's where Bart and Nora Edwards lived and raised that great big family?" she prompts.

"Well, I went to school with Flodina and Ruby Page," he recalls. "They must have been his sisters."

"Why, yes," Hazel says, "they were the two youngest girls. Willie was the oldest child in the family."

"Well, I don't guess I ever knew him," Lynwood says.

"Oh, you did," she insists. "He married Lena Carter, Sam Bell's oldest girl, and they lived over where William and Bessie Ferguson used to live."

"Oh, okay, *now* I know who you're talking about!" he says.

On other occasions, conversations are generated by a question about a particular place.

"Now, Mama," Lynwood asks, "whose old house was that back behind where Freeman Carter's built that restaurant on the Mud Lick road?"

"Is it a big old two-story white house?" she asks.

"Yes, back against the woods there."

"Was it Benton Tucker's place?" she ponders. "No, no, not

Benton—Willie. Willie Tucker, that was Benton's brother. He built
that house after him and Marcella was married."

"I thought Willie and Marcella lived on down closer to Mount
Gilead, near the old Bushong homeplace," Lynwood says.

"No, you're thinking of Ivis Tucker, Willie and Benton and all of
them's daddy," Hazel explains. "That's where they was all raised."

"Well, who lives there now?" Lynwood wants to know.

"Now, Lynwood," she says, "I couldn't tell you. It must be
some of them Tucker children, Jerrell, maybe—he's the oldest."

"Now who did he marry?"

"Well, his first wife was Lizzie Norman, Carl's youngest girl,"
she recalls. "I don't know who he's married to now; she's from
Metcalfe [an adjoining county] is all I know."

At first, each of these conversations was only slightly less cryp-
tic to me than the preceding one. But, eventually, I began to remember names I'd heard before and recognize places I'd seen before, so
that I could follow what was being said, after a fashion. More
important, however, I began to sense a rhythm or a pattern in the
way people talked; it began to sound familiar to me even when I
*didn't* know the people they were talking about or the places they
mentioned. That pattern lay in the orderly linking of names and
places. Rarely were individuals named without mention of who
their relatives were and where they lived, and places (that is,
properties) were invariably identified by the names of their owners.
Recognizing this pattern gave me the key to understanding how
conversation expresses the fundamental structure of Rock Bridgers'
view of their world.

This view is organized around two interlocking elements: the
people who live or have lived within the boundaries of the community and the land they live or lived on. Residents of the neighborhood, past and present, are linked to one another by bonds of
kinship just as their places are joined contiguously on the land. So
when the people of Rock Bridge look around them, they see the
landscape as a complex web of human lives lived on it; they see, in
other words, a genealogical landscape.

Kinship is one of the two basic components of the genealogical
landscape, and the importance of being able to identify an individual's place within a kinship network is clear in all sorts of conversational contexts.[5] Pinpointing where an individual lies on a
genealogical map—that is, in relation, literally, to other people—
reveals his or her identity, just as a constellation is outlined by

drawing lines from star to star on a map of the sky. When individuals who are not members of the conversationalists' families, immediate neighborhoods, or friendship circles are mentioned, however casually, they are almost always given a genealogical label. Minimally that label consists of parents' names. For instance, Lynwood is known as "Willie and Hazel Montell's boy," while Hazel would be called "Chris and Martha Chapman's youngest girl." ("Boy" and "girl" are consistently used in this connection, even when the people they refer to are adults, sometimes advanced in years; this usage emphasizes their identities as the *children* of their parents.) When meeting for the first time, people may ask each oher, "Now who is (or was) your daddy?" Along similar lines, a married woman understands the question "Who *were* you?" as a request for her maiden name or the names of her parents. Occasionally, the names of parents aren't quite enough to make an individual's place in a kinship system clear; when this happens, the conversationalists may undertake the verbal construction of a family tree, naming various relatives—grandparents, brothers and sisters, spouse, and children—to locate the person in question firmly in a family nexus, before the conversation turns back to its original focus. These impromptu genealogies can involve mildly astonishing feats of memory.

"Now, whose son is Charles Strode?" Lynwood wanted to know one afternoon.

"Oh, why, he's Turner's," Hazel said, then corrected herself. "No—Estes's. Estes was Turner's son [i.e., Turner was Charles' grandfather]."

"Are they the Poplar Log bunch?" Lynwood asked, referring to the Strode family from a neighboring community.

"They're *my* bunch," she pointed out, meaning that she considers them as belonging to her branch of the family. "Mammy and Turner was first cousins," she went on, "me and Estes second, so you and Charles is third cousins. They're the Persimmon bunch of Strodes," she concluded, locating them in still another neighboring community.

"Now, Hade [Strode]," she commented, harking back to a name mentioned earlier in the conversation, "his daddy was a half-brother to Uncle Smith who was the daddy of Turner."[6]

Sometimes this genealogical rundown constitutes the whole of a conversation. That is, kinship relations are discussed for their own sake. When that happens, a person's forebears back to great-grandparents may be identified; his or her siblings, their spouses, and their children named; their ages and birth order established; their status as living or dead accounted for; where various members of the family lived recalled; and family complications such as illegitimacy and divorce hashed out.

In these genealogical conversations, people frequently refer not only to an individual's kinship ties but also to his or her "homeplace," suggesting that where people live or have lived is just as significant in establishing personal identity as who their relatives are. And, indeed, the second basic element of the genealogical landscape is the "place"—that is, a house and the acreage surrounding it that constitutes a family's "homeplace." The term "place" is loaded with meaning, suggesting primacy even over the concept of "home"; one speaks of a "place" or a "homeplace" but only rarely of a "home" in connection with a particular house or property. "Place" thus has a special meaning in the community's lexicon, beyond its usual sense of locality: it denotes a piece of property and thus implies a relationship between it and its owner. Second, a "place" is a plot of ground permanently defined not only by legal possession but also by human occupance. It is not just *any* plot of land; it is where people live now or have lived in the past, a fact that is embodied in a house located on the place and in the owner's name being given to the place. In fact, the only parcels of land in the community identified by name are those with houses on them. Even when the houses are destroyed by fire, neglect, or bulldozer, the place names persist. The identification of a place with a house is revealed in the interchangeable use of the terms "so-and-so's house" and "so-and-so's place."

There is a systematic way in which names are assigned to "places" and connections made between places and the people who live on them. First, a place is known by the *owner's* name. It is never given the name of renters or tenants, no matter how long they may have lived there. (In cases of long-term tenancy, neighbors may refer to the house by the tenants' name—e.g., "the Fergusons' "— but they will never call it "the Ferguson place.") Second, a place is identified with the couple who owned it and raised their family there. (Permanent bachelor- or spinsterhood is rare and married couples without children are anomalies.) Sometimes, several generations of a family live successively in the same house; as ownership is transferred from one generation to the next, community residents will begin to use the names of the current owners in referring to the place. Lynwood's homeplace, for instance, was initially known as the Pick Strode place, after its builder, then as the Polk Strode (Pick's son) place. After Chris Chapman married Martha Strode, Polk's daughter, the house was known as the Chris Chapman place and continued to be called that, even after Willie Montell married Chris and Martha's daughter Hazel, likely because Chris lived with them until the family moved out of the house permanently in the mid-1940s.

Occasionally, a couple or a family will move from one house to another. If the first house is left empty, it becomes known as the "old so-and-so place." If, however, it is used as rental property, the house becomes known as the "so-and-so *old* place," in contrast to the new place in which the owners now live. On the northern edge of Rock Bridge, for instance, stands a house, now occupied by renters, that people refer to as the "Josh Miller old place." Josh Miller, who once lived in the house and still owns it, lives across the road.

The house, as the focal point of the place, is not just a material structure but also an evocative symbol of the human relationships—the family ties—lived out in it. This is made clear in numerous references to houses being built by couples after their marriages, and by the consistent descriptions of those houses as places where the couples' children were born and raised. In fact, individuals are frequently identified with the locations of their childhood homes. "She grew up back there behind the Joe Lind Carter place, on what they called the old Ferguson place," Hazel might say. Sometimes when an individual's identity is unclear in conversation, the confusion can be cleared up by specifying where that person grew up. Thus "Where did you grow up?" is a question almost as common as "Now who was your daddy?"

Just as a good deal of talk revolves around genealogy, conversations also focus on the question of where various people in the community spent their early years or their adult lives. The speculation on the question is not idle: I have heard Hazel remark on several occasions, "I'd give anything to know just where my grandmother was raised." By "just where," Hazel means the exact homesite; her grandmother grew up somewhere in the Rock Bridge vicinity, but the specific location remains a mystery. This preoccupation with locating people in space is puzzling to the outsider. But it also reveals the strength of the identification between people and place, intimating that some part of the individual's personal identity is chthonic, bound up with the particular spot on earth where he or she was born and absorbed early impressions.

The connection between people and their places is revealed perhaps most clearly in Hazel's commentary on the landscape during drives around the countryside. She "reads" the landscape in genealogical terms, identifying the houses according to their occupants' family connections. "Now, Sam Bell's middle boy, Lewis, lives there," she will say. Even when she does not actually know who lives in the houses, she can often identify them from the names on their mailboxes perched by the side of the road. "'Tom Carter'— that must be Hubert and Lucille Carter's youngest child; he married a Pettit," she might comment. (Occasionally, when no name is visible from the road, she remarks impatiently, "There ought to be a law that says everybody has to put their name on their mailbox so people will know who lives there!") Empty and abandoned houses are named along with those currently occupied. "That's the old Hunt Smith place, I believe," she'll speculate. During these jaunts, she is comfortable as long as she recognizes the places or names she sees. Once she travels beyond them into unfamiliar territory, however, she feels lost. "Now don't ask me where we are," she'll say. "I know nothing about this neighborhood." Even though it might be not a dozen miles from Rock Bridge, "it might as well be a thousand miles away," she says. The power of the genealogical landscape to shape perception is unmistakable in remarks like, "If I could see a *name*, I'd know *where* I'm at." When she recognizes a name, she relaxes; "Oh, I'm at home in here," she says. The landscape is strange and empty in Rock Bridgers' eyes if they don't know who lives on it, just as people aren't fully recognized until they can be identified with a particular spot on the landscape.

Each homeplace, like each individual, is an autonomous entity. But, like individuals, they are also part of the social fabric of the community. The connections between places analogous to the kinship ties between individuals are the roads that web the neighborhood and operate as both physical and symbolic links among neighbors. The lively local interest that people take in roads reveals their significance as symbols of community as well as actual routes of communication and interaction. Just as the sites of both past and present homeplaces are recognized on the local landscape, people also know the locations of old roadbeds as well as those currently linking various parts of the neighborhood together and connecting it with the world beyond. The significance of roads as community symbols was highlighted in the late 1980s, when residents were anxious to see the community's own names for local roads adopted as the post office converted from the rural route and box address system to a numbered street system. In Rock Bridge, residents successfully challenged the post office after it assigned a family name to a road that they unanimously referred to as the Rock Bridge School Road.

The association of people with place, of kinship with landscape, runs like a leitmotif through conversation in this rural neighborhood. To these two dimensions of the genealogical landscape can be added a third—history, for current residents' knowledge of their neighborhood embraces the past as well as the present. This dimension deepens and enriches residents' sense of identity with their home neighborhood by encompassing not just their personal associations with the land and the people who live there, but the memories of parents, grandparents, and other older family and community members transmitted through the community's oral traditions. That generational memory produces an emotionally powerful sense of place that almost defies articulation. I once asked Lynwood why the Rock Bridge landscape meant so much to him. "You know when you look around," he said simply, "that you're seeing the same things they saw."

For residents of Rock Bridge—and, by extension, of communities all over the rural South—a sense of place is inseparable from a sense of the network of relations, past and present, that bind people in a neighborhood together. They read the landscape as a historical record in which people are related both to each other and to the land itself through their homeplaces which simultaneously shelter and symbolize structured and stable family life. Identifying people with homeplaces is a way of establishing a physical basis for the kinship system that constitutes the social order of the community. The genealogical landscape constructed in conversation, which expresses this sense of interconnectedness of people and land, thus seems to be at the heart of the southern sense of place.

On the surface, this symbolic landscape can be seen as a conceptual counterpart of the old proverb "a place for everything and everything in its place," a snug system that, theoretically, can accommodate everyone and every place. But on another level, it renders a whole class of individuals and their homes virtually invisible and in doing so reveals the grounds for the region's social structure. Because only *owners'* names are given to places, the people who do not own the land they live on are automatically excluded from the genealogical landscape. In this rural community, these are the tenants, black and white, who have lived in small houses on landowners' places and worked as farm laborers or sharecroppers. Their houses might be referred to as being located "on so-and-so's place," but they are never named after their occupants who, after all, often move annually from one place to another. Just as their tenure on the land is not memorialized, their family ties remain unrecorded in the oral annals of community history. This is not to say that the people themselves are unknown as individuals; after all, they have lived and worked alongside the people whose land they farmed. But the tenant system works against the primary principle of the genealogical landscape: the link between people and place. Tenants are not bound to the land through ownership and consequently float freely through the landscape. Because their life histories are not associated permanently with particular places, there is no way to weave them into the community fabric; they are ghostlike figures who wander nameless and placeless through the social landscape, a class apart.

The class distinctions inherent in the genealogical landscape cut across the racial lines usually considered the fundamental divisions in southern society. One explanation for the apparent absence of racial overtones in this local class structure is that since the proportion of black to white residents has historically been very low in this part of Kentucky, race consciousness is consequently less fully blown than in other parts of the South. In principle, this seems plausible, but in fact race relations are just as much an issue here as anywhere else in the region. A more convincing explanation is that the class structure evinced in Rock Bridgers' conversations mirrors the larger southern system of defining class, status, and identity in terms of land ownership: the region's upper class has traditionally comprised large landholders, the lower class, tenants and sharecroppers. This structure, of course, not only incorporates both blacks and whites but has been, historically, at the root of the relationship between them since the system of plantation agriculture that characterized the southern economy from the beginning introduced African slavery, with its enduring sociocultural legacy of race relations, into the region. Thus, blacks and whites alike find their status and identity defined in terms of their relationship with the land as well as each other; racial differences may complicate but do not subvert this basic structure.

The people in Rock Bridge articulate this historical link between land and class by constructing in conversation a genealogical land-scape in which social identity is rooted in the idea of place, both figuratively, in an individual's place in a kinship network, and literally, in a homeplace. The paradox in this symbolic construction is that it reflects an economic system that no longer exists. Although south central Kentucky is still largely rural, its economic base began to change in the 1930s as a result of a variety of social forces, including government-sponsored social welfare programs, rural electrification, improved transportation and communication, a shift from subsistence to cash-crop agriculture, and large-scale out-migration.[7] At present, many residents of the neighborhood, both men and women, have "public" (i.e., wage-paying) jobs. Their ties to the land have dwindled to the raising of small vegetable gardens for family consumption and, perhaps, a "patch" of tobacco, the size of which is subject to strict government regulation. "Places" are bought and sold and subdivided with increasing frequency; old houses slowly collapse in cornfields, or serve as hay barns, or stand as ironic backdrops to new ranch-style brick houses or double-wide trailers. Yet association with a homeplace and its concomitant inte-gration into a kinship network remain the unalterable grounds for the social recognition of an individual as a full-fledged member of the community. The genealogical landscape, which so clearly re-veals the class structure of this rural society, the basis for it, and the traditional mechanism—conversation—by which it is perpetuated, is an anachronism, keeping the past alive in the present. Yet the conversation that keeps that past alive also preserves the basis for community cohesion on a symbolic level long after its economic bases have eroded away.

What began almost as an idle pastime for me—making sense of the talk going on around me—has become unexpectedly a powerful means of understanding regional culture. In listening to that talk, I've discovered that the simple notions of home, of place and family, as revealed in ordinary, everyday conversation, contain in micro-cosm all the complex strands of human relations, economic pat-terns, and historical attitudes that are distinctively southern.

# Regional Culture Studies
# and American Culture Studies

## THOMAS J. SCHLERETH

*In the essay that concludes this anthology, Thomas Schlereth picks up various threads from each of the preceding essays and weaves them into a larger intellectual picture by demonstrating the connections between the study of regional culture and the study of American culture.*

As Barbara Allen's introductory chapter succinctly outlines and the previous essays attest, the concept of region—the idea that one can observe a relative uniformity of certain cultural attitudes, behaviors, and artifacts in place and time—continues to be a useful explanatory model to students of the American experience (see fig. 1). In this concluding essay, I wish to do several things. I will first sketch a collective portrait of the book's authors as regionalists. Next I will offer a brief assessment of the shape, substance, and significance of the types of regional-culture studies we find in their ten essays. I divide this task into two parts: the first identifying common arguments, the second comparing approaches to regional research. In both cases—and throughout my essay—I look for patterns that unite these diverse essays and also interconnect them with parallel trends in past and present American Studies scholarship. Finally, since it is not often that one gets to say the last word, I conclude with brief reflections on some issues not directly addressed in our probes of regional culture and regional consciousness but that the book's essays suggest for an agenda of future research.

Trained as an intellectual historian, I frequently begin a cultural analysis with historiographical, bibliographical, and biographical questions. It seems particularly helpful to begin this way in thinking about the cadre that Barbara Allen labels "regional folklorists." Since she has so comprehensively situated them in a wide bibliographical context, I have thought about their collective intellectual and cultural biography. While they come from many different cultural regions (only two still reside where they were born), they were largely trained at three of American folklore scholarship's academic hearths: the University of Pennsylvania, Indiana University, and the University of California at Los Angeles. Two-thirds of them are "outsiders" to the regions they study. While those regions are widespread (primarily the West, Midwest, upland South, eastern New Jersey), we have no representatives writing on New England and the Southwest, two of the country's oldest regions.

As we would expect from these scholars, each of whom applies a folkloristic perspective to a particular region, participant observation and informal interviews provide much of the data upon which their interpretations are based. This book of essays is, among other things, a book of conversations; and, justly so, since the volume honors a master regional storyteller who has long studied tale and teller, memory and history.

Like Lynwood Montell, several authors orient part of their scholarship on a specific region from the vantage point of their original home place or from a regional frame of reference they know well. Barbara Allen, for example, begins her understanding of Rock Bridge in Kentucky's Upper Cumberland by remembering growing up in the Los Angeles Basin. Charles Martin uses a similar approach to regional study in briefly contrasting the creativity of New York graffiti artists with eastern Kentucky artisans. Polly Stewart's "non-Lower-Eastern shoreness" is still evident to her (and the natives) after more than ten years of residency in the region she studies.

This kind of comparative study has also been common and useful in the American Studies movement. Most often, Europe (read Western Europe) has been the benchmark for assessing our national identity. In the movement's early decades, many works sought to demonstrate how Old World ideas took on a different coloration when transported to the New World. Pioneering texts such as Edward Eggleston's *The Transit of Civilization from England to America in the Seventeenth Century* (1900); *Civilization in the United States*, edited by Harold Stearns (1922), Stanley T. Williams's *The American Spirit in Letters* (1926) and *American Democratic Thought* (1940); Benjamin Spencer's *The Quest for Nationality: An American Literary Campaign* (1957); and Daniel Boorstin's trilogy, *The Americans: The Colonial, The National, and The Democratic Experience* (1959-73), pictured the United States as a new culture, a new consciousness, a new land in contrast to "Old" Europe. In recent times,

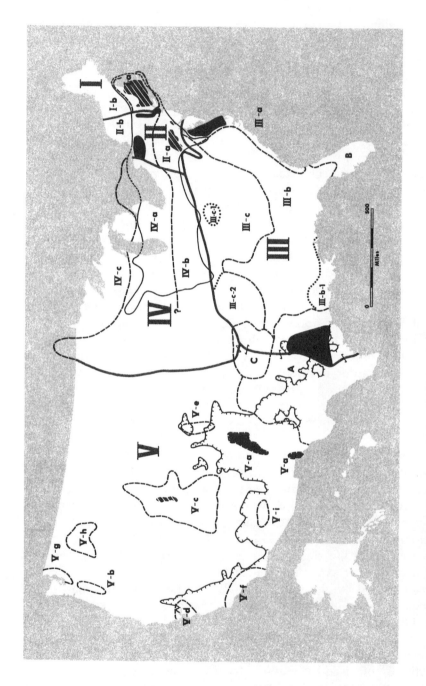

Fig. 1. Culture Areas of the United States. From Wilbur Zelinsky, *The Cultural Geography of the United States* (Englewood Cliffs, N.J.: Prentice-Hall, 1973), pp. 118-19. Courtesy Wilbur Zelinsky and Prentice-Hall, Inc.

First-order cultural boundary
Second-order cultural boundary
Third-order cultural boundary
Documented core area
Presumed or incipient core area

Boundary of Socioeconomic Core Region of North America, ca. 1970
Northern boundary of significant Hispanic-American settlement (after Nostrand)

| REGION | APPROXIMATE DATES OF SETTLEMENT AND FORMATION | MAJOR SOURCES OF CULTURE (listed in order of importance) |
| --- | --- | --- |
| **I. NEW ENGLAND** | 1620-1830 | England |
| I-a. Nuclear New England | 1620-1750 | England |
| I-b. Northern New England | 1750-1830 | Nuclear New England; England |
| **II. THE MIDLAND** | | |
| II-a. Pennsylvania Region | 1682-1850 | England & Wales; Rhineland; Ulster; 19th Century Europe |
| II-b. New York Region, or New England Extended | 1624-1830 | Great Britain; New England; 19th Century Europe; Netherlands |
| **III. THE SOUTH** | | |
| III-a. Early British Colonial South | 1607-1750 | England; Africa; British West Indies |
| III-b. Lowland, or Deep South | 1700-1850 | Great Britain; Africa; Midland; Early British Colonial South; aborigines |
| III-b-1. French Louisiana | 1700-1760 | France; Deep South; Africa; French West Indies |
| III-c. Upland South | 1700-1850 | Midland; Lowland South; Great Britain |
| III-c-1. The Bluegrass | 1770-1800 | Upland South; Lowland South |
| III-c-2. The Ozarks | 1820-1860 | Upland South; Lowland South; Lower Middle West |
| **IV. THE MIDDLE WEST** | | |
| IV-a. Upper Middle West | 1790-1880 | New England Extended; New England; 19th Century Europe; British Canada |
| IV-b. Lower Middle West | 1790-1870 | Midland; Upland South; New England Extended; 19th Century Europe |
| IV-c. Cutover Area | 1850-1900 | Upper Middle West; 19th Century Europe |

| REGION | APPROXIMATE DATES OF SETTLEMENT AND FORMATION | MAJOR SOURCES OF CULTURE (listed in order of importance) |
| --- | --- | --- |
| **V. THE WEST** | | |
| V-a. Upper Rio Grande Valley | 1590- | Mexico; Anglo-America; aborigines |
| V-b. Willamette Valley | 1830-1900 | Northeast U.S. |
| V-c. Mormon Region | 1847-1890 | Northeast U.S.; 19th Century Europe |
| V-d. Central California | (1775-1848) 1840- | (Mexico) Eastern U.S.; 19th Century Europe; Mexico; East Asia |
| V-e. Colorado Piedmont | 1860- | Eastern U.S.; Mexico |
| V-f. Southern California | (1760-1848) 1880- | (Mexico) Eastern U.S.; 19th & 20th Century Europe; Mormon Region; Mexico; East Asia |
| V-g. Puget Sound | 1870- | Eastern U.S.; 19th & 20th Century Europe; East Asia |
| V-h. Inland Empire | 1880- | Eastern U.S.; 19th & 20th Century Europe |
| V-i. Central Arizona | 1900- | Eastern U.S.; Southern California; Mexico |
| **REGIONS OF UNCERTAIN STATUS OR AFFILIATION** | | |
| A. Texas | (1690-1836) 1821- | (Mexico) Lowland South; Upland South; Mexico; 19th Century Central Europe |
| B. Peninsular Florida | 1880- | Northeast U.S.; the South; 20th Century Central Europe; Antilles |
| C. Oklahoma | 1890- | Upland South; Lowland South; aborigines; Middle West |

Americanists have begun to compare America with other national regions such as Canada and hemispheric regions like Central America as well as world regions such as Asia. The obvious, but important, point here is that area studies (national and regional) are usually done best, not in a historical or geographical vacuum, but in a cross-cultural and comparative perspective.

Barre Toelken recognizes this in his use of the works of Yanagita Kunio, a Japanese folklorist not widely known among American scholars.[1] Kunio's concept of "invisible culture" is an idea that might serve as an appropriate subtitle for this volume, a point about which more later. If Kunio acts as a guide for Toelken, who inspires the others? In addition to respected veterans of folklore research (Richard Dorson, Henry Glassie), cultural geography (Fred Kniffen, Wilbur Zelinsky), and American Studies (John Kouwenhoven, V.L. Parrington), two others serve as gurus for our regionalists: Suzi Jones, with her theory of regionalization, and William Jansen, with his esoteric-exoteric factor.

What further can we say about our essayists? What else do they and their articles have in common? I am struck by two of their interests.

As Allen alerts us in her introduction, our stable of authors is deeply interested in the role that the natural environment plays in regional culture and consciousness. Rightly so. Natural resources, climate, flora and fauna, weather, figure prominently in their work as it has in the efforts of American Studies students (art, literature, geography, history) of the American land and landscape.[2] What is particularly intriguing about this book's research is that much of it rests on *water* (not land) for its environmental base. To wit: Barnegat Bay, Cohansey Aquifer, Mullica River, the Ozark National Scenic Riverways, the Current River, Chesapeake Bay and its Eastern Shore, the Green and the Ohio rivers. And, if the point can be stretched, might we not include tornadoes, "drowning" gravestones, and tall tales of the lack of precipitation in arid central Oregon and its opposite in the state's rainy Olympic peninsula. All rightful tribute, in my mind, to the man who wrote *"Don't Go up Kettle Creek": Verbal Legacy of the Upper Cumberland* (1983)—Lynwood Montell.

A second, more pervasive concern is with violence, a topic often neglected (other than in accounts of military conflict) in American history. In the preceding pages, we learn how personal violence, civil disorder, and domestic or community conflict can be a cause and/or consequence of regional identity: the mass murder and two lynchings which occur in the lower Eastern Shore; the Almo "Massacre" on the Utah-Idaho border; the Ku Klux Klan terrorism, the feuds of the Birger and Shelton gangs, and the 1922 Herrin Massacre in the Egypt region of southern Illinois. Richard Meyer recalls Oregon's frontier violence in epitaphs such as that for William Moody in the Eagle Valley cemetery near Richmond: "Murdered by his pretended friends." Even William Lightfoot's hero, Arnold Shultz, dies "officially of heart disease, unofficially in the regional lore of either 'bad' whiskey or poison administered by white musicians jealous of his musicianship."

Such attention to what the historian Richard M. Brown has called "the dark side of the American tradition" is, of course, entirely appropriate in a volume dedicated to a man who wrote *Killings: Folk Justice in the Upper South* (1986).[3] It is also to be applauded because Americanists and Americans have far too often ignored internal domestic conflict. Both have been victims of what members of the National Commission on the Causes and Prevention of Violence have called "a historical amnesia" regarding "the sheer commonplaceness of conflict and violence in our past."[4]

While Progressive historians such as Charles Beard, Carl Becker, Frederick Jackson Turner, and Vernon Parrington did depict the American past in terms of conflicting economic and political interests—Patriots versus Tories, Federalists versus Anti-Federalists, Democrats versus Whigs, populists versus plutocrats—the vast majority of American historiography has been consensual. Only since the 1960s have we admitted to the drama and the dimensions of personal conflict and public violence in the American historical psyche.

One reason for this is that scholars tended to think about the topic in national terms. But as Richard Hofstadter once pointed out in *American Violence*, very little of public conflict in this country has been insurrectionary.[5] That is, most of our public violence has taken the form of action by one group of citizens against another group, rather than a group of citizens against the state. More often than not, American conflict and violence has been regional rather than national.

A brief sampler of the historical forms violence and conflict have assumed in American culture includes: religious and ethnic conflict (Philadelphia nativist riots in 1844, or the New Orleans anti-Italian riot in 1891); antiradical and police violence (Centralia, Washington, in 1919, or the Detroit Massacre in 1932); family feuds (Hatfield-McCoy on the Kentucky–West Virginia border, 1873-88; Sutton-Taylor in DeWitt and other Texas counties, 1869-77; Grahams-Tewksbury in Arizona, 1886-92); vigilantism (the San Francisco Vigilance Committee of 1856); and lynchings (the famous Paris, Texas, 1893 lynching, only one of the more than 4,950 that took place in the country from 1882 to 1927). Such a survey of American civil strife, of course, does not begin to catalog local and regional examples of conflicts such as urban riots, agrarian uprisings, assassinations, ethnic rivalries, religious vendettas, or labor-versus-industry struggles.

This book's authors understandably struggle with questions about proper definitions of their topic and method. So do researchers in American Studies. In the case of American Studies (my practical preference showing), part of the debate has been over which nomenclature is best: "American Civilization," "American Thought and Culture," "American Studies," or "American Culture Studies" (my preference showing in the title of my essay).[6]

The regional folklorists in this volume seek to clarify mega-issues such as "region" and "regionalism." More definitional attention, however, is paid to questions of "popular," "vernacular," and "folk" regions, as well as the meanings of "regional culture" and "regional consciousness." Here there is no need to repeat the useful discussions of these terms as we find them in the Toelken, Stewart, Coggeshall, and Allen essays. I would note, however, that several of our essayists are more interested in the definition of regional consciousness than that of regional culture. The regional "state of mind," as Stewart identifies it; "a regional sense of self," Allen calls it; or, in Meyer's language, "a region's collective self-concept" intrigues us most. In each case, regional consciousness is a dynamic rather than a static state. Following Suzi Jones, Coggeshall and Allen convert the noun "region" into the verb "regionalize" to emphasize the transforming and (sometimes) transformed nature of regional identity. The result is a paradigm named "regionalization."[7]

Regionalization may prove a useful analytical tool in the future regional research of both folklorists and Americanists. If so, it prompts me to wonder how it might be compared with modernization, another explanatory model much in vogue with certain American Studies students.[8] Could regionalization serve as a counter

Fig. 2. A new regional U.S.A. From: Stanley D. Brunn, *Geography and Politics in America* (New York: Harper & Row, 1974), p. 423. *Courtesy Stanley D. Brunn.*

point covering term (to be juxtaposed to modernization theory's homogenizing tendencies) to keep us honest about the definite (and hence defining) gender, racial, ethnic, generational, and class lines that engender—despite modernization's juggernaut—cultural patterns that may harbor insularity and xenophobia as well as a resistance to national assimilation and acculturation? Perhaps.

Before leaving the word world of regional nomenclature, a remark about American regional place names is in order (see fig. 2). Occasionally they are noted above—Summer Shade and Bugtussle, Karnak and Thebes, Posen and Tamaroa—but their analysis is not prominent. Other regionalists have argued that we can learn much about settlement history, population movements, cultural identity and attitudes, and human-land relationships by examining patterns of language, and dialects—vocabularies, grammars, the variations in pronunciations and meaning of words—writing systems, and the many other aspects of place names.

As Randall Detro and others have traced, the comprehensive

study of the American vernacular tongue began in the 1920s with the work of H.L. Mencken and Hans Kurath.[9] In 1928 Kurath initiated the *Linguistic Atlas of the United States and Canada*, a project that is still many years from completion and one that demonstrates the correlation of language characteristics with settlement history, source areas of settlers and regional culture and consciousness.[10]

Both the American Studies movement and American folklorists have deep linguistic and literary roots. Folklorists, however, have usually paid more attention to American place names. Not so, ironically, American Studies scholars, despite their heavy concentration in departments of English. On American Studies syllabi, one occasionally finds reference to such classics as George Stewart's *Names on the Land* (1967) and his *American Place Names: A Concise and Selective Dictionary for the Continental United States of America* (1970), but we do not often see the influential work of Kurath, much less recent contributions by Randall A. Detro, Harold B. Allen, or E. Bagley Atwood.[11]

While our authors are not as taken with place names (as one might expect), they are assuredly absorbed with the meaning(s) of place. What motivates several of them is the possibility of identifying, classifying, and understanding what could be said to be distinctive about a regional place. This quest for cultural distinctiveness, of course, has also been a perennial theme in American cultural history (for example, Hector St. John de Crevecoeur, "What Then Is This New Man, the American?" *Letters from an American Farmer,* 1782) and in American Studies scholarship (for example, Charles W. Eliot, *American Contributions to Civilization and Other Essays,* 1907). In the latter case, a sample list of acknowledged texts would include: Bliss Perry, *The American Mind* (1912); Van Wyck Brooks, *America's Coming of Age* (1915); George Santayana, *Character and Opinion in the United States* (1920); D.H. Lawrence, *Studies in Classic American Literature* (1922); William Carlos Williams, *In the American Grain* (1925); Constance Rourke, *American Humor, A Study in National Character* (1931); Geoffrey Gorer, *The American People: A Study in National Character* (1948); David Riesman et al., *The Lonely Crowd: A Study of the Changing American Character* (1950); and David Potter, *People of Plenty: Economic Abundance and the American Character* (1954).

In American Studies historiography (as the last four subtitles suggest), such writings have been labeled as part of a "national character" school of interpretation. This is because their purpose, stated or not, has been to explain the collective weltanschauung of an entire nation.[12] Such works attempt to make a case for a distinctive, some would argue, novel, American identity. While they do not necessarily agree on which character traits constitute the national character—a pluralistic egalitarianism, a sense of cultural or artistic inferiority, a nonideological pragmatism, an inductive, experimental frame of mind, a fascination with technology, or a preference for democratic social and political theory are only some of their explanations for American exceptionalism—they are united in the belief that (1) a national character exists, and (2) scholars willing to think with a synoptic perspective can discover and describe this national ethos.[13]

At first glance, national character scholars appear to have little common cause with regional folklorists. In the national-character school's ambitious attempts to synthesize all historical evidence (mostly documentary but occasionally oral and material data), American regions are usually dissolved or homogenized. These metahistorians, painting the national portrait with the broad brush strokes of a Tocqueville, Whitman, or Turner have little use for regional history or its regional locale. So what is the connection? Let me suggest a few.

National character interpreters and regional folklorist researchers are one in the pursuit of the varied dimensions of a particular geographical entity. Each seeks to find out what's special about a particular area or place and what might make it exceptional. To make a comparison, in the same way that John Kouwenhoven asks in a classic American Studies essay, "What's American about America?" Erika Brady wants to know "What's Missourian (or Ozarkian)" about the people and place of the Current River.[14] Both are interested in collective identity.

Folklorists and Americanists seeking character traits, whether in a nation or a region, often share a common tool, the "esoteric-exoteric factor," proposed by William Jansen, cited directly by Stewart, and used as analytic probe in almost all of our essays. The "us-them" dichotomy explains much in regional studies. We might say that the search for cultural exceptionalism, national or regional, automatically posits an "other": other nation(s) or other region(s). Several authors (particularly Hufford, Brady, Coggeshall, and Stewart) use the esoteric-exoteric factor to demonstrate how regional groups perceive themselves by making reference to how they perceive other groups and how they imagine *other* groups perceive them. So does Lynwood Montell, in *The Saga of Coe Ridge: A Study in Oral History* (1970). American national character scholarship operates under similar assumptions. In fact, a small subfield of American Studies research concerns itself with issues of how "others see us."[15] As I noted above, Western Europe (especially Britain) has frequently served as the "other" in order to demonstrate American cultural distinctiveness. If, however, the national character approach reestablishes itself in American Studies scholarship, we may anticipate wider cross-cultural comparisons of America with Asian and African countries. Perhaps a place to watch this will be in scholars' interpretations of American cultural history in the context of the Columbian Quincentary which will conclude in 1992.

In calling attention to the widespread use of the us-them methodology, I move into another aspect of my commentary. Are there other interpretive strategies in the preceding essays that connect them one with another as well as with parallel themes in American Studies? I notice three: (1) a preference for *mentalité* over mind in cultural investigation; (2) a delight in exploring cultural dualisms; and (3) a willingness to consider material culture as not merely a reflection of human activity but an act of cultural behavior.

In opening his discussion of folklore and reality in the American West, Barre Toelken cites Yanagita Kunio's concept of the "invisible culture"; that is, the culture of "everyday people who 'perform' their culture to each other on the live vernacular level and who thus seldom achieve notoriety or acclaim . . . these are the housewives, fishermen, farmers, tradespeople, artisans, longshoremen, children, and the like." The previous pages are peopled with such individuals—Hazel Montell, Ed Hazelton, Reub Long, Ralph Kelsich, Chester Cornett, and more. Charles Martin and William Lightfoot use specific individuals within the invisible culture to demonstrate the roles that regional tradition and personal innovation play in human creativity. In Lightfoot's example of Arnold Shultz we have an instance of how influential the supposedly "invisible" culture can be. Shultz's "thumb picking," as Lightfoot traces it, developed as a regional musical tradition and became a part of our national culture.

Other authors use family history as the social unit by which to study invisible culture. Many of the conversations Allen listened to are long verbal (as well as geographical) genealogies with occasional Faulkneresque touches (Fig. 3) as to which Rock Bridge families

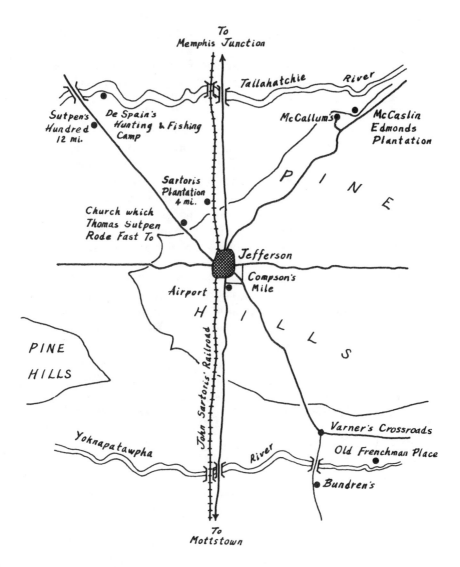

Fig. 3. Yoknapatawpha County, Mississippi. From Charles S. Aiken, "Faulkner's Yoknapatawpha: Geographical Fact into Fiction," *Geographical Review* 67 (1977): 8. *Courtesy American Geographical Society.*

have done what, when, and, of course, where. Family lineage is similarly important to Lightfoot's biographical account; the family cemetery provides the artifacts for Meyer's Oregon regional identity; and Martin shows the importance of consanguinity, particularly brothership, as in that of Cody and Otis Jacobs, in Appalachian folk arts. Kith and kin figure strongly as well in the ethnic coal patches of Coggeshall's carbon-copy towns.

Coggeshall's hyphenated ethnic Americans—the Polish-American Egyptians, Italian-American Egyptians, and the Slovakian-American Egyptians—along with this volume's heavy emphasis on themes of cultural pluralism and occupational diversity, prompt me to see the essayists as more interested in American *mentalities* than in the American *mind*. To be sure, folklorists have always championed the folk, but here we see a more diverse scholarly populism, one cognizant that culture, not even regional or subregional culture, is never monolithic, static or singular.

Here we have another parallel with the American Studies movement. In its early decades, academic phrenologists probed for the contours that revealed the cognitive pattern of the American mind. In this quest for a single, holistic explanation for the American national experience, American Studies scholars produced many examples: Bliss Perry, *The American Mind* (1912); Joseph Dorfman, *The Economic Mind in American Civilization*, in three volumes (1946-49); Henry Steele Commager, *The American Mind: An Interpretation of American Thought and Character Since the 1880s* (1950); and Stow Persons, *American Minds: A History of Ideas* (1958). By the 1970s, however, this perspective came under serious challenge from many sides. In contrast to much earlier work, which tended to emphasize broad floating currents of thought in America, another orientation—in debt to developments in social history, minority studies, ethnography, women's studies, folklore and folklife, family history, and popular culture studies—stressed the immediate, particularistic, tangible, pluralistic everyday environments and activities of ordinary people.[16] In this preference for *mentalité* over mind, some advocated a name change for the field. Jay Mechling, among others, called for "a new mode of approach," one better termed "American *Culture* Studies" than American Studies.[17] Barbara Allen and I think of regional culture studies, as described in the introductory essay and applied elsewhere in the book, in an analogous way.

In the desire to achieve a more democratic, plural, proletarian cultural analysis, a variety of American scholars—folklorists, historians, literary critics, anthropologists—continue to be aware that American culture appears to be a culture of contradictions.[18] Michael Kammen has been particularly insightful in suggesting how polarity and paradox are useful frames of reference for investigating America; how bifocalism and double-consciousness pervade American ideals; and American culture history is shot through with binary patterns. In Kammen's estimate, we are a "people of paradox" and "a contrapuntal civilization."[19]

So are our regions. "Us-them" and "them-us" perspectives partially influence their cultural dichotomies, as we have seen in the regional antagonisms between "Baltimoreans" and Eastern Shoremen. A centuries-old tension between Hamiltonian centralism and federal sovereignty versus Jeffersonian localism and states' rights conditions another aspect of regional doubleness: Jesse ("Buck") Asbridge versus the National Park Service. Erika Brady summarizes this cultural doubleness best: "Perhaps the culture of any region is best sought in such clusters of contradiction, rather than in simple enumeration of characteristics." Of her own case study, she writes, "The attitudes of Ozark trappers reveal contradictions which illuminate significant cultural tensions of the region: conservatism versus modernity, rural values opposed to but caught within urban-controlled power and economy, and ethical questions involving appropriate relations between men, animals, and the environment."

Henry Adams's epigrammatic recognition, in *The Education of Henry Adams* (1918), of "Life, that double thing" likewise appears in our articles. The complexity of human affairs is evident, for example, in Stewart's multiple versions of who did what to whom in the Richardson-Armwood case. Was it conspiracy? rape? robbery? murder? A parallel conundrum (death of natural causes? bad whiskey? the poison of jealous white musicians?) remains as to Arnold Shultz's demise. Finally, what are we to believe about the Almo Massacre? Perhaps a comprehensive construction of regional reality includes both the conclusions of historians such as Brigham Madsen and vernacular accounts by inter-mountain pioneers.

Here, in one sense, we American Studies people are back on familiar territory—especially given our interest in myths and symbols, facts and fictions.[20] Toelken rightly points up the limitations of Henry Nash Smith's *Virgin Land: The American West as Symbol and Myth* (1950) while acknowledging the role that myths and symbols play in regional identity.[21] Other essayists use specific symbols—

the Barnegat Bay sneakbox, Oregon frontier cemeteries, ethnic foodways, the overland wagon, the Pioneer Mother—to enter regional culture and summarize regional consciousness.

These symbols are artifacts. In studying them, our authors contribute to many inquiries: American Studies, folkloristic research, regional analysis, and material-culture studies. As Simon Bronner and I have described elsewhere, American studies and material-culture studies have strikingly parallel histories.[22] While both have roots in the latter decades of the nineteenth century, it is in post–World War II America that they expanded.

One approach several of this volume's scholars take toward the material culture evidence they examine is informed by performance ethnography. Intrigued by the many unexplored interconnections between material and mind, these scholars apply a "performance" or "phenomenological" mode of analysis to artifacts.[23] Such researchers argue that the human processes involved in conceiving, making, perceiving, using, adapting, decorating, exalting, loathing, and abandoning objects are intrinsic elements of human experience, and such experience, not just the object, is what the material-culture student should strive to comprehend. To performance theorists, the human processes of creation, communication, and conduct are the important features of material-culture research.[24]

In his attempt to get into the minds of artifact makers, for example, Charles Martin applies performance theory to vernacular architecture. By studying the "performance" extant in traditional artifacts, he has attempted to recreate the shapes of patterned behavior behind the objects. In the enterprise, he sought answers to questions such as, From whom do traditional artists get their ideas? What do they do with such ideas between the time they learn them and the time they produce an object? An interest in process and performance as well as product and persons also informs how and why sneakboxes are used, Ozark fur trapping is done, and the "Travis touch" is played.

With the exception of Charles Martin and John Coggeshall our essayists do not include material-culture research on regional structures. While one of the deans of American vernacular architecture and regional studies, Fred Kniffen, is cited, we do not talk much of how regional culture has often conditioned regional constructions: for example, the New England connecting barn, the California bungalow, or the Midwest Prairie School residence. We hope the coauthor of *Kentucky Folk Architecture* (1976) will forgive this omission.

We also recognize that there are other important aspects of regional study not included here. Although Washington Irving and John Steuart Curry are mentioned, no one deals directly with "high style" literary or artistic regionalism. The former topic has long been a mainstay in American Studies scholarship, the latter a more recent interest in the movement.[25] A cultural geography perspective is also not represented here, although this chapter's assorted cartography hints at some of its methods for doing regional research.[26]

The preceding essays, while never intending to cover all aspects of American regionalism, offer several directions for future study of the topics. A close reading of their arguments and approaches suggests an agenda of ideas that other regionalists might pursue further.

For instance, the work of Coggeshall and Martin prompts us to recognize how complicated the concept of cultural diffusion (standard hardware in most regionalists' tool chests) can become, especially during historical eras of "modernization."[27] What in regional culture can be said to be indigenous? What can be identified as imported? How is regional culture exported? assimilated? acculturated? Meyer and Toelken's tales of Oregon odysseys cause us to question who is native and who is auslander? Who is insider and who is outsider? Whose region is it anyway? Those who came first? Those who settled next? Those who wrote the first local histories? Those who passed on the local lore? Those who call themselves regional folklorists?

Stewart and Danielson prompt us to consider how crises can forge regional consciousness. Might there be other applications of their insights? While court trials ostensibly mitigate crisis, personal or communal, such may not always be the case. Consider how the Haymarket (1886), the Scopes (1925), the Sacco-Vanzetti (1927), or the Scottsboro Boys (1932, 1935) trials may have influenced regional consciousness. How might these court cases have been shaped by their regional venues?

Following Danielson's discussion of midwestern tornados, might there be a certain cult of catastrophe that contributes to a regional psyche? What would a detailed study of the Great Plains drought of 1888-92, or the southern tornado outbreak in 1884, or the famous eastern blizzard of 1888, or the Galveston tidal wave of 1900 (the worst natural disaster in North America, claiming between six and eight thousand lives), or the Great Lakes hurricane of 1913, or the 1927 "Deep'n as it come" Mississippi River flood tell us?[28] Think also of major fires and their consequences—Chicago (1871), Boston (1872), New York (1860), Philadelphia (1888), Baltimore (1904), San Francisco (1906).

The 1871 Chicago conflagration assuredly shaped the city's collective and, to a certain extent, its regional identity. City fathers later commemorated the fire on their city flag (marked as one of its four red stars), and historians of the city have used it as a turning point in many of their interpretations of the Midwest metropolis. We, however, have not usually perceived cities as regions. Perhaps we should. John Adams (and many New Englanders since) thought of Boston as the "hub of the universe," a domain even he recognized to be larger than New England; Mencken felt the same way about Baltimore—the opinions of the Eastern Shoremen notwithstanding. Throughout American history, cities as diverse as Chicago, Denver, Salt Lake City, Des Moines, Atlanta, Philadelphia, and Los Angeles have been regional capitals, not only of what the Census Bureau now calls the Standard Metropolitan Statistical Area but also of regional hinterlands stretching beyond their administrative, judicial, or political jurisdictions. Communication networks—urban newspapers (recall the *Baltimore Sun* in the Stewart study) and, in the twentieth century, electronic media—shape, sell, and stereotype this regional consciousness. To note three Midwest examples: William Allen White's *Emporia Daily and Weekly Gazette* in Kansas; the *Des Moines Register* (the only major daily in Iowa with a circulation that includes the entire state); and Colonel Robert M. McCormick's *Chicago Tribune*, claiming with typical Chicago bravado to be "The World's Greatest Newspaper," covering all of "Chicagoland" (McCormick's term), encompassing northern Illinois, southern Wisconsin, and northern Indiana.

Boundaries between urban and rural regionalisms are, assuredly, always problematic. Much regional consciousness, as several of our essayists show, is a state of mind, an individual and communal perception, not something defined by voting districts, state borders, or coinages such as Metroplex or Michiana. It's in the mind, or, as in Allen's journeys through Rock Bridge, it's in the mind's eye and ear. Allen's genealogical map, a personal and collective palimpsest continually enriched with almost every journey and conversation, makes me think of other maps we too carry around in our heads. Various social scientists—for example, cognitive psychologists, environmental researchers, and cultural geographers—frequently call these cartographies of the mind "mental maps." The basic elements of the concept are nicely summarized in Donald Meinig's essay, "The Beholding Eye: Ten Versions of the Same Scene."[29] Another application of the idea is found in Peter Orlean's plotting of the mental maps of numerous individuals living in Los Angeles. In a comparative study (fig. 4), he notes that the residents of Avalon, a black community near Watts, have a restricted view of the city centered on their neighborhood and routes to the city center. The middle-class suburban residents of Northridge, on the other hand, have a collective mental map of the city largely focused on the subregion of the San Fernando Valley.[30]

How can one sum up what has been undertaken in these collected essays on American regional cultures and regional consciousness, written in honor of an American regionalist, Lynwood Montell? Of course, it cannot be done in any succinct way.

What can be said is that these essays are plural and pluralistic, as is the American Studies movement. They are also as rich in ethnographic detail and in use of oral testimony as the best in American folklore scholarship. The essays stand in a long research tradition that includes the regional studies of Odum, Moore, Dorson, Paredes, Glassie, and, Montell.

Our authors' collective work might be compared to the stained-glass window that John Coggeshall offers us as an artifactual metaphor for his Illinois coal-mining ethnic Egyptians. In these essays we find a unity of regional-studies theory within a diversity of regional-research practice. The twin concepts of culture and consciousness serve as the window's frame, in which are suspended multifaceted and multicolored panels (for example, gender, race, status, religion) of various regional identities, delimited and interconnected by the lead alloys of historical experience and contemporary social interaction. The window sill is a physical environment as diverse as the continent. A layer of glass covers the two sides of the window encrusted with the patina of historically evolved regional folk expressions. As I hope I have shown, the window's insights reflect and refract with the work of American Studies researchers doing area research through other fenestrae. The window has its dark recesses—homicides, lynchings, massacres; it also has its joyous visions: guitar playing, log-pen building, and mink trap-

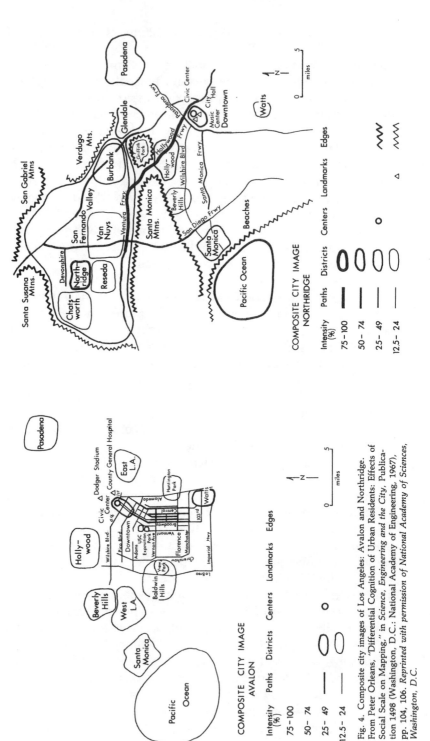

Fig. 4. Composite city images of Los Angeles: Avalon and Northridge. From Peter Orleans, "Differential Cognition of Urban Residents: Effects of Social Scale on Mapping," in *Science, Engineering and the City,* Publication 1498 (Washington, D.C.: National Academy of Engineering, 1967), pp. 104, 106. *Reprinted with permission of National Academy of Sciences, Washington, D.C.*

ping. In its many contrasting lights we find cultural ambiguities and contradictions. Best of all, however, this mosaic of regional empires made visible is full of folks, folks and their vernacular expressions of regional consciousness and creativity—as written, remembered, performed, and crafted.

# Notes

ALLEN: REGIONAL STUDIES IN FOLKLORE SCHOLARSHIP

1. Howard W. Odum and Harry Estill Moore, *American Regionalism: A Cultural-Historical Approach to National Integration* (New York: Holt, Rinehart & Winston, 1938), 2.

2. Quoted by Rupert Vance, "Region," *International Encyclopedia of the Social Sciences*, ed. David L. Sills (New York: Macmillan, 1968), 379.

3. Odum and Moore, *American Regionalism*, 16, my emphasis.

4. Vance, "Region," 377-78.

5. Louis Wirth, "The Limitations of Regionalism," in *Regionalism in America*, ed. Merrill Jensen (Madison: Univ. of Wisconsin Press, 1951), 391.

6. Brian Goodall, "Region," *Dictionary of Human Geography* (New York: Facts on File, 1987).

7. George W. Pierson, "The Obstinate Concept of New England: A Study in Denudation," *New England Quarterly* 28 (1955): 12.

8. Stanbery is quoted in Odum and Moore, *American Regionalism*, 2; Richard M. Dorson, *Land of the Millrats* (Cambridge: Harvard Univ. Press, 1981), 6; James Shortridge, "Vernacular Regions in Kansas," *American Studies* 21 (1980): 90; Rita Moonsammy, David S. Cohen, and Lorraine E. Williams, Introduction to *Pinelands Folklife* (New Brunswick, N.J.: Rutgers Univ. Press, 1987), 1; Archie Green, "Reflexive Regionalism," *Adena* 3 (1978): 11.

9. William Lightfoot provides a good overview of the history of regionalism and regional folklore studies in "Folklore of the Big Sandy Valley of Eastern Kentucky" (Ph.D. diss., Indiana Univ., 1976), 7-38. His survey reveals that while the collection and study of regional folklore has a long history in American folklore scholarship, it has up until the present remained a minor stream in that scholarship. The relative neglect of regional folklore is also apparent from a cursory review of the current textbooks of American folklore. Jan Brunvand, in his *Folklore: A Study and Research Guide* (New York: St. Martin's, 1976), makes no mention of region, nor is the subject addressed in Richard M. Dorson's *Folklore and Folklife: An Introduction* (Chicago: Univ. of Chicago Press, 1972), Barre Toelken's *The Dynamics of Folklore* (Boston: Houghton Mifflin, 1979), or Elliott Oring's *Folk Groups and Folklore Genres* (Logan: Utah State Univ. Press, 1986). Brunvand, in his *Introduction to American Folklore*, 3d ed. (New York: Norton, 1986) mentions region briefly in a discus-

sion of various folklore genres, but does not treat the subject separately. Nor is there a comprehensive bibliography of American regional folklore studies. The bibliography at the end of Richard M. Dorson's *Buying the Wind: Regional Folklore in the United States* (Chicago: Univ. of Chicago Press, 1964) is extensive but, more than a quarter-century later, outdated.

10. The literature dealing with the folklife movement is extensive. Influential early works are Sigurd Erixon, "An Introduction to Folk Life Research or Nordic Ethnology," *Folkliv* 14-15 (1950-51): 5-15, and "European Ethnology in Our Time," *Ethnologia Europaea* 1, no. 1 (1967): 3-11; Ronald H. Buchanan, "A Decade of Folklife Study," *Ulster Folklife* 10 (1965): 63-75; and Alexander Fenton, "An Approach to Folklife Studies," *Keystone Folklore Quarterly* 12 (1967): 5-21. Don Yoder deals with the application of the folklife concept in the United States in "The Folklife Studies Movement," *Pennsylvania Folklife* 13, no. 2 (July 1963): 43-56, and "Folklife Studies in American Scholarship," in *American Folklife,* ed. Don Yoder (Austin: Univ. of Texas Press, 1976), 3-18. Robert Wildhaber compiled "A Bibliographic Introduction to American Folklife," published in *New York Folklore Quarterly* 21 (1965): 259-302, of which a little more than two pages is devoted to "Regional Folklore" (277-80). A comprehensive treatment of the intellectual history of American folklore scholarship is Simon Bronner's *American Folklore Studies: An Intellectual History* (Lawrence: Univ. Press of Kansas, 1986).

11. Good discussions of the history of regions as ideas in American culture are Fulmer Mood's "The Origin, Evolution, and Application of the Sectional Concept, 1750-1900" and Vernon Carstensen's "The Development and Application of Regional-Sectional Concepts, 1900-1950," in *Regionalism in America,* 5-98 and 99-118. A history of the idea of region in European, especially British, geographical scholarship is E.W. Gilbert's "The Idea of the Region," *Geography* 45 (1960): 157-75.

One of the first areas of the country to emerge in national consciousness as a cultural region was the Appalachians, especially the southern mountains. In *All That Is Native and Fine: The Politics of Culture in an American Region* (Chapel Hill: Univ. of North Carolina Press, 1983), David Whisnant describes how outsiders have perceived and manipulated that local regional culture beginning about the turn of the twentieth century. Another example of regional consciousness from this period is described by Portia Lee in "Victorious Spirit: Regional Influences in the Architecture, Landscaping and Murals of the Panama Pacific International Exposition" (Ph.D. diss., George Washington Univ., 1984).

12. A case in point of how the idea of folklore limited approaches to the study of regional folk culture is the southern mountains. The focus of folklorists' attention there was on surviving lore from the Old World as perpetuated by a particular ethnic group, the Scots-Irish. These survivals were, oddly enough, *explained* in terms of place—i.e., the isolation imposed on the residents of the mountains by terrain which hampered transportation and communication. But the relationship of culture to place *stops* there; there is no consideration of the dynamic ways in which place and response to place shaped folk culture.

13. John McNab Currier, "Contributions to the Folk-Lore of New England," and Mrs. Fanny D. Bergen, "On the Eastern Shore," *Journal of American Folklore* 2 (1889): 291-94 and 296-300; John G. Bourke, "Popular Medicine, Custom, and Superstitions of the Rio Grande," *Journal of American Folklore* 7 (1894): 119-46; James Mooney, "Folk-Lore of the Carolina Mountains," *Journal of American Folklore* 2 (1889): 95-104; and Adelene Moffat, "The Mountaineers of Middle Tennessee," *Journal of American Folklore* 4 (1891): 314-20.

14. The regional journals were *Southern Folklore Quarterly* (1937) and *Western Folklore* (which originated as the *California Folklore Quarterly* in 1942). The state folklore journals included the *Kentucky Folk-Lore and Poetry Magazine* (1926), succeeded by *Bulletin of the Kentucky Folk-Lore Society* in 1931 and *Kentucky Folklore Record* (1955), which merged with *Southern Folklore Quarterly* in 1988 to become *Southern Folklore;* the *Tennessee Folklore Society Bulletin* (1934); *Hoosier Folklore Bulletin* (1942), succeeded by *Hoosier Folklore* (1946) and *Midwest Folklore* (1951), recently revived as *Midwestern Folklore* (1986); *New York Folklore Quarterly* (1945), followed by *New York Folklore* (1976); *New Mexico Folklore* (1946); and *Pennsylvania Folklife* (1949). Several more state and regional journals appeared in the 1950s and 1960s, including *North Carolina Folklore* (1954), *Keystone Folklore Quarterly* (1956), *Northeast Folklore* (1958), and *Northwest Folklore* (1965). The Texas Folklore Society initiated the *Publications of the Texas Folklore Society* in 1916 and established it as an annual publication in 1922. Much of the material published on regional folklore during this time period appears in the bibliography at the end of Dorson, *Buying the Wind.*

15. Cecil J. Sharp, *English Folksongs from the Southern Appalachians*, 2 vols. (New York: Oxford Univ. Press, 1917). Frank C. Brown's vast collections were eventually compiled and published as *The Frank C. Brown Collection of North Carolina Folklore*, 7 vols., Newman Ivey White, gen. ed. (Durham, N.C.: Duke Univ. Press, 1952-64); other examples of publications stemming from collecting within a state are Emelyn E. Gardner's *Folklore from the Schoharie Hills, New York* (Ann Arbor: Univ. of Michigan Press, 1937) and Harold Thompson's *Body, Boots, and Britches: Folktales, Ballads and Speech from Country New York* (Philadelphia: Lippincott, 1939). Vance Randolph's work as a folklorist has been documented by Robert Cochran in *Vance Randolph: An Ozark Life* (Urbana: Univ. of Illinois Press, 1985).

16. Harry M. Hyatt, *Folk-Lore from Adams County, Illinois* (New York: Alma Egan Hyatt Foundation, 1935); Louise Pound, *Nebraska Folklore* (Lincoln: Univ. of Nebraska Press, 1959), an anthology of essays originally published in the 1930s and 1940s; Grace Partridge Smith, "Folklore from 'Egypt,'" *Journal of American Folklore* 54 (1941): 48-59.

The emphasis on the study of folklore within state boundaries continues to the present, as witnessed in two recent publications: David S. Cohen, *Folklore and Folklife of New Jersey* (New Brunswick, N.J.: Rutgers Univ. Press, 1983), and Marta Weigle and Peter White, *The Lore of New Mexico* (Albuquerque: Univ. of New Mexico Press, 1988). This continuing emphasis is particularly evident in public sector folklore and folklife programs at the state level, in which the politics of funding dictate the folklorist's mandate to preserve and present the folklore and folklife of a state.

17. This link between ethnic settlement and regional culture in the United States permeates much of the scholarship on American cultural regions. See, e.g., Wilbur Zelinsky's *Cultural Geography of the United States* (Englewood Cliffs, N.J.: Prentice-Hall, 1973), esp. 20-22. Three of the five regions represented in Richard Dorson's *Buying the Wind* are characterized in terms of the ethnic groups who inhabit them ("Pennsylvania Dutchmen," "Louisiana Cajuns," and "Southwest Mexicans"). The same relationship is posited in Linda Keller Brown and Kay Mussell's *Ethnic and Regional Foodways in the United States: The Performance of Group Identity* (Knoxville: Univ. of Tennessee Press, 1984). Weigle and White's *Lore of New Mexico* is also organized largely along ethnic group lines.

18. Prospectus for "Regional American Folklore" and letters from Stith Thompson to Levette J. Davidson, University of Denver Archives. The project was dropped in 1952.

19. Green, "Reflexive Regionalism," 5.

20. Carl von Sydow, "Geography and Folk-Tale Oikotypes," in *Selected Papers on Folklore* (Copenhagen: Rosenkilde and Bagger, 1948), 44-59.

21. Herbert Halpert, "American Regional Folklore," *Journal of American Folklore* 60 (1947): 355-66.

22. Michael C. Steiner has described the rise of regionalism in the 1930s in "Regionalism in the Great Depression," *Geographical Review* 73 (1983): 430-46. Walter Prescott Webb's *The Great Plains* appeared in 1931 (Boston: Ginn). Derwent Whittlesey comments on the rising interest in regionalism among American geographers during this period in "The Regional Concept and the Regional Method," in *American Geography: Inventory and Prospect*, ed. Preston E. James and Clarence F. Jones (Syracuse, N.Y.: Syracuse Univ. Press, 1954), 25-26; see also Howard W. Odum's *Southern Regions of the United States* (Chapel Hill: Univ. of North Carolina Press, 1936), and Donald Davidson, *The Attack on Leviathan: Regionalism and Nationalism in the United States* (Chapel Hill: Univ. of North Carolina Press, 1938). The seminal work of the Southern Agrarians was *I'll Take My Stand: The South and the Agrarian Tradition*, by Twelve Southerners (New York, Harper, 1930); Benjamin Botkin describes a meeting on southwestern regional literature in 1933 and refers to other such meetings in Virginia in 1931 and Montana in 1932 in "The New Mexico Round Table on Regionalism," *New Mexico Quarterly* 3 (1933): 152-59. The emergence of the mission of the Federal Writers' Project is explained by Monty Noam Penkower in *The Federal Writers' Project: A Study in Government Patronage of the Arts* (Urbana: Univ. of Illinois Press, 1977), 17-30. Among the books in the 28-vol. American Folkways Series were Jeannette Bell Thomas, *Blue Ridge Country*, and Wallace Stegner, *Mormon Country* (New York: Duell, Sloan and Pearce, 1942); Harnett Kane, *Deep Delta Country* (New York: Duell, Sloan and Pearce, 1944); and Gertrude Atherton, *Golden Gate Country* (New York: Duell, Sloan and Pearce, 1945). The proceedings of the University of Wisconsin conference were published as *Regionalism in America* in 1951. Wayland D. Hand makes reference to the Western Folklore conferences in his foreword to *Idaho Folklife: Homesteads to Headstones*, ed. Louie W. Attebery (Salt Lake City: Univ. of Utah Press, and Boise: Idaho Historical Society, 1985), viii.

23. An excellent assessment of Botkin's work as a folklorist is Jerrold Hirsch's "Folklore in the Making: Benjamin A. Botkin," *Journal of American Folklore* 100 (1987): 3-38. A bibliography of Botkin's publications is appended to *Folklore and Society: Essays in Honor of Benjamin A. Botkin*, ed. Bruce Jackson (Hatboro, Pa.: Folklore Associates, 1966).

24. Botkin's interest in regions is reflected in the various compendia of regional folklore he edited in the 1940s and 1950s, published as *A Treasury of New England Folklore: Stories, Ballads, and Traditions of the Yankee People* (New York: Crown, 1947); *A Treasury of Southern Folklore: Stories, Ballads, Traditions, and Folkways of the People of the South* (New York: Crown, 1949); *A Treasury of Western Folklore* (New York: Crown, 1951); and *A Treasury of Mississippi River Folklore: Stories, Ballads, and Folkways of the Mid-American River Country* (New York: Crown, 1955).

25. Richard M. Dorson, *Bloodstoppers and Bearwalkers: Folk Traditions of the Upper Peninsula* (Cambridge: Harvard Univ. Press, 1952), 2.

26. Richard M. Dorson, *American Folklore* (Chicago: Univ. of Chicago Press, 1959).

27. Ibid., 74-75.

28. Americo Paredes, *"With His Pistol in His Hand": A Border Ballad and Its Hero* (Austin: Univ. of Texas Press, 1958).

29. Green, "Reflexive Regionalism," 4. The most systematic expression of the "new folkloristics" is in "Toward New Perspectives in Folklore," ed. Americo Paredes and Richard Bauman, *Journal of American Folklore* 84 (1971); reprinted as *Toward New Perspectives in Folklore* (Austin: Univ. of Texas Press, 1972).

30. Suzi Jones, "Regionalization: A Rhetorical Strategy," *Journal of the Folklore Institute* 13 (1976): 105-20.

31. Ibid., 107.

32. Fred Kniffen, "Louisiana House Types," *Annals of the Association of American Geographers* 26 (1936): 179-93, and "Folk Housing: Key to Diffusion," *Annals of the Association of American Geographers* 55 (1965): 549-77; Henry Glassie, *Pattern in the Material Folk Culture of the Eastern United States* (Philadelphia: Univ. of Pennsylvania Press, 1968). Among Terry Jordan's numerous publications dealing with folk cultural materials are *Texas Log Buildings: A Folk Architecture* (Austin: Univ. of Texas Press, 1978) and *Texas Graveyards: A Cultural Legacy* (Austin: Univ. of Texas Press, 1982). Other treatments of folk architecture in regional settings are Henry Glassie's *Folk Housing in Middle Virginia: A Structural Analysis of Historical Artifacts* (Knoxville: Univ. of Tennessee Press, 1975); Howard W. Marshall's *Folk Architecture in Little Dixie: A Regional Culture in Missouri* (Columbia: Univ. of Missouri Press, 1981); and John Michael Coggeshall and Jo Anne Nast's *Vernacular Architecture in Southern Illinois* (Carbondale: Southern Illinois Univ. Press, 1988). Terry Jordan and Lester Rowntree note that folk cultures have historically been defined by geographers in material-culture terms; see their *The Human Mosaic: A Thematic Introduction to Cultural Geography*, 2d ed. (New York: Harper and Row, 1972), 228.

33. Hans Kurath, *Linguistic Atlas of New England*, (Providence, R.I.: Brown Univ. Press, 1939-41). Kurath described the linguistic atlas methodology in

"Dialect Areas, Settlement Areas, and Cultural Areas in the United States," in *The Cultural Approach to History,* ed. Caroline Farrar (New York: Columbia Univ. Press, 1940), 331-45. An equally ambitious project on American regional speech is the multivolume *Dictionary of American Regional Speech,* edited by Frederick G. Cassidy, the first volume of which appeared in 1985 (Cambridge: Harvard Univ. Press).

34. Joseph W. Brownell, "The Cultural Midwest," *Journal of Geography* 59 (1960): 81-85; Ruth Hale, "A Map of Vernacular Regions in America" (Ph.D. diss., Univ. of Minnesota, 1971); John Shelton Reed, "The Heart of Dixie: An Essay in Folk Geography," *Social Forces* 54 (1976): 925-39; Terry Jordan, "Perceptual Regions in Texas," *Geographical Review* 68 (1978): 293-307; Wilbur Zelinsky, "North America's Vernacular Regions," *Annals of the Association of American Geographers* 70 (1980): 1-16; E. Joan Wilson Miller, "The Ozark Culture Region as Revealed by Traditional Materials," *Annals of the Association of American Geographers* 58 (1968): 51-77; Halpert, "American Regional Folklore," 356.

35. W.F.H. Nicolaisen, "The Mapping of Folk Culture as Applied Folklore," *Folklore Forum Bibliographic and Special Series* 8 (1971): 26-30; "Folklore and Geography: Towards an Atlas of American Folk Culture," *New York Folklore Quarterly* 29 (1973): 3-20; "Surveying and Mapping North American Culture," *Mid-South Folklore* 3, no. 2 (1975): 35-40; "The Folk and the Region," *New York Folklore* 2 (1976): 143-49; "Variant, Dialect, and Region: An Exploration in the Geography of Tradition," *New York Folklore* 6 (1980): 137-50.

36. Jones, "Regionalization," 110. Yi-Fu Tuan, *Topophilia: A Study of Environmental Perception, Attitudes, and Values* (Englewood Cliffs, N.J.: Prentice-Hall, 1974). Two essays that focus specifically on "oral literature"—i.e., folklore—as expressive of environmental perception and attitudes are Edmunds V. Bunkse, "Commoner Attitudes toward Landscape and Nature," *Annals of the Association of American Geographers* 68 (1978): 551-66, and a response to Bunkse by Hong-key Yoon in "Commentary: Folklore and the Study of Environmental Attitudes," *Annals of the Association of American Geographers* 69 (1979): 635-39.

37. Several publications have resulted from these projects, including Howard W. Marshall and Richard E. Ahlborn, *Buckaroos in Paradise: Cowboy Life in Northern Nevada,* Publications of the American Folklife Center, no. 6 (Washington: Library of Congress, 1980); Lyntha Scott Eiler, Terry Eiler, and Carl Fleischhauser, *Blue Ridge Harvest: A Region's Folklife in Photographs* (Washington: American Folklife Center, Library of Congress, 1981); and Mary Hufford, *One Space, Many Places: Folklife and Land Use in New Jersey's Pinelands National Reserve* (Washington: American Folklife Center, Library of Congress, 1986). Moonsammy, Cohen, and Williams, *Pinelands Folklife,* also stems from the Pinelands project. Included in the Folklife Center's mandate from the U.S. Congress was the preservation of *regional* cultures, among other aspects of American folk culture.

38. Three quite different but intriguing approaches to the study of regional folk culture as reflecting response to place are Roger Welsch, *Shingling the Fog and Other Plains Lies* (Chicago: Swallow Press, 1972); Margaret Yocom, "Regionalism, Negative Definitions, and the Suburbs: Folklife in Northern Virginia,"

*Folklore and Folklife in Virginia* 3 (1984): 57-83; and Timothy Cochrane, "Place, People and Folklore: An Isle Royale Case Study," *Western Folklore* 46 (1987): 1-20. Jay Mechling proposes a new theoretical approach to the study of regional culture in "If They Can Build a Square Tomato: Notes toward a Holistic Approach to Regional Studies," in *Prospects: An Annual of American Cultural Studies,* ed. Jack Salzman, vol. 4 (1979), 59-77.

This recent emergence of interest in regionalism among folklorists parallels a general interest in the subject among a variety of scholars. Meetings focusing on the topic include the American Studies Association convention in Memphis in 1983, whose theme was "Regions and Regionalism" and the "Regionalism: Concepts and Applications" conference at Baylor University in 1987. A number of regional studies centers sprang up in the 1970s and 1980s at universities around the country, among them the Center for the Study of Southern Culture at the University of Mississippi, the Center for Great Plains Studies at the University of Nebraska, the Center for New England Studies at the University of Massachusetts at Amherst, the Rocky Mountains Culture Studies Center at the University of Wyoming, and the Sacramento Valley Studies Center at the University of California, Davis. The *Journal of Regional Cultures* (Bowling Green, Ohio) first appeared in 1981, dedicated to "describing and analyzing all aspects of regional cultures, their impact on the larger culture and its impact on them." And regionalism continues to be treated in scholarly, governmental, and popular books. Among the more recent are Raymond Gastil's *The Cultural Regions of the United States* (Seattle: Univ. of Washington Press, 1975); *American Regionalism: Our Economic, Cultural, and Political Makeup* (Washington: Cong. Quarterly, 1980); Joel Garreau's *The Nine Nations of North America* (New York: Houghton Mifflin, 1981); and Michael Bradshaw's *Regions and Regionalism in the United States* (Jackson: Univ. Press of Mississippi, 1988).

## TOELKEN: FOLKLORE AND REALITY IN THE AMERICAN WEST

1. Yanagita Kunio's works remain mostly untranslated; the most useful single work describing his theories and approaches in English is J. Victor Koschmann, Oiwa Keibo, and Yamashita Shinji, eds., *International Perspectives on Yanagita Kunio and Japanese Folklore Studies,* Cornell University East Asia Papers, no. 37 (Ithaca, N.Y.: Cornell Univ. Press, 1985).

2. Fred Kniffen, "On Corner-Timbering," *Pioneer America* 1 (Jan. 1969): 1.

3. Rhys Isaac, *The Transformation of Virginia, 1740-1790* (Chapel Hill: Univ. of North Carolina Press, 1982); John Vlach, "The Shotgun House: An African Cultural Legacy," *Pioneer America* 8 (Jan.-July 1976): 47-70.

4. Henry Nash Smith, *Virgin Land: The American West as Symbol and Myth* (New York: Vintage Books, 1950), 178.

5. For further discussion of these verses and other similar songs and legends, see Barre Toelken, "Folklore in the American West," in Thomas Lyon, sr. ed., *A Literary History of the American West* (Fort Worth: Texas Christian Univ. Press, 1987), 29-67.

6. Jan Harold Brunvand, *The Vanishing Hitchhiker: American Urban Legends and Their Meanings* (New York: Norton, 1981), 1-17. Elliott Oring holds that it is the "truth status," not the factual accuracy, of a legend that is negotiated in the narration of such a story. See his essay, "Folk Narratives," in Elliott Oring, ed., *Folk Groups and Folklore Genres* (Logan: Utah State Univ. Press, 1986), 121-45, esp. 125.

7. Francis Haines, "Goldilocks on the Oregon Trail," *Idaho Yesterdays* 9 (Winter 1965-66): 26-30.

8. Austin Fife and Alta Fife, *Saints of Sage and Saddle: Folklore among the Mormons* (Bloomington: Indiana Univ. Press, 1956; repr., Univ. of Utah Press, 1980), 64. A parallel story is given by the Fifes on p. 145 in which the young woman has dark hair, but the note on p. 350 indicates that there are four other versions in which the girl is blond and blue-eyed.

9. A widely used school history text mentions the Almo incident without qualification as recently as 1966: Floyd R. Barber and Dan W. Martin, eds., *Idaho in the Pacific Northwest* (Caldwell, Idaho: Caxton Printers, 1966), 118.

10. Brigham Madsen, *The Shoshoni Frontier and the Bear River Massacre* (Salt Lake City: Univ. of Utah Press, 1985), 101.

11. Clyde A. Milner II, "The Shared Memory of Montana Pioneers," *Montana: Magazine of Western History* 37 (Winter 1987): 2-13.

12. William Lynwood Montell, *Killings: Folk Justice in the Upper South* (Lexington: Univ. Press of Kentucky, 1986).

13. Barbara Allen, "The Heroic Ride in Western Popular Historical Tradition," *Western Historical Quarterly* 19 (Nov. 1988): 397-412.

14. Barry Holstun Lopez, *Of Wolves and Men* (New York: Charles Scribner's, 1978), 71.

15. I discuss tall tales briefly in *The Dynamics of Folklore* (Boston: Houghton Mifflin, 1979), 112, 118, 345-48. See also Susan Mullin, "Oregon's Huckleberry Finn: A Münchhausen Enters Tradition," *Northwest Folklore* 2 (1967): 19-25; Jan Harold Brunvand, "Len Henry: North Idaho Münchhausen," *Northwest Folklore* 1 (1965): 11-19; Stephen Dow Beckham, *Tall Tales from the Rogue River: The Yarns of Hathaway Jones* (Bloomington: Indiana Univ. Press, 1974); Roger Welsch, *Shingling the Fog and Other Plains Lies: Tall Tales of the Great Plains* (Chicago: Swallow, 1972).

16. Suzi Jones, "Regionalization: A Rhetorical Strategy," *Journal of the Folklore Institute* 13 (1976): 105-20.

17. A number of Reub Long's favorite yarns are to be found in E.R. Jackman and R.A. Long, *The Oregon Desert* (Caldwell, Idaho: Caxton Printers, 1964), esp. 347-51, 389-90; the whitewashed rat story is found on pp. 133-34.

## DANIELSON: TORNADO STORIES IN THE BREADBASKET

A shorter form of this essay was presented in a panel, "Regional Experience and Narrative Expression," at the American Folklore Society meeting, Albuquerque, N.M., Oct. 25, 1987. My thanks to Christopher Antonsen for permitting me to quote from his paper, "Tornado Lore in the Midwest," delivered at the same meeting, and from our discussions concerning his examination of tornado narratives in central Illinois.

1. L. Frank Baum, *The Wonderful Wizard of Oz and the Marvelous Land of Oz*, (1900; repr., New York: Parents' Magazine, 1964), 3.

2. See chap. 30, "Summer Storm," in Laura Ingalls Wilder, *These Happy Golden Years* (New York: Harper and Row, 1971), 251-58.

3. "A 'Water-Spout' Near Iowa City: May 1859," in David M. Ludlum, *Early American Tornados, 1586-1870* (Boston: American Meteorological Society, 1970), 120.

4. For the tornado in tall-tale tradition, see, for example, John Henry Faulk, "Joe Whilden, One of the People," in *And Horns on the Toads*, ed. Mody C. Boatright, Wilson M. Hudson, and Allen Maxwell, Publications of the Texas Folklore Society, no. 29 (Dallas: Southern Methodist Univ. Press, 1959), 48-51; George L. Jackson, "Cyclone Yarns," *Prairie Schooner* 1, no. 2 (April 1927): 158-60; Howard C. Key, "Twister Tales," in *Madstones and Twisters*, ed. Mody C. Boatright, Wilson M. Hudson, and Allen Maxwell, *Publications of the Texas Folklore Society*, no. 28 (Dallas: Southern Methodist Univ. Press, 1958), 52-68; Roger Welsch, *Catfish at the Pump: Humor and the Frontier* (Lincoln: Univ. of Nebraska Press, 1982), 78-79, *Shingling the Fog and Other Plain Lies* (Chicago: Swallow, 1972), 22-26, and "Tornado Tales," in *A Treasury of Nebraska Pioneer Folklore* (Lincoln: Univ. of Nebraska Press, 1966), 156-58. For ballads, see "The Sherman Cyclone," in William A. Owens, *Texas Folk Songs*, ed. William A. Owens, *Publications of the Texas Folklore Society*, no. 23 (Dallas: Southern Methodist Univ. Press, 1950), 128-31.

5. I have formally interviewed some twenty individuals at length concerning either their personal experiences in a tornado or stories they have heard about tornadoes. Their ages ranged from about twenty to eighty and they all had grown up in Kansas or Illinois. I have participated in innumerable conversations about the topic, from childhood on, and in the past half-year have paid special attention to twister accounts, sometimes deliberately eliciting them through my own informal questions.

6. Walter Prescott Webb, *The Great Plains* (Boston: Ginn, 1931), 3-26, passim.

7. Joel Garreau, "The Nine Nations" and "The Breadbasket," in *The Nine Nations of North America* (Boston: Houghton Mifflin, 1981), 1-13, 328-61, passim.

8. Ibid., 333.

9. Peter Miller, "Tornado!" *National Geographic*, 171, no. 6 (June 1987), 705 (map).

10. John Edward Weems, *The Tornado* (Garden City, N.Y.: Doubleday, 1977), 34-35.

11. Ibid., 37.

12. Miller, "Tornado!" 705; Weems, *Tornado* 71; Stan Gibilisco, *Violent Weather: Hurricanes, Tornadoes, and Storms* (Blue Ridge Summit, Pa.: Tab Books, 1984), 132.

13. Weems, *Tornado*, 70.

14. Ibid., 71.

15. Interview with Mark Esping, August 6, 1987, Lindsborg, Kansas.

16. Ibid.

17. Interview with Tom Kintner, October 7, 1987, Champaign, Illinois; collected from an unnamed drop-in visitor during Esping interview.

18. Writes Christopher Antonsen in his examination of tornado lore in central Illinois: "A straw through a telephone pole and cars carried twenty miles with the driver unharmed are motifs of tornado lore which are familiar to nearly every Midwesterner in one variation or another." He then cites two typical narratives he collected in his research during the spring of 1988: "A tornado came through town and took the roofs off some apartment buildings and sucked the water out of the pool, but inside the apartments a book that was left open was still on the same page, untouched." "One time there was a tornado in Tolono and it came down and went right past. I was real scared. Hell, yes. I was in the basement! But it didn't do anything. But I heard of a time one blew a penny into the side of a brick wall and it got imbedded there. I think it's still there, but I don't remember where it was" (Christopher Antonsen, "Tornado Lore in the Midwest," unpublished ms.).

19. Typical sources for such accounts are W.W. Daniells, *The Wisconsin Tornadoes of May 23, 1878* (n.p., n.d.), and Weems, *Tornado*, 66-69. Community, county, and state histories from the region often note such details in their descriptions of weather phenomena.

20. W.J. Humphreys, *Weather Rambles* (Baltimore: Williams and Wilkins, 1937), 7, 11.

21. Wilder, *These Happy Golden Years*, 257-58.

22. See, e.g., "Tornado Oddities," in John L. Stanford, *Tornado: Accounts of Tornadoes in Iowa* (Ames: Iowa State Univ. Press, 1977), 23-25.

23. "An interview with Mrs. John Steuart Curry, Conducted by Bret Waller," in *John Steuart Curry* (Lawrence: Univ. Press of Kansas, 1970), 8.

24. See Laurence E. Schmeckebier, *John Steuart Curry's Pageant of America* (New York: American Artists Group, 1943), 111-13.

25. Ibid., 110.

26. Ibid., 115-16.

27. Interview with Clare Barkley, September 23, 1987, Urbana, Illinois. Compare the following detail from the description of a central Kansas tornado in 1905: "Mr. and Mrs. O.S. Ellvin were carried on their bed a distance of 520 feet and laid down without being injured" (Ruth Bergin Billdt and Elizabeth Jaderborg, eds., *The Smoky Valley in the After Years* [Lindsborg, Kans.: Lindsborg News-Record, 1969], 211-12).

28. Axel Olrik's classic article, "Epic Laws of Folk Narrative," reprinted in *The Study of Folklore*, ed. Alan Dundes (Englewood Cliffs, N.J.: Prentice-Hall, 1965), 129-41, discusses the importance of major tableau scenes in traditional oral literature, among other narrative traits.

29. See Donald McDonald, "A Visual Memory," *Scottish Studies* 22 (1978): 1-26; also see Barbara Allen and Lynwood Montell, *From Memory to History: Using Oral Sources in Local Historical Research* (Nashville: AASLH, 1981), 33-35.

30. Writes Barre Toelken, in his discussion of "reliable lies": "each local tall

tale normally has some germ of truth in it, usually by capturing some key feature of the region in hyperbolic description" (Toelken, *The Dynamics of Folklore* [Boston: Houghton Mifflin, 1979], 345).

31. Gibilisco, *Violent Weather*, 123.

32. Stanley Vestal, *Short Grass Country* (New York: Duell, Sloan and Pearce, 1941), 136.

33. C. Warren Thornthwaite, "Climate and Settlement in the Great Plains," in *Climate and Man: Yearbook of Agriculture* (Washington: Department of Agriculture, 1941; repr., Detroit: Gale Research, 1974), 180. See also Welsch, *Shingling the Fog*, 13-14, for an amusing personal-experience account of radical weather changes in Nebraska, and *Catfish at the Pump*, 40.

34. Weather lore comprises the second largest category in William E. Koch's collection, *Folklore from Kansas: Customs, Beliefs, and Superstitions* (Lawrence: Regents Press of Kansas, 1980), superseded only by the category, "Prevention and Cure of Illnesses and Injuries" (see p. 414).

35. *1981 Kansas State Network Weather Calendar* (n.p. 1981). The calendar includes weather maps, traditional weather signs, forecasting tips, temperature statistics for the Wichita area for each date, weather safety suggestions, and a list of "Tornado Safety Rules."

HUFFORD: THE BARNEGAT BAY SNEAKBOX

I would like especially to acknowledge Pinelands Folklife Project fieldworkers Tom Carroll, Nora Rubinstein, and Elaine Thatcher, whose contributions to the Pinelands Folklife Project are now housed at the Archive of Folk Culture, American Folklife Center, Library of Congress, for interview materials cited in the article. Conversations over the past decade with Gerald Parsons, folklorist, duck hunter, sneakbox owner, and reference librarian at the American Folklife Center, have greatly enriched my understanding of and appreciation for the social rites of outdoorsmanship. My husband, Steven Oaks, deserves much gratitude for critical readings of earlier drafts. I also wish to thank Anthony Hillman for permission to use his drawing of the Barnegat sneakbox.

Most of all, thanks are due to the Barnegat Baymen, makers and perpetrators of sneakboxes, who have so generously given of their time and knowledge.

1. Wilbur Zelinsky, *The Cultural Geography of the United States* (Englewood Cliffs, N.J.: Prentice-Hall, 1973), 112-13.

2. William E. Lightfoot, "Regional Folkloristics," in *Handbook of American Folklore*, ed. Richard M. Dorson (Bloomington: Indiana Univ. Press, 1983), 183-93.

3. Jonathan Berger and John W. Sinton, *Water, Earth, and Fire: Land Use and Environmental Planning in the New Jersey Pine Barrens* (Baltimore: Johns Hopkins Univ. Press, 1985).

4. See Suzi Jones, "Regionalization: A Rhetorical Strategy," *Journal of the Folklore Institute* 13 (1976): 105-20.

5. Heda Jason advances the view of items on the landscape as thresholds

to other realms in "Jewish Near-Eastern Numskull Tales: An Attempt at Interpretation," *Asian Folklore Studies* 31, no. 1 (1972): 1-39. Katharine Young develops the notion in *Taleworlds and Storyrealms: The Phenomenology of Narrative* (Dordrecht: Martinus Nijhoff, 1987).

6. Nathaniel H. Bishop, *Four Months in a Sneak-Box* (Boston: Lee and Shepard, 1879), 4.

7. John Holloway, interview with author, April 1979, Parkerstown, N.J.

8. Ed Hazelton, Bill Cranmer, Eppie Falconburg, and Hurley Conklin, interview with author, March 1987, Manahawkin, N.J. All quoted speech is from this recording session unless otherwise indicated.

9. George Heinrichs, interview with Elaine Thatcher, Oct. 1, 1983, New Gretna, N.J.

10. Sam Hunt, interview with Christopher Hoare, April 28, 1978, Waretown, N.J.; cited in David Steven Cohen, *The Folklore and Folklife of New Jersey* (New Brunswick, N.J.: Rutgers Univ. Press, 1983), 122.

11. Ed Hazelton, interview with author, Jan. 23, 1986, Manahawkin, N.J.

12. Anthony Hillman, interview with author, Sept. 1980, Seaville, N.J. Hillman, a local artist and carver of traditional Barnegat style decoys, lives at 1818 Shore Road in Seaville, N.J. 08230.

13. Berger and Sinton, *Water, Earth, and Fire*, 54; Henry R. Hegeman, "The Barnegat Bay Sneakbox," *New Jersey Outdoors* (Sept.-Oct., 1977): 29.

14. Harry Shourds, interview with author, March 1984, Manahawkin, N.J.

15. Bishop, *Four Months in a Sneak-Box*, 9-10; Joe Reid, interview with Thomas Carroll, Nov. 16, 1983, Waretown, N.J.; Heinrichs, interview with Thatcher, Oct. 1, 1983; Pemberton H. Drinker, "Sneakboxes," *Wooden Boat* 20 (Jan.-Feb., 1978): 23-26; George Heinrichs, interview with author, Sept. 1979, New Gretna, N.J.

16. Mihaly Csikszentmihalyi and Eugene Rochberg-Halton, *The Meaning of Things: Domestic Symbols and the Self* (London: Cambridge Univ. Press, 1981), 92.

17. Erving Goffman, *The Presentation of Self in Everyday Life* (New York: Anchor Books, 1959), 109.

18. Bishop, *Four Months in a Sneak-Box*, 8.

19. Heinrichs, interview with author, Sept. 1980, New Gretna, N.J.

20. Heinrichs, interview with Thatcher, Oct. 1, 1983, New Gretna, N.J.

21. Heinrichs, interview with author, Sept. 1979, New Gretna, N.J.

22. John Chadwick, interview with author, Sept. 1980, Barnegat, N.J.

23. For a discussion of the importance of taking animal "others" in the building of identity among Asturian mountain children in northern Spain, see James Fernandez, "The Mission of Metaphor in Expressive Culture," in *Persuasions and Performances: The Play of Tropes in Culture* (Bloomington: Indiana Univ. Press, 1986), 28-70.

24. Drawing on Lauri Honko's concept of landscape features as "milieu dominants" that bear on regional traditions ("Four Forms of Adaptation of Tradition," *Studia Fennica* 26 [1981]: 19-33), Timothy Cochrane explores the

cultural significance of milieu dominants that are animals, in "Folklore and the Geographical Character of Two Natural Parks" (Paper delivered at the American Folklore Society meeting, Albuquerque, Oct. 1987).

25. Hurley Conklins, interview with Mary Hufford, April 1979, Manahawkin, N.J.

26. Heinrichs, interview with Thatcher, Oct. 1, 1983, New Gretna, N.J.

27. Ed Hazelton, interview with Tom Carroll and Nora Rubinstein, Nov. 4, 1983, Manahawkin, N.J.

28. Robert Suralik, interview with Mary Hufford, May 1980, Bayville, N.J.

29. Gerald Parsons advanced and developed the notion of the salt marsh as a liminal zone, both socially and geographically, in "Commercial Hunting of Freshwater Railbirds: An Ethnographic Perspective" (Paper delivered before the Maryland Ornithological Association, Upper Marlboro, Md., Fall 1987).

30. See Susan Stewart, *On Longing: Narratives of the Miniature, the Gigantic, the Souvenir, the Collection* (Baltimore: Johns Hopkins Univ. Press, 1984).

31. Barbara Kirshenblatt-Gimblett, "Authoring Lives" (Paper delivered at the American-Hungarian Folklore Conference on Life History as Cultural Construction and Performance, Budapest, Aug. 1987).

32. For more on the significance of miniatures constructed by the elderly, see Mary Hufford, Marjorie Hunt, and Steven J. Zeitlin, *The Grand Generation: Memory, Master, Legacy* (Seattle: Univ. of Washington Press, 1987).

33. On aspects of the relationship between folklife and regional planning, see Mary Hufford, *One Space, Many Places: Folklife and Land Use in New Jersey's Pinelands National Reserve* (Washington: American Folklife Center, Library of Congress, 1986).

34. *Comprehensive Management Plan for the Pinelands National Reserve and Pinelands Area* (New Lisbon, N.J.: New Jersey Pinelands Commission, 1980).

35. See Daniel LeDuc, "In Pinelands, A Way of Life Is in Peril," *Philadelphia Inquirer*, Sunday, April 5, 1987, and the following articles by William J. Watson for *The Press* (Atlantic City, N.J.): "Pinelands Preservation Threatens a Lifestyle," July 20, 1987; "Pinelands Shellfishermen See Way of Life Fading Fast," Aug. 16, 1987; "New Jersey Drives Pineys to Southern States," Sept. 21, 1987; "Development, Change Threaten Pinelands Culture," Oct. 19, 1987; "Don't Pine for Them: A Lifestyle Is Dying in the Pine Barrens, But Its Death Bell Tolls for Thee," Nov. 8, 1987.

BRADY: TRAPPING AND IDENTITY IN THE OZARKS

I am grateful to the Eastern National Park and Monument Association, who awarded me a Herbert E. Kahler Research Fellowship to pursue the investigation on which this article is based. Thanks also are due to U.S. Congressman Bill Emerson of Missouri's Eighth District, and his staff members in Washington and Cape Girardeau; and to Arthur Sullivan, Superintendent of the Ozark National Scenic Riverways, National Park Service, Van Buren, Missouri, and staff members James P. Corless and Alex Outlaw. Above all my gratitude goes to the members of the Ninth District of the Missouri Trappers Association under the leadership of Kenneth Wells, whose cooperation made this study possible.

1. An Act to Provide for the Establishment of the Ozark National Scenic Riverways in the State of Missouri, United States Code 16 460m-4(b).

2. Memorandum from Regional Director, Midwest Region, U.S. Department of the Interior, to Acting Director, National Park Service, July 21, 1983, concerning implementation of 36 Code of Federal Regulations 2.2. In a letter to Congressman Emerson cited in the plaintiff's brief in *Missouri Trappers Association vs. Donald Paul Hodel et al.* (filed May 21, 1987, in the U.S. District Court for the Eastern District of Missouri, Southeastern Division, no. S 86-0193C(D), p. 13), former U.S. Congressman Ichord confirmed that the intention of the language of the enabling legislation had been to include trapping. The letter, dated Sept. 9, 1986, reads in part, "I can assure you that I would not have supported, much less sponsored, legislation that would have the effect of prohibiting trapping—a practice that is so much a part of the Ozark tradition and way of life."

3. Arthur L. Sullivan, Superintendent, Ozark National Scenic Riverways, "A Report on Trapping within the Ozark National Scenic Riverways," in response to a request from U.S. Congressman Bruce F. Vento, Subcommittee on National Parks and Recreation, and U.S. Congressman Bill Emerson, Eighth District, Missouri, p. 13. Report dated May 1, 1986.

4. Bill Smith, "Ozark Trappers Caught in Clamp of Ban," *St. Louis Post-Dispatch*, Oct. 26, 1986, p. 1A.

5. Bobcat and gray fox are the only species trapped in more abundant numbers in the Ozark Plateau zoographic region than any other portion of the state. Frank W. Sampson, *Missouri Fur Harvests*, Terrestrial Series, no. 7 (Jefferson City: Missouri Department of Conservation, 1980), 50-56.

6. Arthur L. Sullivan, Superintendent, Ozark National Scenic Riverways, "A Report on Trapping," 20-21.

7. Milton D. Rafferty, *The Ozarks: Land and Life* (Norman: Univ. of Oklahoma Press, 1980), 138. I have often heard legends concerning de Soto from individuals throughout the southeast Missouri Ozarks, and legends of lost mines of gold and silver are still common.

8. Quoted in Louis Huck, *A History of Missouri*, vol. 1 (Chicago: Donnelley, 1908), 34.

9. For records of French fur merchants in a major early port on the Mississippi, see Regional History Collection, Southeast Missouri State University, Ste. Genevieve Archival Records, microfilm.

10. See, for example, F.B. Green Store and Census, Carter Co., 1832-, Western Historical Manuscript Collection, Univ. of Missouri-Columbia.

11. *Monk's History of Southern Missouri and Northern Arkansas*, 8-11, quoted in Carl O. Sauer, *Geography of the Ozark Highland of Missouri* (Chicago: Univ. of Chicago Press, 1920), 151.

12. Such moralistic descriptions of animal behavior may be found in W. Hamilton Gibson, *Camp Life in the Woods and the Tricks of Trapping and Trap Making*

(New York: Harper, 1881), 154-219, and in *The Art of Trapping* (Chicago: A.B. Schubert, 1917), 93-107.

13. Woods-Holman Family Papers, folder 2; William H. McMurtrey, Crawford Co. [Arkansas] to William Woods, Caldedonia, Missouri, May 24, 1831, Western Historical Manuscript Collection, Univ. of Missouri-Columbia.

14. Rudolf Bennitt and Werner O. Nagel, "A Survey of the Resident Game and Furbearers of Missouri," *University of Missouri Studies* 12, no. 22 (1937).

15. For a detailed discussion of Ozark agriculture, see Rafferty, *The Ozarks*, 140-71.

16. Kenneth Wells, interview with author, Salem, Mo., Oct. 10, 1987. Conversations are transcribed from tape recorded interviews made in the course of the trapping investigation. Copies of these tapes will be deposited at the Western Historical Manuscript Division of the Univ. of Missouri-Columbia and the Archive of Folk Culture at the Library of Congress on completion of the project. Access will be restricted until 1995.

17. Ibid. I have observed that trappers do indeed contact the Department of Conservation with their observations concerning wildlife population. During 1987-88, I myself was asked by a trapper to notify the Department about a recent outbreak of distemper among raccoon in Carter County. When I did so, I was told that this was the first indication of the spread of the sickness from mid-Missouri, where it had become a serious problem, to the southern region.

18. This resentment and the contrasting attitudes toward the Riverways it represents is more fully explored in my article "Debatable Land: Frontier versus Wilderness in the Ozark National Scenic Riverways," in *The Folklife Annual, 1988-89* (Washington: Library of Congress, 1989, 46-57).

19. Robert Flanders, Introduction to *A Connecticut Yankee in the Frontier Ozarks: The Writings of Theodore Pease Russell*, ed. James F. Keefe and Lynn Morrow (Columbia: Univ. of Missouri Press, 1988).

20. Ernest Gibbs, interview with author, Salem, Mo., May 16, 1987.

21. Ralph Kelsick, interview with author, Grandin, Mo., June 30, 1987.

22. I have heard this widely repeated; in addition, it is quoted in a privately published how-to book by Thomas ("Doug") Curtis, *Trapping the Missouri Ozarks* (Cassville, Mo., 1982), 231.

23. Ibid., 213.

24. Kelsick interview.

25. Ibid.

26. From the handwritten manuscript of an unpublished manual on trapping.

27. Douglas Flannery, interview with author, Jackson, Mo., January 19, 1986.

28. Curtis, *Trapping*, 215.

29. Born in the town of Grandin near the Current River, Judge Wangelin was a well-known storyteller and local character. He was sympathetic to trappers as representatives of an Ozark tradition familiar to him since boyhood. Within days of the decision, he was hospitalized with cancer; he died in early June of 1987.

30. These bills were H.R. 2122 in 1984, H.R. 103 in 1986, and H.R. 137 in 1987.

STEWART: REGIONAL CONSCIOUSNESS AS A SHAPER OF HISTORY

1. Stories of the out-of region hunter can be found in a variety of regional settings, where they serve to mark identity boundaries between insiders and outsiders. See Jan Howard Brunvand, *Curses! Broiled Again! The Hottest Urban Legends Going* (New York: Norton, 1989), 138-41.

2. William Hugh Jansen, "The Esoteric-Exoteric Factor in Folklore," *Fabula: Journal of Folktale Studies* 2 (1959): 205-11; reprinted in *The Study of Folklore*, ed. Alan Dundes (Englewood Cliffs, N.J.: Prentice-Hall, 1965), 43-51.

3. Alan Dundes, "The Number Three in American Culture," in *Every Man His Way: Readings in Cultural Anthropology*, ed. Alan Dundes (Englewood Cliffs, N.J.: Prentice-Hall, 1968), 401-24.

4. Ibid., 159.

5. Edward Hall, *The Silent Language* (Garden City, N.Y.: Doubleday, 1959).

6. See also Trudier Harris's fine *Exorcising Blackness: Historical and Literary Lynching and Burning Rituals* (Bloomington: Indiana Univ. Press, 1984). Arthur F. Raper, *The Tragedy of Lynching* (1933; repr., New York: Arno, 1969).

7. Quotation from the *Salisbury Times*, Oct. 20, 1931. It seems clear that the International Labor Defense League used the Lee case to bring to national attention the need to end Jim Crowism. Because of developments in the Lee case, the ILD helped establish legal precedents for black civil rights in Maryland and elsewhere thirty years before these became customary. For example, it got the Lee case transferred out of the Shore on the argument that no black could receive a fair trial there; it invalidated Lee's first trial on the argument that blacks had been excluded from the jury pool; and it challenged his second trial on the argument that blacks, while included in the pool, had not been selected to serve on the jury.

8. This and all subsequent quotations are from the confidential files of the Folklore Archives at Salisbury State University. The interviews were conducted with the understanding that narrators' anonymity would be protected.

9. John R. Wennersten, "Tidewater Somerset: A County History, 1850-1976" (manuscript), 392.

MEYER: IDENTITY IN OREGON'S PIONEER CEMETERIES

Various portions of this essay were first presented in abbreviated form at two separate venues: A Symposium on Heritage Cemeteries in British Columbia, Victoria, B.C., April 1987; and the Annual Meeting of the American Folklore Society, Albuquerque, New Mexico, Oct. 1987. Special thanks for help along the way to Addie Dyal, Lotte Larsen, and Walt Stempek.

1. Histories and interpretations of this movement exist in abundance as well as varying quality. The most comprehensive and contextually useful studies remain David Lavender, *Land of Giants: The Drive to the Pacific Northwest, 1750-1950* (Garden City, N.Y.: Doubleday, 1958); Dorothy O. Johansen and

Charles M. Gates, *Empire of the Columbia: A History of the Pacific Northwest*, rev. ed. (New York: Harper and Row, 1967); Malcolm Clark, Jr., *Eden Seekers: The Settlement of Oregon, 1818-1862* (Boston: Houghton Mifflin, 1981); and Gordon B. Dodds, *The American Northwest: A History of Oregon and Washington* (Arlington Heights, Ill.: Forum Press, 1986).

2. For an overview of this process see the introduction to my *Cemeteries and Gravemarkers: Voices of American Culture* (Ann Arbor, Mich.: UMI Research Press, 1989), 1-6.

3. Barre Toelken, "In the Stream of Life: An Essay on Oregon Folk Art," in *Webfoots and Bunchgrassers: Folk Art of the Oregon Country*, ed. Suzi Jones (Salem: Oregon Arts Commission, 1980), 15.

4. Some of the most vivid descriptions of these burials may be found in the various accounts of pioneer women. See in particular Fred Lockley, *Conversations with Pioneer Women*, comp. and ed. Mike Helm (Eugene, Oreg.: Rainy Day Press, 1981); and Kenneth L. Holmes, ed., *Covered Wagon Women: Diaries and Letters from the Western Trails*, 7 vols. (Glendale, Calif.: Arthur H. Clark, 1983-87).

5. Holmes, *Covered Wagon Women*, 5: 39-135. Joaquin Miller, from "By the Sun-Down Seas," in *Poems* (Boston: Roberts Brothers, 1882), 133; cf. Miller's comment in a speech given at the 1905 Lewis and Clark Exposition in Portland: "It is a sad story. There was but one graveyard that hot, dusty, dreadful year of 1852, and that graveyard reached from the Missouri to the Columbia" (quoted in Holmes, *Covered Wagon Women*, 4: 13).

6. See Lewis A. McArthur and Lewis L. McArthur, *Oregon Geographic Names*, 5th ed. (Portland: Oregon Historical Society, 1982).

7. The only useful field guide to Oregon's pioneer cemeteries is a document entitled *Oregon Cemetery Survey*, compiled in 1978 under the direction of Robert Gormsen for the Oregon Department of Transportation. Rumors of a revised and expanded version of the *Survey* in the offing have surfaced from time to time, but as of this writing it has not yet appeared.

8. The first published city directories in Oregon, appearing in the decades of the 1860s and 1870s, contain numerous entries for marble carvers in each of these cities. As early as the 1850s, however, "signed" stones by carvers such as William Young of Portland began to appear in Willamette Valley cemeteries. By the 1870s the products of local carvers were also being erected in cemeteries in southern and eastern Oregon.

9. Background information on these confrontations, and indeed on many of the individuals commemorated on these stones, is readily available in any number of sources, e.g., Howard McKinley Corning, ed., *Dictionary of Oregon History* (Portland: Binfords and Mort, 1956).

10. An account of this bizarre accident may be found in Howard McKinley Corning, *Willamette Landings: Ghost Towns of the River*, 2d ed. (Portland: Oregon Historical Society, 1973), 24-25.

11. Both notations (Sept. 18, 1890, and Oct. 11, 1893) are from the sexton's records, Lone Fir Cemetery, Portland, Oreg. See Wythle F. Brown and Lloyd E. Brown, comps., *Records of Lone Fir Cemetery* (Portland: Genealogical Forum of Portland, Oregon, 1981).

12. Annual meetings of the exclusive Oregon Pioneer Association, held between its organization in 1873 and demise in 1951, resembled in many fashions class reunions, with members paying particular allegiance to their emigration year.

13. Terry G. Jordan, *Texas Graveyards: A Cultural Legacy* (Austin: Univ. of Texas Press, 1982), 7.

COGGESHALL: THE REGIONALIZATION OF ILLINOIS'S EGYPT

The fieldwork for this study developed from a research project on the region's architectural history sponsored by the Illinois Humanities Council and the Southern Illinois University (Carbondale) Museum, written and directed by Jo Anne Nast. After an initial survey, communities representing several ethnic groups were selected for more concentrated study in 1986. Participant observation and informal interviews provided the information.

1. Paul Claval, "The Region as a Geographical, Economic, and Cultural Concept," *International Social Science Journal* 112 (1987): 170.

2. Suzi Jones, "Regionalization: A Rhetorical Strategy," *Journal of the Folklore Institute* 13 (1976), 118.

3. John Allen, *Legends and Lore of Southern Illinois* (Carbondale: Southern Illinois Univ. Press, 1963), 40.

4. Thomas Barton, "Physical Geography," in *Southern Illinois: Resources and Potentials of the Sixteen Southernmost Counties*, Executive Committee on Southern Illinois (Urbana: Univ. of Illinois Press, 1949), 5-6.

5. Allen, *Legends*, 41-42; see also Herbert Halpert's comments in Richard M. Dorson, *Buying the Wind: Regional Folklore in the United States* (Chicago: Univ. of Chicago Press, 1964), 295-97.

6. Paul Angle, *Bloody Williamson: A Chapter in American Lawlessness* (New York: Knopf, 1952), 72.

7. Malcolm Brown and John Webb, *Seven Stranded Coal Towns: A Study of a Depressed Area* (Washington: GPO, 1941; repr., New York: DaCapo, 1971), 110.

8. Ibid., 1.

9. McAlister Coleman, *Men and Coal* (Toronto: Farrar and Rinehart, 1943; repr., New York, Arno, 1969), 285.

10. Ibid., 60.

11. Ibid., 118-20; see Angle, *Bloody Williamson*, for the details of the event.

12. Brown and Webb, *Seven Stranded Coal Towns*, xx, 110; Herman Lantz and J. S. McCrary, *People of Coal Town* (Carbondale: Southern Illinois Univ. Press, 1958; repr., London: Arcturus Books, 1971), 38.

13. Angle, *Bloody Williamson*, 136-37, 144-45.

14. Ibid., 150-54.

15. Brown and Webb, *Seven Stranded Coal Towns*, 1-2; Coleman, *Men and Coal*, 6.

16. Paul W. Gates, *The Illinois Central Railroad and Its Colonization Work* (Cambridge: Harvard Univ. Press, 1934), 318-22.

17. Ibid., 323.

18. M. Ksycki, DuBois, August 1, 1987.

19. Gates, *Illinois Central Railroad*, 322.

20. Ibid., 322-23.

21. C. Pelcyznski, DuBois area, June 13, 1987.

22. J. Wojtowicz, DuBois, July 3, 1987.

23. M. Ksycki, DuBois, June 13, 1987.

24. See John M. Coggeshall and Jo Anne Nast, *Vernacular Architecture in Southern Illinois: The Ethnic Heritage* (Carbondale: Southern Illinois Univ. Press, 1988), 113-33.

25. Angle, *Bloody Williamson*, 138.

26. A. Calcaterra, Herrin, June 12 and July 2, 1987.

27. A. Calcaterra, Herrin, June 12, 1987.

28. T. Calcaterra and A. Calcaterra, Herrin, July 2, 1987.

29. A. Calcaterra, Herrin, June 12, 1987.

30. A. Calcaterra and T. Calcaterra, Herrin, June 12, 1987.

31. By the 1930s, chain stores had undermined the stores' prices, and they closed.

32. A. Calcaterra, June 19, 1987.

33. Resident, Herrin, June 26, 1987.

34. Ibid.

35. A. Calcaterra, Herrin, July 2, 1987.

36. Ibid.; see also Coggeshall and Nast, *Vernacular Architecture*, 154-55.

37. A. Calcaterra, Herrin, June 19, 1987.

38. T. Calcaterra and A. Calcaterra, Herrin, July 2, 1987; see also Brown and Webb, *Seven Stranded Coal Towns*, 48.

39. Resident, Dowell, July 14, 1987; H. Azeling, Royalton, July 15, 1987.

40. Resident, Colp, July 10, 1987.

41. M. Connor and A. Sepeczi, Royalton, July 15, 1987.

42. Ibid.

43. Resident, Colp, July 10, 1987; resident, Dowell, July 14, 1987; resident, Colp, July 10, 1987.

44. H. Azeling, A. Sepeczi, M. Connor, and H. Azeling, Royalton, July 15, 1987.

45. H. Azeling, Royalton, July 15, 1987.

46. See Coggeshall and Nast, *Vernacular Architecture*, 163-81.

47. Resident, Colp, July 10, 1987; resident, Dowell, July 14, 1987; see also Coggeshall and Nast, *Vernacular Architecture*, 176-77.

LIGHTFOOT: A REGIONAL MUSICAL STYLE

1. George O. Carney, ed., *The Sounds of People and Places: Readings in the Geography of American Folk and Popular Music* (Lanham, Md.: Univ. Press of America, 1987), xviii.

2. Paul Oliver, liner notes to LP album *Blind Boy Fuller with Sonny Terry and Bull City Red*. Blue Classics No. 11, n.d.

3. D.K. Wilgus, "On the Record," *Kentucky Folklore Record* 7 (1961): 126; Charles K. Wolfe, *Kentucky Country: Folk and Country Music of Kentucky* (Lexington: Univ. Press of Kentucky, 1982), 109.

4. Merle Travis and Tommy Flint provide further commentary on these characteristics in *Mel Bay Presents the Merle Travis Guitar Style* (Pacific, Mo.: Mel Bay Publications, 1974); Arthur J. Maher offers a brief but informative discussion of the style in "Travis Techniques: The Educated Hands of Merle Travis: They Do Things Their Own Way," *Guitar World* 1 (1980): 19-20.

5. Mose Rager, tape-recorded interview with author, Aug. 3, 1979, Drakesboro, Ky.

6. Kentucky's land regions are presented in P. Karan and C. Mather's *Atlas of Kentucky* (Lexington: Univ. Press of Kentucky, 1977), 9; the maps of Kentucky rivers are also helpful (156-57).

7. Otto A. Rothert, *A History of Muhlenberg County* (Louisville: John P. Morton, 1913), 338; Harrison D. Taylor, *Ohio County, Kentucky, in the Olden Days: A Series of Old Newspaper Sketches of Fragmentary History* (Louisville: John P. Morton, 1926), 120.

8. Helen Bartter Crocker, *The Green River of Kentucky* (Lexington: Univ. Press of Kentucky, 1976), 11.

9. Ibid., 12-15.

10. Katie Dee and Sherrill Johnson, tape-recorded interview with author, Aug. 13, 1979, Owensboro, Ky.

11. Rothert, *History of Muhlenberg County*, 389.

12. Crocker, *Green River*, 34.

13. Rothert, *History of Muhlenberg County*, 398.

14. Washington Irving, "The Early Experiences of Ralph Ringwood," in *Wolfert's Roost*, vol. 27 of *The Complete Works of Washington Irving*, ed. Roberta Rosenberg (Boston: Twayne, 1979), 157.

15. Ibid., 168-69.

16. McDowell A. Fogle, *Fogle's Papers: A History of Ohio County, Kentucky* (Evansville, Ind.: Unigraphic, 1970), 332.

17. Ibid., 286, 432.

18. Jerry Long, *Early Settlers of Ohio County, Kentucky, 1799-1840* (Utica, Ky.: McDowell Publications, 1983), 15, 46, 73.

19. Ella Shultz Griffin, tape-recorded interview with author, Aug. 9, 1979, Hartford, Ky.

20. Fogle, *Fogle's Papers*, 433.

21. Hiriam Rogers, tape-recorded interview with author, Aug. 9, 1979, Cromwell, Ky.

22. Claud Baltzell, tape-recorded interview with author, June 13, 1980, Columbus, Ohio.

23. Ella Shultz Griffin, tape-recorded interview with author, June 22, 1978, Hartford, Ky.

24. Previous surveys of Shultz's life include Keith Lawrence, "The Greatest (?) Guitar Picker's Life Ended before Promise Realized," *John Edwards Memorial Foundation Quarterly* 17 (1981): 3-8; Wolfe, *Kentucky's Country*, 112-14;

and William E. Lightfoot, "It All Goes Back to Arnold Shultz," *Merle Travis Newsletter* 2 (1988): 6-7. With a few slight modifications, the Lawrence article has been reprinted as "Arnold Shultz: Godfather of Bluegrass?" in *Bluegrass Unlimited* 24 (1989): 39-43; the earlier piece remains the better of the two.

25. Baltzell interview.

26. William E. Lightfoot, "Mose Rager of Muhlenberg County: 'Hey, c'mon bud, play me a good rag.'" *Adena* 4 (1979): 18.

27. Ibid., 23.

28. Ibid., 19-20.

29. James Rooney, *Bossmen: Bill Monroe and Muddy Waters* (New York: Dial, 1971), 22.

30. Griffin interview, 1978; Lawrence, "Greatest (?) Guitar Picker's Life Ended," 4.

31. Raymond Kessinger, tape-recorded interview with author, Dec. 29, 1977, Beaver Dam, Ky.

32. Malcolm Walker, tape-recorded interview with author, June 21, 1978, Owensboro, Ky.

33. John Walker, tape-recorded interview with author, Nov. 27, 1978, Owensboro, Ky.

34. Phyllis Karpp, *Ike's Boys: The Story of the Everly Brothers* (Ann Arbor: Pierian Press, 1988), 7.

35. The history and structure of "Cannonball Rag," which in many ways embodies the history and structure of Travis picking, are discussed in William E. Lightfoot, "The 'Cannonball Rag,'" *Merle Travis Newsletter* 2 (1988): 5-6 (part 1) and 3:1 (1990): 3-6 (part 2).

36. Lawrence, "Greatest (?) Guitar Picker's Life Ended," 6.

37. Shelby ("Tex") Atchison, tape-recorded interview with author, Aug. 9, 1979, Cromwell, Ky.

38. Forrest ("Boots") Faught, tape-recorded interview with author, June 22, 1978, Hartford, Ky.

39. Lightfoot, "Mose Rager," 25.

40. Kessinger interview.

41. Malcolm Walker interview.

42. Griffin interview, 1978.

43. Lawrence, "Greatest (?) Guitar Picker's Life Ended," 8.

44. Leon Mosely, tape-recorded interview with author, Dec. 29, 1977, Beaver Dam, Ky.

45. Kennedy Jones, tape-recorded interview with author, Oct. 24, 1978, Cincinnati, Ohio.

46. Merle Travis, "Merle Travis Remembers: The Fingerpickers of Muhlenberg County, Ky.," *Guitar World* 1 (1980): 17-18. A somewhat more detailed analysis of the influence of local pickers on Travis can be found in Lightfoot, "Mose Rager."

47. The best sources of information on Travis's career are Mark Humphrey's interviews with Travis appearing in *Old Time Music* 6-7 (1981-82): 6-10, 14-18, 20-24.

48. Lawrence, "Greatest (?) Guitar Picker's Life Ended," 8.

49. Paul Oliver, *The Story of the Blues* (New York: Penguin, 1978), 22.

50. Lightfoot, "Mose Rager," 11-12.

51. Mosely interview.

MARTIN: CONSTRAINTS IN THE FOLK ARTS OF APPALACHIA

1. John Kouwenhoven, *Arts in Modern American Civilization* (New York: Norton, 1967).

2. Others have observed the lack of an easily definable tradition of "art" in Appalachia. See, for example, Jack Weller, *Yesterday's People* (Lexington: Univ. of Kentucky Press, 1965), 132; Elmora Messer Matthews, *Neighbor and Kin: Life in a Tennessee Ridge Community* (Nashville: Vanderbilt Univ. Press, 1965), xxi; Richard A. Ball, "The Southern Appalachian Folk Subculture as a Tension-Reducing Way of Life," 74, in John D. Photiadis and Harry K. Schwarzweller, eds., *Change in Rural Appalachia: Implications for Action Programs* (Philadelphia: Univ. of Pennsylvania Press, 1970); and Harry K. Schwarzweller, James S. Brown, and J.J. Mangalan, eds., *Mountain Families in Transition: A Case Study of Appalachian Migration* (University Park: Pennsylvania State Univ. Press, 1971), 62.

3. See, for example, Herbert Read, *Art and Society* (New York: Schocken, 1966), 33, 41, and 43. Walter Gropius also noted that "artistic design is neither an intellectual nor a material affair, but simply an integral part of the stuff of life," in *The New Architecture and The Bauhaus* (Cambridge: MIT Press, 1965). William A. Haviland states in *Cultural Anthropology* (New York: Holt, Rinehart and Winston, 1981) that no culture is known to lack an aesthetic manifested in at least some form of art (372).

4. Charles E. Martin, "The Manton Cornett Farm: Shelter and Symbol," *Appalachian Heritage* 10 (Winter-Spring 1982): 114-28.

5. Charles E. Martin, "Howard Acree's Chimney: The Dilemma of Innovation," Pioneer America 15 (March 1983): 35-49.

6. Cody Jacobs, interview with author, Knott County, Ky., May 1, 1981.

7. Otis Jacobs, interview with author, Knott County, Ky., May 9, 1981.

8. Ethereal explanations for creativity appear to be used by a wide variety of artists from folk to pop. Hilda Bolling, a Knott County quilter, first saw the pattern to her "Dreamboat" quilt in her dreams (*Troublesome Creek Times,* May 1, 1985). The singer Michael Jackson invokes a similar source of inspiration: "I woke up from my sleep and I had this song. . . . They just come out of nowhere" (*Rolling Stone* [Jan. 31, 1985], 20).

9. Crafus Watson, interview with author, Knott County, Ky., April 13, 1981.

10. Benny Moore, interview with author, Floyd County, Ky., Jan. 19, 1984. See also Matthews, *Neighbor and Kin*, 83.

11. Ernst Kris, *Psychoanalytic Explorations in Art* (New York: International Universities Press, 1962), 63. For a view that quilt tops are not "paintings," see

Geraldine N. Johnson, "'Plain and Fancy': The Socioeconomics of Blue Ridge Quilts," *Appalachian Journal*, 10 (Autumn 1982): 35 n. 5.

12. Michael Owen Jones, *The Handmade Object and Its Maker* (Berkeley: Univ. of California Press, 1975), 48. (This book has recently been revised and issued as *Craftsman of the Cumberlands: Tradition and Creativity* [Lexington: Univ. Press of Kentucky, 1989]). For an exhaustive and insightful examination into Chester Cornett's work in particular, and folk art in general, see Jones's "Chairmaking in Appalachia: A Study in Style and Creative Imagination in American Folk Art" (Ph.D. diss., Indiana Univ., 1970). Samples of Cornett's work and methodology are depicted in Herb E. Smith, *Hand Carved*, 16mm (Whitesburg, Ky.: Appalshop Films, 1981).

13. The family as the center around which all other aspects of Appalachian cultural life revolve has been widely observed. Among the sources used in formulating the following discussion are: Rena Gazaway, *The Longest Mile* (Garden City, N.Y.: Doubleday, 1969); Bruce Ergood and Bruce E. Kuhre, eds., *Appalachia: Social Context Past and Present* (Dubuque, Iowa: Kendall/Hunt, 1978); Photiadis and Schwarzweller, *Change in Rural Appalachia*; Allen Batteau, ed., *Appalachia and America: Autonomy and Regional Dependence* (Lexington: Univ. Press of Kentucky, 1983); John B. Stephenson, *Shiloh: A Mountain Community* (Lexington: Univ. of Kentucky Press, 1968); Patricia Beaver, *Rural Community in the Appalachian South* (Lexington: Univ. Press of Kentucky, 1986); George L. Hicks, *Appalachian Valley* (New York: Holt, Rinehart and Winston, 1976), 37; Berton H. Kaplan, *Blue Ridge: An Appalachian Community in Transition* (Morgantown: Appalachian Center, West Virginia Univ., 1971); Frank S. Riddle, *Appalachia: Its People, Heritage, and Problems* (Dubuque, Iowa: Kendall/Hunt, 1974); David H. Looff, *Appalachia's Children: The Challenge of Mental Health* (Lexington: Univ. Press of Kentucky, 1971).

14. Recent evidence of the persistence of politics in education was outlined in Mary Ann Roser, "5th District Schools Ripe for Change, Report Says," *Lexington Herald-Leader*, Sept. 5, 1986.

15. This informant agreed to an interview provided she could remain anonymous.

16. For a brief biography and a description of Simon Rodia and Creek Charlie's work, see Elinor Lander Horwitz, *Contemporary Folk Artists* (Philadelphia and New York: Lippincott, 1975), 118-26, 132-37. Edgar Tolson's life and work appear in David Crum, "Portrait of a Folk Craftsman," *Lexington Herald-Leader*, July 25, 1982; David Holwerk, "Whittlin' Man," *Louisville Courier-Journal Magazine*, March 14, 1979; Elinor Lander Horwitz, *Mountain Crafts, Mountain People* (Philadelphia and New York: Lippincott, 1974), 57-60; and Owensboro Museum of Fine Art, *Unschooled Talent: Art of the Home-Taught and Self-Taught from Private Collections in Kentucky* (Owensboro, Ky.: Owensboro Museum of Fine Art, 1979).

17. Anonymous informant cited in note 15.

18. Erich Neumann, *Creative Man*, Bollingen Series 61:2 (Princeton: Princeton Univ. Press, 1979), 250-51.

ALLEN: THE GENEALOGICAL LANDSCAPE

1. David Potter comments on "the relation between the land and the people" in the South in "The Enigma of the South," *Yale Review* 51 (1961): 142-61.

2. This conversational pattern can be found in rural neighborhoods in other American regions; Larry Danielson, for instance, has told me that conversations in his home community in Kansas often revolve around genealogy. What makes the pattern described here distinctive is its reflection of the larger context of regional social structure.

3. See, for instance, B.A. Botkin, "Folk and Folklore," in *Culture in the South*, ed. W.T. Couch (Chapel Hill: Univ. of North Carolina Press, 1934), 570-93. Charles Joyner updates Botkin's argument that a significant, and over-looked, source of information about the South is its folk culture in "The South as a Folk Culture: David Potter and the Southern Enigma," in *The Southern Enigma: Essays on Race, Class, and Folk Culture*, ed. Walter J. Fraser, Jr., and Winfred B. Moore, Jr. (Westport, Conn.: Greenwood Press, 1983), 157-67.

4. All the conversations reported here, unless otherwise noted, are re-constructions of actual exchanges or hypothetical examples modeled on hundreds of conversations heard over the past ten years. They are, to the best of my ability, faithful in content, structure, style, tone, and diction to the originals.

5. Recent works that deal with the family in rural southern society include Stephen William Foster, *The Past Is Another Country: Representation, Historical Consciousness, and Resistance in the Blue Ridge* (Berkeley: Univ. of California Press, 1988); Robert C. Kenzer, *Kinship and Neighborhood in a Southern Community: Orange County, North Carolina, 1849-1881* (Knoxville: Univ. of Tennessee Press, 1987); Patricia Duane Beaver, *Rural Community in the Appalachian South* (Lexington: Univ. Press of Kentucky, 1986); and John Egerton, *Generations: An American Family* (Lexington: Univ. Press of Kentucky, 1983). See also Elmora Matthews, *Neighbor and Kin: Life in a Tennessee Ridge Community* (Nashville: Vanderbilt Univ. Press, 1966); and Rupert Vance, "Regional Family Patterns," *American Journal of Sociology* 53 (1948): 426-29, reprinted in *Regionalism and the South: Selected Papers of Rupert Vance*, ed. John Shelton Reed and Daniel Joseph Singal (Chapel Hill: Univ. of North Carolina Press, 1982), 149-54.

6. Lynwood Montell and Hazel Montell, Rock Bridge, Ky., tape-record-ed conversation, Feb. 27, 1988.

7. Lynwood Montell describes these developments for the Upper Cum-berland region in the final chapter of *"Don't Go up Kettle Creek": Verbal Legacy of the Upper Cumberland* (Knoxville: Univ. of Tennessee Press, 1983). Jack Temple Kirby deals with large-scale changes in the South during this period in *Rural Worlds Lost: The American South, 1920-1960* (Baton Rouge: Louisiana State Univ., 1987).

SCHLERETH: REGIONAL AND AMERICAN CULTURE STUDIES

1. J. Victor Koschman, Oiwa Keibo, and Yamashita Shinji, eds. *International Perspectives on Yanagita Kunio and Japanese Folklore Studies*, Cornell University East Asia Papers, no. 37 (Ithaca: Cornell University Press, 1985).

2. Christopher L. Salter, "Recent Views of the American Landscape," in *Sources for American Studies*, edited by Jefferson B. Kellogg and Robert H. Walker (Westport, Conn.: Greenwood Press, 1983), 418-24.

3. Richard Maxwell Brown, *Strain of Violence: Historical Studies of American Violence and Vigilantism* (New York: Oxford Univ. Press, 1975).

4. Hugh D. Graham and Ted R. Gurr, eds., *Violence in America: Historical and Comparative Perspectives. A Report to the National Commission on the Causes and Prevention of Violence* (Washington: GPO, 1969).

5. See Richard Hofstadter and Michael Wallace, eds., *American Violence: A Documentary History* (New York: Vintage Books, 1971), on American historians' past myopia toward domestic violence; also see Bernard Sterusker, *Consensus, Conflict, and American Historians* (Bloomington: Indiana Univ. Press, 1975).

6. For summaries of the debate, see three essays by Robert Sklar: "American Studies and the Realities of America," *American Quarterly* (hereafter cited as *AQ*) 22 (1970): 597-605; "Cultural History and American Studies: Past, Present, and Future," *American Studies: An International Newsletter* (hereafter cited as *ASI*) 11 (Autumn 1971): 3-9; "The Problem of an American Studies 'Philosophy': A Bibliography of New Directions," *AQ* 27 (Summer 1975): 245-62.

7. Suzi Jones, "Regionalization: A Rhetorical Strategy," *Journal of the Folklore Institute* 13 (1976): 105-20.

8. For a useful review of the concept of modernization, see S.N. Eisenstadt, "Studies of Modernization and Sociological Theory," *History and Theory* 13 (1974): 225-52. For applications of the modernization concept to America's past, see Richard D. Brown, "Modernization and the Modern Personality in Early America, 1600-1865: A Sketch of a Synthesis," *Journal of Interdisciplinary History* 2 (Winter 1971): 201-28, and *Modernization: The Transformation of American Life, 1600-1865* (New York: Hill and Wang, 1976) pp. 3-22.

9. Randall A. Detro, "Language and Place Names" (chap. 6), in *This Remarkable Continent: An Atlas of United States and Canadian Society and Cultures*, ed. by John F. Rooney, Jr., Wilbur Zelinsky, and Dean R. Louder (College Station: Texas A&M Univ. Press, 1982), 121-48; Richard B. Sealock and Pauline A. Seely, *Bibliography of Place-Name Literature, United States and Canada*, 2d ed. (Chicago: American Library Association, 1967).

10. H.L. Mencken, *The American Language*, 4th ed. (New York: Knopf, 1936); *Supplement I* (New York: Knopf, 1945); *Supplement II* (New York: Knopf, 1948); Hans Kurath, *Word Geography of the Eastern United States* (Ann Arbor: Univ. of Michigan Press, 1949).

11. Randall A. Detro, "Generic Terms in the Place Names of Louisiana, An Index to the Cultural Landscape" (Ph.D. diss., Louisiana State Univ., 1970); Harold B. Allen, *The Linguistic Atlas of the Upper Midwest*. 2 vols. (Minneapolis: Univ. of Minnesota Press, 1973); E. Bagley Atwood, *The Regional Vocabulary of Texas* (Austin: Univ. of Texas Press, 1962).

12. David M. Potter, "The Quest for the National Character," in *The Reconstruction of American History*, ed. John Higham (New York: Harper and Row, 1962), 197-220.

13. In his anthology, *The Contrapuntal Civilization: Essays toward a New Understanding of the American Experience* (New York: Crowell, 1971), Michael Kammen presents a useful summary of additional essentially single-factor explanations for the essence of the American character: "the intellectual inheritance of western Europe (Ralph Barton Perry); the English tradition of liberty, which has produced distinctive political institutions (Hans Kohn); the Anglo-Saxon tradition of law, language, religion, and customs (Louis B. Wright); the process and psychological impact of immigration (Marcus L. Hansen, Oscar Handlin, Geoffrey Gorer); the interplay of inheritance and environment (Henry Steele Commager); economic abundance (David Potter); immigration and abundance in tandem (Henry Bamford Parkes); migration and mobility (George W. Pierson); the westward movement of the frontier (Frederick Jackson Turner and Ray Billington); 'the American dream'—the desire for liberty, opportunity, and land (James Truslow Adams); the universal passion for physical prosperity (Harold Laski); freedom of enterprise (Louis Hacker); the democratic faith or dogma (Ralph H. Gabriel and Gerald Johnson); 'the American conscience'—the dominant body of opinion (Roger Burlingame); our mode of conformity (David Riesman); generosity and the philanthropic impulse (Merle Curti); our modes of child-rearing (Margaret Mead); and the antithesis between highbrow and lowbrow (Van Wyck Brooks), to mention only a few."

14. John Kouwenhoven, *The Beer Can by the Highway: Essays on What's American about America* (New York: Doubleday, 1961).

15. An early example of this scholarship is J.G. Brooks, *As Others See Us; A Study of Progress in the United States* (New York: Macmillan 1908), and an excellent regional anthology is B.L. Pierce, ed., *As Others See Chicago: Impressions of Visitors, 1673-1933* (Chicago: Univ. of Chicago Press, 1933). For other titles, see "Collections of Narrative and Travels," in *Harvard Guide to American History* (Cambridge: Harvard Univ. Press, 1960).

16. Gene Wise presents the most comprehensive summary to date of this trend toward greater American Studies populism and pluralism in his essay " 'Paradigm Dramas' in American Studies: A Cultural and Institutional History of the Movement," *AQ* 31 (1979): 312-37.

17. Jay Mechling, Robert Merideth, and David Wilson, "American Culture Studies: The Discipline and the Curriculum," *AQ* 25 (1973): 363-89; Gene Wise, "Some Elementary Axioms for an American Culture Studies," *Prospects* 4 (1979): 517-47.

18. A sampler of such interpretations would include: Erik Erikson, *Childhood and Society,* 2d ed. rev. (New York: Norton, 1963), 285-96; John Steinbeck, *America and Americans* (New York: Viking, 1966), 29-34; James F. Muirhead, *The Land of Contrasts: A Briton's View of His American Kin* (London: John Lane, 1898), 7-23; W.E.B. Du Bois, *The Souls of Black Folk: Essays and Sketches* (Chicago: A.C. McClurg, 1903), 1-12; Ralph Barton Perry, *Characteristically American* (New York: Knopf, 1949), 3-20; William A. Clebsch, *From Sacred to Profane America* (New York: Harper and Row, 1968), 1-14; Richard Chase, *The American Novel and Its Tradition* (New York: Doubleday, 1957), 1-11; Marvin Meyers, *The Jacksonian Persuasion: Politics and Belief* (Stanford: Stanford Univ. Press, 1957), 24-41; Reinhold Niebuhr, *The Irony of American History* (New York: Scribner's Sons, 1952), 1-16; Gregory Bateson,

"Morale and National Character," in *Civilian Morale*, ed. Goodwin Watson (New York, Boston: Houghton Mifflin, 1942), 71-91; Alpheus T. Mason, "The Federalist—A Split Personality," *American Historical Review* 57 (April 1952): 625-43.

19. See note 13 and Michael Kammen, *People of Paradox: An Inquiry Concerning the Origins of American Civilization* (New York: Knopf, 1973), 273-98.

20. Bruce Kuklich, "Myth and Symbol in American Studies," *AQ* 24 (1972): 435-50. Also see Cecil Tate, *The Search for Method in American Studies* (Minneapolis: Univ. of Minnesota Press, 1973).

21. Other well-known American Studies applications of the myth-and-symbol approach include: John William Ward, *Andrew Jackson: Symbol for an Age* (New York: Oxford Univ. Press, 1955); Leo Marx, *The Machine in the Garden* (New York: Oxford Univ. Press, 1964); and Alan Trachtenberg, *Brooklyn Bridge: Fact and Symbol* (New York: Oxford Univ. Press, 1960).

22. Simon J. Bronner, *American Folklore Studies: An Intellectual History* (Lawrence: Univ. Press of Kansas, 1986); Thomas J. Schlereth, ed., *Material Culture Studies in America* (Nashville: AASLH, 1982).

23. Classic examples of performance studies include: G. Ewart Evans, *Ask the Fellows Who Cut the Hay* (London: Faber, 1956); James Spradley, *You Owe Yourself a Drunk: An Ethnography of Urban Nomads* (Boston: Little, Brown, 1970); Richard Horwitz, *Anthropology toward History: Culture and Work in a 19th-Century Maine Town* (Middletown, Conn.: Wesleyan Univ. Press, 1978). Thomas Adler, following Edmund Husserl, summarized the phenomenological position as applied to folk artifacts in his essay, "Personal Experience and the Artifact: Musical Instruments, Tools, and the Experience of Control," in *American Material Culture and Folklore: A Prologue and a Dialogue* (Ann Arbor: UMI Research Press, 1985), 103-18.

For discussions of phenomenology's relation to time in history, see Edmund Husserl, *Cartesian Meditations: An Introduction to Phenomenology*, trans. Dorian Carins (The Hague: Nijhoff, 1960), 33-43; Donald M. Lowe, "Intentionality and the Method of History," in *Phenomenology and the Social Sciences*, ed. Maurice Natanson (Evanston, Ill.: Northwestern Univ. Press, 1973), 11-14; C.D. Keys, "Art and Temporality," *Research in Phenomenology* 1 (1971): 63-73.

24. Dell Upton, "Toward a Performance Theory of Vernacular Architecture: Early Tidewater Virginia as a Case Study," *Folklore Forum* 12 (1979): 173-95; Adler, "Personal Experience and the Artifact," 103.

25. For example, see Hannah Logasa, *Regionalism in the United States: A Subject List* (Boston: Little Brown, 1942); Carey Williams, *The New Regionalism in American Literature* (Seattle, 1930); on American regional art, see Matthew Baigell, *The American Scene: American Painting in the 1930s* (New York: F.A. Praeger, 1974); Bernard Karpel, ed., *The Arts in America*, 4 vols. (Washington, D.C.: Smithsonian Institution 1979), and Alan Gussow, *A Sense of Place, The Artist and America* (New York: Saturday Review Press, 1972).

26. A fine overview of recent work in American cultural geography is Pierce Lewis's essay, "Learning from Looking: Geographic and Other Writing about the American Landscape," in *American Culture, A Research Guide*, ed. Thomas J. Schlereth (Lawrence: University of Kansas Press, 1985), pp. 35-56; for

an excellent compendium of recent American cartography, see *This Remarkable Continent: An Atlas of the United States and Canadian Society and Cultures*, ed. John F. Rooney, Wilbur Zelinsky, and Dean R. Louder.

27. Tension between the regional and the modern are explored, in part, in several of the essays in *Regions of the United States*, ed. John Fraser Hart (New York: Harper and Row, 1972); also see Brown, *Modernization*, pp. 120-21, 170-73, 183-85.

28. A model study for such regional research is Pete Daniel, *Deep'n as It Come: The 1927 Mississippi River Flood* (New York: Oxford Univ. Press, 1977).

29. In Donald Meinig, ed. *The Interpretation of Ordinary Landscapes* (New York: Oxford Univ. Press, 1979), 33-48; on mental mapping, see Peter Gould and Rodney White, *Mental Maps* (Baltimore: Penguin, 1974).

30. Peter Orleans, "Differential Cognition of Urban Residents: Effects of Social Scale on Mapping," in *Science, Engineering, and the City*, Publication 1498 (Washington: National Academy of Engineering, 1967), pp. 103-17.

# Contributors

BARBARA ALLEN, a native Californian, received her training in folklore at UCLA. Since 1981 she has taught in the American Studies Department at the University of Notre Dame. Her major research interest is the relationship between folklore and history, as reflected in her publications *From Memory to History: Using Oral Sources in Local Historical Research* (with Lynwood Montell), *Homesteading the High Desert*, and articles in folklore and oral history journals.

ERIKA BRADY has been investigating the Ozark fur trade since 1986. A native of Washington, DC, she holds degrees in folklore from Harvard-Radcliffe, UCLA, and Indiana University, and has worked at the American Folklife Center at the Library of Congress. She is currently Assistant Professor of Folk Studies at Western Kentucky University.

JOHN M. COGGESHALL, although born in Boston, grew up in the coal-mining region of southern Illinois. Coggeshall received a Ph.D. in anthropology from Southern Illinois University (Carbondale), and currently serves as an assistant professor of anthropology at Clemson University. Coggeshall's publications include *Vernacular Architecture in Southern Illinois* (with Jo Anne Nast), and articles on American folklore and on prisoner culture appearing in the *Journal of American Folklore, Anthropology Today,* and *Southern Folklore Quarterly.*

LARRY DANIELSON received his Ph.D. in Folklore and American Studies from Indiana University in 1972. He is associate professor in the English Department, University of Illinois, Urbana-Champaign. His research interests, which include ethnic folklore in the U.S., paranormal legend and belief, and the relationship between oral history and traditional verbal art, are represented in a variety of publications.

MARY HUFFORD received the Ph.D. in folklore at the University of Pennsylvania in 1989. Since 1982 she has been a folklife specialist at the American Folklife Center, Library of Congress. From 1983 to 1985 she directed the Pinelands Folklife Project, a field study designed to assist regional planners in setting policies that protect traditional lifeways as well as natural resources in the Pinelands National Reserve. She is the author of *One Space, Many Places: Folklife and Land Use Planning in New Jersey's Pinelands National Reserve.*

WILLIAM E. LIGHTFOOT, a native of western Kentucky, attended Western Kentucky University, the University of Kentucky, and Indiana University, where he received a Ph.D. in folklore in 1976. He taught at the Ohio State

University from 1974 to 1980; since 1980 he has been a member of the English Department of Appalachian State University in Boone, North Carolina. Interested primarily in the relationships between folk and popular music, Lightfoot is working on book-length studies of Lulu Belle and Scotty Wiseman, Tex Atchison and the Prairie Ramblers, and the evolution of the Merle Travis guitar style.

CHARLES MARTIN received a master's degree in folk studies from Western Kentucky University and a Ph.D. in folklore from Indiana University. He is the author of the award-winning *Hollybush: Folk Building and Social Change in an Appalachian Community*, as well as numerous articles on folk art and material culture. He has taught at Alice Lloyd College and Transylvania University in Kentucky.

RICHARD E. MEYER, Professor of English at Western Oregon State College, completed his undergraduate work at Northwestern University and his graduate training at the Universities of Washington and Oregon. Besides publications in English and American literature, he has written on American outlaw folklore and various aspects of folk material culture. He is the editor of *Cemeteries and Gravemarkers: Voices of American Culture* (1989), and chairs the Cemeteries and Gravemarkers Section of the American Culture Association.

THOMAS J. SCHLERETH received his graduate education in history at the University of Wisconsin and the University of Iowa. Since 1972 he has been a member of the American Studies faculty at the University of Notre Dame. He is the author of numerous books and articles on material culture studies, including *Material Culture Studies in America* (1982) and *Victorian America: Transformations of Everyday Life, 1876-1915 (1990).*

POLLY STEWART has been teaching folklore, comparative mythology, and Chaucer at Salisbury (Maryland) State University since 1973. She earned a Ph.D. at the University of Oregon in 1975. She produced the Eastern Shore Folklife Festival (1976), the Maryland Folklife Festival (1978) and the Delmarva Folklife Festival (1983), and did fieldwork and presentation for festivals in Utah and Idaho (1979, 1980, 1981). Beyond teaching and public-sector folklife programming, her folklore interests include folksong, verbal style in folk narrative, and the relation of regionalism to local history.

BARRE TOELKEN is Professor of English and History at Utah State University, where he is director of the Folklore Program and of the American Studies Graduate Program. He is past president of the American Folklore Society, former Editor of the *Journal of American Folklore,* and a member of the Folklore Fellows. He was appointed by Congress to a five-year term on the Board of Trustees of the American Folklife Center in the Library of Congress (1985-1990).